T_EX
Applications, Uses, Methods

ELLIS HORWOOD SERIES IN COMPUTERS AND THEIR APPLICATIONS
Series Editor: IAN CHIVERS, Senior Analyst, The Computer Centre, King's College, London, and formerly Senior Programmer and Analyst, Imperial College of Science and Technology, University of London

Series continued at back of book

T_EX
Applications, Uses, Methods

MALCOLM CLARK B.A., M.Sc.
User Support Manager
Research Computer Unit, Imperial Cancer Research Unit, London
formerly Imperial College Computing Centre, London

ELLIS HORWOOD
NEW YORK   LONDON   TORONTO   SYDNEY   TOKYO   SINGAPORE

First published in 1990 by
ELLIS HORWOOD LIMITED
Market Cross House, Cooper Street,
Chichester, West Sussex, PO19 1EB, England

A division of
Simon & Schuster International Group

Printed and bound in Great Britain
by Hartnolls, Bomdin

British Library Cataloguing in Publication Data

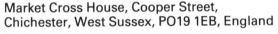

Applications, Uses, Methods
(Ellis   Horwood   Series   in   Computers   and
theirApplications).
CIP catalogue record for this book is available from the
British Library.
ISBN 0–13–912296–6

Library of Congress Cataloging-in-Publication Data available

Contents

Preface

TeX88 (or more whimsically, TeXeter), was the third European TeX conference. It took place at the University of Exeter on 18 th–20 th July, 1988. The two previous conferences had taken place in 1985 at Como, Italy, and in 1986 at Strasbourg, France.

TeX88 attracted over 140 participants, mainly from Europe, but also from the Middle East and North America. We were fortunate and privileged to be hosts to so many of our colleagues who share our enthusiasm for things TeXnical. Organising conferences is not an occupation to be taken lightly, and the smooth running of TeX88 has much to do with the skills and ability of the local organiser, Cathy Booth, and to Ewart North's steadying influence. It all went remarkably well. Even the notoriously unreliable local weather failed to react to the provocation of a steam train and river boat excursion.

It is disappointing that not all the papers were available in their entirety. But all the papers are represented by at least an abstract. Two of them require further comment. A version of Brüggeman-Klein and Wood's paper was published in 'Electronic Publishing – origination, dissemination, design', under the same title. It is printed here by permission of John Wiley Publishers. I felt that the readership of the proceedings and the journal were sufficiently distinct that it was valuable to present it here. The 'Polish paper' of Jackowski, Hołdys and Ryćko was not given at the conference, since the authors were unable to be present. However it is sufficiently important to be given an airing at a European TeX conference. I look forward to greater participation from eastern Europe at future conferences – and before too long to European TeX conferences in eastern Europe.

The proceedings were prepared from author's submissions – from disk, email, and even from real manuscripts. They were TeXed on TeXpert systems' Macintosh Plus with Textures, using custom built TeX macros. With the sole exception of Alois Heinz' paper they were typeset on the University of London's Linotronic 300, using ArborText's DVILASER/PS to convert the dvi file; the fonts were the bit-mapped Computer Modern fonts generated by either Philip Taylor or Andrew Trevarrow. Alois Heinz' paper was typeset on an LN300 at Linotype in Cheltenham, driven directly from a Macintosh and using Blue Sky's POSTSCRIPT outline Computer Modern fonts. The index was prepared by Richard Raper et al. of Indexing Specialists.

A work like this is a joint effort. I was helped and supported by many people: the authors themselves; Martin Powell of the University of London

Computer Centre ('purveyors of distinctive typesetting to the University'); Mike Winthrop of Linotype; Philip Taylor and Sebastian Rahtz; Marek Ryćko; and Hubert Partl. Equally significant, none of this would have been possible without Don Knuth.

A number of the TeX macros referred to in this volume have been placed in the Aston Archive. The macros will doubtless find there way to other servers and archives. Details will be found in future editions of TUGBOAT and TeXline. The macros involved are those of Hoenig, Olivier, Ramek, Brüggeman-Klein and Wood, and Jackowski, Hołdys and Ryćko. If you cannot access the macros in an archive, contact me directly for further details.

The copyright of all material remains with the individual authors, *except* for the work of Brüggeman-Klein and Wood, where the copyright is that of John Wiley and Sons.

Many names are trademarks: these include TeX and $\mathcal{AMS}$-TeX (American Mathematical Society); METAFONT (Addison Wesley); *Textures* (Blue Sky Research); the ubiquitous Unix (AT&T Technologies); Macintosh (Apple Computer Inc); and many many more, for whose omission here and consequent lack of acknowledgement we apologise.

Lastly: one of TeX's strengths is in its user groups: in the fact that many people are prepared to put time and effort into the world of TeX. There are a number of user groups. Join one and enjoy TeX even more!

●DANTE
Research Centre
University of Heidelberg
Im Neuenheimer Feld 293
D-6900 Heidelberg 1
FRG

●NTG
Kees van der Laan
Rekencentrum RUG
Landleven 1
NL-9700 AV Groningen
The Netherlands

●GUTenberg
c/o IRISA
Campus Universitaire de Beaulieu
F-25042 Rennes Cedex
France

●Nordic TeX Users
c/o Roswitha Graham
Royal Institute of Technology
S-100 44 Stockholm
Sweden

●UK TeX Users Group
c/o Computing Service
Aston University
Aston Triangle
Birmingham B4 7ET
UK

●TUG
TeX Users Group
PO Box 9506
Providence
RI 02940
USA

Malcolm Clark

Chapter 1
An Introduction to TeX for New Users

Alan Hoenig

This paper presents a brief overview of the TeX typesetting system. Amateurs, novices, and new users are often slighted at user group meetings like this. This does them and TeX no good, and I am pleased to have the opportunity to make brief remarks of an introductory nature about TeX. The remarks will be so brief that I cannot possibly deliver a tutorial on the use of TeX, but I will instead strive for an overview, with special attention to TeX's idiosyncrasies.

1.1   What is this thing called TEX?

TEX is a computer typesetting system. You hand it some words, figures, equations, tables and so on, and later, at the end of the TEX life cycle, it delivers to you your copy in typeset form. If your printer is capable of sufficient resolution, your printed, TEXed document will be suitable to give to your printer. He will then make plates from it using a photographic process and then embark on the manufacturing process of printing.

This simple description makes TEX sound like some super-'word processing' program, but this is an unfortunate analogy for several reasons. First of all, TEX concerns itself with typographic niceties which are all but ignored by traditional word processing and desktop publishing software. The niceties which I most appreciate are *kerns* and *ligatures*. A kern is special spacing added or subtracted to the normal space between letters to improve the appearance of some word. One of the best examples of kerning is TOYOTA. A ligature is a special single character used to represent two or more characters. In Roman fonts, common ligatures include ff, fi, fl, ffi, and ffl. Compare 'ff' with 'ff'.

TOYOTA	**officious affluent riffraff**
TOYOTA	**officious affluent riffraff**
Kerning	Ligatures in practice.

Figure 1. Kerns and ligatures illustrated.

One other nicety is TEX's proficiency in setting mathematical and technical text. In most cases, TEX properly adjusts the spacing so the math looks as pleasing as possible.

$$\pi \approx \frac{63}{25}\left(\frac{17+15\sqrt{5}}{7+15\sqrt{5}}\right)$$

$$\int_0^\infty \sin^{2n}\theta\, d\theta 0 = \frac{(2n)!}{2^{2n}(n!)^2}\pi$$

$$\frac{2}{\pi} = \sqrt{\frac{1}{2}}\cdot\sqrt{\frac{1}{2}+\frac{1}{2}\sqrt{\frac{1}{2}}}\cdot\sqrt{\frac{1}{2}+\frac{1}{2}\sqrt{\frac{1}{2}+\frac{1}{2}\sqrt{\frac{1}{2}}}}\cdots$$

$$\int_a^b f(x)\, d[x] = \sum_{a<n\leq b} f(n)$$

Figure 2. TEX does mathematics. All these formulas relate to the computation of the constant π.

Another difference between TEX and ordinary word processors lies in the nature of their 'life cycles'. Office word processing is a simple two-stage process: (1) enter the text; and (2) print it.

> 1.   Enter text.
> 2.   Print document.

Figure 3. The word processing life cycle.

The TEXing of any document calls for *three* steps with associated substeps along the way.

1 Prepare a file containing your text: interspersed among it are the various and sundry TEX commands.
2 Run this file through the TEX program. TEX produces a special file which you will need for the next step.
   –But first, go back to step 1 to fix anything that TEX did not like.
3 Run the file from the last step by your printer. You will need a special program to do this – a so-called printer *device driver* which can translate the TEX typesetting commands into a form familiar to your printer.
   –You may want to run the file from step 2 through a *previewer* program, which is like a device driver, except that it shows you your typeset document on the some sort of terminal screen.

> 1.   Prepare TEX source file.
> 2.   Run source through TEX.
> 2a.   Fix errors and bugs.
> 3.   Print document.
> 3a.   Preview document before printing.

Figure 4. The TEX life cycle.

It seems as if a bit more work is involved with TEX than, say, with WordStar. A complete TEX system involves several different programs working in concert.

TEX does involve extra work, and the reason for this lies in the very of essence of typesetting itself. There are truly an infinite number (at least!) of formats that people need for professionally typeset documents. Furthermore, decisions about where to place typeset elements on a page may depend on material that comes after it. (Proper line breaking of the first line of a paragraph may well depend upon all the words in the paragraph. In an extreme case, the last word of the paragraph may influence the setting of the first line!)

It is the contention of most hard-core users of TEX that no word processing program or desktop publishing program can typeset as well as TEX. Most word processing programs do not give you an infinite set of options from which to

\		begins a command
{	}	grouping symbols
	$	toggle in and out of math modes
^	_	super- and sub-script indicators
	&	tab
	%	begins non-printing comment
	#	place holder in alignment

Figure 5. T_EX special characters.

choose. Their menus and command structures are limited to a high number, to be sure, but a number which is still limited.

1.2   Commanding T_EX

T_EX works by digesting a file containing the text of your document together with commands that mean something to the T_EX program. T_EX's commands consist of descriptive words which more-or-less indicate their purpose. You might suppress the indentation of a paragraph, for example, by including something like

`\noindent   It was the best of times...`

at the beginning of the paragraph. The 'noindent' part of the command is pretty self-explanatory, and the backslash that precedes it tells T_EX that this is a command, and not part of the text. After all, you might someday want to typeset

`noindent It was the best of times...`

and T_EX needs some way to differentiate between the two cases. The backslash, then, is a reserved symbol to T_EX, as are a few other such special characters. The special command symbols were chosen because they are used infrequently, but if you do need any of them, there are commands to generate them.

Some commands, such as those controlling font changes, are to take effect over some portion of your document. We use curly braces '{' and '}' to delimit that portion. If we want to use giant type, we would specify

`It was the {\giant best} of times...`

to generate

It was the best of times...

in our document. I have previously told T_EX that `\giant` is to represent this large, bold-face type style.

The signal to T_EX to start a new paragraph is a blank line in your text file. Merely indenting your text will *not* do it (Figure 6).

T_EX's repertoire of commands is exceptionally rich. Commands exist to adjust the dimensions of the printed page, the size and style of type font, the addition of space, and much, much more. In addition to commands of

Input to TEX (right way)   ⟶   Output from TEX

```
      One one one one one one
one one one one one one one one
one one one one one one one one
one one one one one one one one
one one.
```
One one one one one one
one one one one one one one one
one one one one one one one one
one one one one one one one one
one one.

```
      Two two two two two two
two two two two two two two two
two two two two two two two two
two two two two two two two two
two two two two.
```
Two two two two two two
two two two two two two two two
two two two two two two two two
two two two two two two two two
two two two two.

Input to TEX (wrong way)   ⟶   Output from TEX

```
      One one one one one one
one one one one one one one one
one one one one one one one one
one one one one one one one one
one one.
      Two two two two two two
two two two two two two two two
two two two two two two two two
two two two two two two two two
two two two two.
```
One one one one one one
one one one one one one one one
one one one one one one one one
one one one one. Two two two two
two two two two two two two two
two two two two two two two two
two two two two two two two two
two two two two two two.

Figure 6. Blank lines on input signify a new paragraph to TEX.

a 'traditional' nature, TEX commands include many that are less traditional – commands that control iterations of a loop, if-then tests, and so forth. Of crucial importance is the fact that simpler TEX commands can be strung together to form new commands. We call these built-up commands *macros*. On one level, you might create your own \newchapter command by beginning a new page, skipping down a third of the page, suppressing indentation on the first line, and typesetting the first word of the text in small caps. But the real importance of macros is that you can define a command, and then redefine it for an entirely new effect *without* otherwise altering your document. An example follows.

I might typeset the theorem

Theorem. There is no royal road to typesetting. Typesetting is an inherently difficult and time consuming occupation.

via the command

```
\theorem  There is no...
```

An editor or layout designer could generate the output

> *Theorem.* **There is not royal road to typesetting. Typesetting is an inherently difficult and time consuming occupation.**

without changing my document file at all! What needs to be changed is my definition of the \theorem command, but that can be done in a separate, auxiliary file which contains the definitions of all my macros. Publishers, for example, can exploit this by shipping off the author's text files for traditional copy editing while the macro files are shipped to the layout designer who will implement the design scheme.

There is another advantage to TₑX's command structure. Since the command is independent of the text it is possible to change the text secure in the knowledge that we have not altered the typeset appearance of the document in any fundamental way. This is not always the case with other computer typesetting systems, which would require relaying out of the text after certain revisions. Using a macro written by Tom Rokicki, this paragraph has been set by

\droppedcap There is another ...

But if I want to revise this paragraph to begin *Another advantage of TₑX is...*, I may leave the command, revise the text, and run it through TₑX one more time. TₑX puts the dropped cap in place (this time an 'A'), and automatically wraps the text around it.

1.3   A working TₑX system

The only thing common to all TₑX systems is the TₑX program itself, although your TₑX and my TₑX may in fact differ to the extent that our programs have been compiled to run under different operating systems on different computers. It is likely that a TₑX version exists for your particular computer system, but if not, not to worry. TₑX is in the public domain, which means you can obtain a listing of the program (it was written originally in the high-level language, PASCAL, and has also been translated in to the C language), implement your own system peculiarities, compile it, and run it. Lots of wizards can advise you on the exact procedure.

You will also need a text editor to prepare your document file. TₑX does not really care which one you use, so long as your file contains only ASCII printable characters. This is no problem for almost any word processor or text editor.

Finally, you will need two programs to translate TₑX's output into the forms acceptable to your output devices. A *previewer* lets you examine your document on your monitor before you instruct your *printer driver* to run off a hard copy for you.

Of course, you will also need the appropriate computer and printing equipment. Do not forget them.

1. TEX
2. Text editor
3. Screen previewer
   Printer driver
4. Proper Hardware

Figure 7. The components of a working TEX system.

1.4   TEXnical matters

I hope I have piqued your interest in TEX. If so, your next question should be: 'How do I learn more about TEX?'

The TEX bible is *The TEXbook* (Knuth, 1986), whose author is also the author of TEX. Essentially everything to be known about TEX is in this volume.

Lamport (1986) describes a vast macro package called LATEX. Its author, Leslie Lamport, created hundreds of new TEX commands by chaining primitive TEX commands together in very clever ways. Many people feel that the LATEX commands are easier to use than raw TEX, but you pay a slight price in that your layout options are limited. It is important to remember that if you use LATEX you are still using TEX.

One of the best introductions to TEX itself is the Personal TEX manual (Spivak, 1985), a particularly lucid and articulate primer written by Michael Spivak. He has also written about a macro package, AMS-TEX, (Spivak, 1986) which is of particular interest to mathematicians.

With its headquarters in the United States, the TEX Users Group (TUG), provides a forum for communication between TEX users. This organization publishes a newsletter, TUGboat, in which members pass along news, new macros, and notification of meetings such as this. Its address is:

TEX Users Group,
P.O. Box 9506,
Providence,
Rhode Island 02940,
USA

Apart from its purely utilitarian virtues, TEX is a rich system. You may use it casually, or you can let it challenge and stretch you till you think you will surely break, but I suspect you will never settle for anything less again.

Bibliography

Donald E. Knuth, 1986, *The TEXbook*, Addison Wesley Publishing Company, Reading, Mass., 483pp.

Leslie Lamport, 1986, *The LATEX Document Preparation System*,   Addison Wesley Publishing Company, Reading, Mass., 242pp.

Michael Spivak, 1985, *PC TEX Manual*, Personal TEX, Inc., Mill Valley, CA.

Michael Spivak, 1986, *The Joy of TEX*, Addison Wesley Publishing Company, Reading, Mass., 290pp.

Alan Hoenig
John Jay College
City University of New York
New York City
USA

Chapter 2
T_EX and Good Design – are they Compatible?

Bill Noble & Rachel Ganz

This paper is a highly personal view of style filters. It describes the implementation of (and rationale behind) a style filter called VarTeX. VarTeX is an implementation of TeX intended to enforce design discipline on authors.

2.1   The background

In 1982, I was working for Inmos, a largeish company which produced a wide range of documents to support its memory and microprocessor products. I had just been given the job of turning the original text for these documents into typeset, printed and bound manuals. I wanted to ensure that all the documents produced by Inmos were in a recognisable house style, whether they were produced by a technical author, an electronics engineer or a managing director. To achieve this I engaged, at enormous expense to Inmos, a team of London graphic designers to produce an exciting and original style.

My first attempt at implementing this style was an education. Was it really necessary to mark up each page of raw text by hand, to indicate to the typesetter how the text should be laid out? Why could the typesetter not understand my simple, idiot proof instructions? Why did I have to spend so much of my time checking every letter, of every word, of every page, of every galley to ensure the typesetter had not modified the text. And was the typesetter trying to make a point when he inserted into the typeset galley a comment I had scrawled "Please don't typeset this comment...". The 100 page *Occam Programming Manual* took over a month to produce. I vowed this would be the last time I produced a manual this way.

It seemed odd that a technically advanced company like Inmos should produce its documentation this way. There had to be a better way of doing things. A way which would fully automate the typesetting process. There was!

I set about specifying what I wanted this, as yet unknown, system to do.

2.2   The design filter

My view of document production was (and still is) that a document should be written by an author, and then passed through a 'design filter' before being typeset and printed. The design filter ensures that no matter who writes a document it is laid out in the correct company style. The important point here is that the writing and layout of a manual are two separate tasks. It is only by taking the layout of a manual away from an author that it is possible to impose a uniform style. Also, it is not reasonable to expect every user of the system to know sufficient details of the page grid and typographic style to lay out each page correctly.

The design filter must be capable of automatically laying out the pages of a manual according to predefined rules. It should provide authors with a level of abstraction above the nitty-gritty of layout and type style considerations. To make sure that the design and company style remains pre-eminent, in spite of the many users of the package, means severely constraining an authors' ability to change layout and type style conventions.

To enable books to be automatically layed out involves defining various attributes of a book, which apply to all books. For example, many books have chapters. Therefore, one can reasonably talk about the idea of a chapter, without defining a particular chapter within a particular book. One can even talk about chapters in relation to books which do not appear to have any, by calling them one chapter books. Equally, one can talk about indented paragraphs without specifying the amount of indentation. These are the 'abstractions' of the book. By that I mean that they can be applied to books in general, without any need to know about the implementation.

The design filter therefore must provide a set of abstractions which can be associated with blocks of text to indicate the structure or 'function' intended.

2.3   The choice of system

I now had a list of requirements for the system I was looking for:

- it must provide a mechanism for defining abstractions;
- it must be able to cope with the wide range of documents that we would want to produce;
- it must be able to implement the exciting and unusual page layout we had spent so much money on;
- it must be able to produce typeset output without any re-keying of text;
- it must run on a VAX/VMS computer and drive non-graphics terminals.

There were very few systems which could satisfy all these requirements. Indeed the choice was quickly narrowed down to one. TEX also had the advantage that it was free.

2.4   VarTEX

TEX had the ability to do all the things I wanted. However, it was not simply a matter of mounting the system and running it. I still needed a macro package which would implement the abstractions. This macro package would be used by a wide variety of people (from secretary to managing director). So it had to be easy to use.

Inmos already had an in-house word processor package called 'Compose', running on a VAX/VMS computer, with which everyone was familiar. This was a simple `roff`-like system. I knew that people would object if I did not provide, in the new system, all the facilities which were currently in Compose. However, I wanted to ensure that all the documents produced on the system fitted into a recognisable house style. I wanted to keep a consistent, elegant company image, by forcing people to produce documents according to the correct style. This meant I could not implement a feature for feature look-a-like.

The requirements for the macro package were:

- simple logical commands;
- equal or greater facilities than the Compose package;
- the ability to layout documents according to a specific design style;
- the ability to force a consistent style on the many people who use the package;
- the ability to implement new abstractions easily.

The LaTeX macro package was investigated as a possible solution to these problems. Unfortunately, it was unable to satisfy two of the requirements, since there was no easy way of implementing the complicated page layout requirements of our expensive designer page style, and LaTeX gives too much flexibility to authors. The solution was to write a new macro package (currently called VarTeX) which would cope with the complexities of current (and hopefully future) page layouts.

2.5   Implementing abstractions

In keeping with my desire to implement a style filter I decided to write VarTeX so that the available macros represented abstractions rather than 'low level' TeX commands. In theory, this would enable authors to remain blissfully ignorant of the page layout, while at the same time having the ability to specify sufficient information for the document to be layed out correctly.

The first implementation of VarTeX was based around the Inmos style for reference manuals.

2.6   Ease of use

To make the macro interface as easy to use as possible, I used commands made up of concatenated English words, in a consistent style, rather than mnemonics. Thus, \begintable and \beginlist were paired off by \endtable and \endlist. Four categories of command were allowed:

- single letter commands such as '$' and '&';
- simple commands without parameters such as '\newpage';
- simple commands with parameters enclosed within curly brackets such as '\heading{This is a heading}';
- block command pairs such as '\beginindent{...} ... \endindent'.

2.7   Style packages

To be able to cope with different document styles it is necessary to wrap up the abstraction implementations in style packages. A style package defines the layout and typography for a particular document style. Style packages have been written for A4 reference manuals, A5 reference manuals, letters, invoices, brochures, flyers etc. Each package provides an appropriate implementation for every abstraction. This makes it possible to use the same text in a manual and in a press release. If an abstraction is not appropriate for a particular style (e.g., '\beginchapter' in a press release), a suitable conversion of the abstraction takes place (in this case converting the chapter name to a simple heading).

Of course there are some abstractions which are specific to one type of style package (for example a '\beginaddress' abstraction in a letter style package). This is unavoidable. The aim is to ensure that every style package will be able to cope with every abstraction (even if this means ignoring it entirely). To select a particular style, authors insert a '\documentstyle{...}' command at the top of the document. The document will then be laid out accordingly.

2.8   Example abstractions

The following are fairly typical of the abstractions provided by the current version of VarTEX. In the examples below the implementation described is for the A4 reference manual style designed for one of my clients, Meiko Ltd.

2.8.1   Headings

The '\chapter{...}' command implements the abstraction for the start of a new chapter. This does the following:

- forces the chapter to start on a new right hand page;
- outputs a blank left hand page with an enlarged company logo placed in the middle of the page, *if* the previous page was a right hand page ;
- creates a special chapter page, with the chapter number and chapter name in a large bold font;
- adds the chapter name and number to a table of contents file;
- makes the chapter name the running header for right hand pages;
- forces a page break.

2.8.2   Highlighted text

The '\warning{...}' command implements an abstraction for text which is to be highlighted as a warning. This has the following effects:

- starts a new paragraph;

- places a graphic warning symbol in the margin, ranged right, *if* illustrations are allowed – if illustrations are not allowed the word 'WARNING' is placed in the margin;
- sets the parameter to the command, the text of the warning, in a bold font;
- forces a paragraph break.

2.8.3   Imposing conventions

Abstractions are particularly useful for imposing conventions such as the appearance of a company name or logo. For example, the company name could be defined as '\company'. When the document is typeset, the '\company' command causes the company name to be set entirely in lower-case, in a fixed upper and lower-case format, or appear as a logo depending on the context. If the standard changes (or the company name changes) it is trivial to redefine the command.

2.8.4   Saving time

My favourite abstraction is the one used for defining functions, procedures, and commands. It is very powerful and very easy to use.

The '\begindefinition{...}{...}{...}...\enddefinition' abstraction takes three parameters:

- the name of the function or item;
- the parameters to the function (this can be left blank);
- a summary of the purpose of the function or item.

Every call to '\begindefinition' does the following:

- starts a new page;
- puts the function name in the footer of each page;
- puts the function name in the contents file;
- puts the function name in the index;
- puts the function name in a large bold font in the margin at the top of the page;
- makes the function summary a bold heading at the top of the page;
- creates a synopsis section. This consists of a 'Synopsis' heading in the margin and a combination of the function name and parameter list in the main body to define the parameters the function takes;
- forces the text following the '\begindefinition' command to start a new paragraph;
- adds the name, parameters, and summary to a command summary file which will later be formatted to produce a facts card.

To achieve all of this all the author needs to do is type:

```
\begindefinition {a}{b}{c}
Explanation
\enddefinition
```

It is likely that definitions will be handled differently in different style packages. Authors need only concern themselves with the 'function' of the text not the implementation.

2.9   The evolution of abstractions

Originally VarTEX had a minimal collection of abstractions. The aim was to provide as small and as simple a system as possible. However as needs arose it has been necessary to add to this collection. The current implementation of VarTEX has over 80 abstractions.

2.10   The problems

Having shown what you can do with VarTEX and what it is for, I would now like to talk about all the things that are wrong with it and why I would do it a different way next time.

2.10.1   Design faults

Firstly, the design faults. As I said earlier, I started from the position of providing all the facilities given by Compose. This included features like emboldening and italicising text. I had naively assumed there was a recognised policy on which font would be used where, and that the authors would stick to it. Of course it turned out that some people highlighted points in bold, whilst others used italic, and the whole system lost the consistency that had been intended. This was not a good start. Had I had any sense (or the hindsight I now have), I would have created an abstraction called 'highlight', or something similar, and encouraged people to use that instead.

2.10.2   Missing abstractions

A consistently recurring problem was what to do when an author requested a new abstraction. Although I attempted to keep the number of abstractions down to a minimum, there were always more in the minds of the authors, and, unsurprisingly, they did not appreciate being limited by a system that they knew could do more than was apparent at the front end.

An author, for example, might be dealing with an entirely new class of item, such as pull-down menus. They quite reasonably want a new abstraction which enables them to talk about menus. Now there are two possible ways of handling such requests:

- generate new abstractions on demand;
- insist that the author works within the current constraints of the system.

Given the resources I had available it was not possible to generate new abstractions on demand. At least not in a time scale that would satisfy everyone. Also my experience with implementing abstractions in a rush was that they were not properly thought out. It takes a good deal of thought to ensure that abstractions are implemented in a compatible and consistent style.

Quite often it was possible to create the effect the author wanted with the existing abstractions.

Unfortunately some authors could see another option. They knew that VarTeX was simply a macro package sitting on top of TeX. Badly disciplined authors, peeved at not being able to do precisely what they wanted, would write their own TeX macros. This of course destroyed to a large extent the raison d'etre of VarTeX. It is interesting that, when the Compose system was all that was available, authors were prepared to accept the limitations of the system. Unfortunately, TeX has this incredible range of possibilities, and no-one can bear to see them wasted. Anyone can borrrow the manual, write a macro, and feel elated at having created something themselves, rather than merely fitting in with the comparatively limited tools provided by VarTeX.

As soon as authors are able to design their own page layouts anarchy prevails, and it becomes impossible to maintain a consistent house style.

This brings me to the provocative title of this paper 'TeX and good design – are they compatible?'. It is my contention that any system which provides individual authors with complete control of page layout and typographic decisions, cannot possibly be compatible with the goals of good design.

2.11 Conclusion

Even if authors can be dissuaded from dabbling in TeX it is still not possible to create a style filter which imposes the correct style on all documents. A determined author can abuse the system by choosing an abstraction which is inapropriate for a given task.

Perhaps my next paper should be called 'Authors and good design – are they compatible'!

Abstractions and style packages are marvellous if used in a disciplined manner. They provide sophisticated facilities to ease the burden of writing documents whilst at the same time laying out documents automatically in an agreed and consistent manner. For authors who wish to do their own thing, abstractions and style packages are frustratingly constraining.

As a system implementer I have found no other system which comes close to TEX for the richness of its facilities. It provides me with nearly all the layout and typographic flexibility I need. What I need is a front end to TEX which stops authors from accessing this flexibility directly.

Bill Noble & Rachel Ganz
Vardas
88 North Road
St Andrews
Bristol BS6 5AJ
UK

Chapter 3
Whither TEX?
Why Has TEX Not Taken Over
the World . . . ?

Malcolm Clark & Cathy Booth

TEX is a high quality document preparation system that predates
the current interest in 'desktop publishing'. It is a highly flexible
typesetting package – a markup language – which has been implemented on a wide variety of systems, and which uses a range of
output devices, including typesetters, laser printers and dot matrix.

This paper charts some of the relevant aspects of the background and growth of TEX from mainframes to micros. It describes
the original motivations behind TEX, and the mixed blessings of its
public domain status in relation to its current standing in the 'desktop publishing' arena.

The elements of TEX have found favour with developers of
other text processing systems. Several such advantages are illustrated, together with some drawbacks, whether actual or merely
pre-supposed. Our intention is to draw an up-to-date picture of
TEX and its influences, and give an idea of its future directions
in a world populated with many tools for document preparation,
maintenance, formatting and mastering.

3.1   The world according to T_EX

T_EX was intended from the outset as a publishing tool. Not as a desktop publishing tool, since at the time (late 1970's) the desktop would have been rather large. T_EX began life on mainframe computers, and only as minis and micros have become more powerful has it been available on these smaller machines. It therefore comes from a batch processing background.

Like the other document preparation tools of this antiquity, troff and *Scribe*, T_EX is still mainly a batch-oriented tool. It is wise to remember that in many ways it may be regarded as a 'software tool'. Knuth designed it to aid his own writing of *The Art of Computer Programming*. Without *The Art of Computer Programming* there would be no T_EX. Knuth's well-known aim was to provide something with which to 'create masterpieces of the publishing art' (Knuth, 1979, 1986a).

One of the most remarkable aspects of T_EX's growth was its steadfast adherence to the public domain. It therefore has some affinities to Kermit, the file transfer protocol, and the editor Emacs. Knuth assigned the trademark 'T_EX' to the American Mathematical Society, but has consistently made public the contents of the program (Knuth, 1986b). It is probably the best-known large program (certainly one of the best documented – and very definitely the best documented public domain software). This means, of course, that all T_EX's algorithms are there for all to see, and use.

Having assigned it to the public domain, nobody is making much money out of T_EX itself. This is not to say that no-one is making any money. There is the world of difference between a program, and a program implemented on any given machine. The use of T_EX in the academic world has ensured that lots of work has been done for free – or at least, rather cheaply. There are also implementations of T_EX which are sold commercially. The cost covers the effort of porting and tuning the software to a particular operating system – and support.

3.2   The function of T_EX

As outlined above, the function of T_EX is to assist in the creation of master-pieces of the publishing art. Essentially this means books. Since the American Mathematical Society was early in its support of T_EX, realising that many mathematicians would relish direct creation of their own papers (and inciden-tally help to reduce the time and effort which the Society had to expend to typeset such papers), scientific papers have always been a key area. These two areas have similarities.

A book is expected to have a similar style throughout. One chapter will have much the same form and structure as the others. Of course the overall structure of the book may be similar to the structure of others in the same series. If a 'house-style' can be defined, then T_EX can help to maintain that style consistently. The fact that TEX is a markup language offers many advantages in traditional publishing. The similarity between articles in a journal and chapters in a book is close. The notions of consistent style are equally important. To a rather limited extent TEX also encourages consistency of notation (something about which mathematicians are often rather lax). Theses also fall into this general area, and of course TEX is well able to handle them. There is a difference though. Assuming that we are dealing mainly with the academic world, we can note that the authors of books and scholarly articles could probably expect secretarial help, while the authors of theses, being impecunious research students, probably have to type in the text of their theses themselves (or get their spouse to do it). This has helped to create a coterie of very clever TEXperts, who want to do rather complicated things (and with TEX too).

In the general scientific and technical area, TEX can have few peers. It is true that there are areas which TEX does not address directly: chemistry is not as straightforward as it ought to be, and of course this impinges directly on medicine, the life sciences and some areas in engineering. Some aspects of physics are poorly served too. The deficiencies turn out to be mainly shortcomings in the availability of particular symbols, not in TEX's capabilities to handle particular disciplines. Of course, the bulk of mathematics (and computer science too), is remarkably well served by TEX.

By chance or design, it turns out that TEX is also suitable for foreign (non-English) text. Diacriticals are provided very easily. It is a reflection of the supremacy of US software (like it or not!) that accents, and diacriticals in general, are very poorly served. In order to penetrate European markets, some manufacturers have paid lip service in this area, usually by replacing some symbols by others, which are supposed to represent national characteristics. There is seldom a 'general' solution. Since English (thankfully) does not employ accents, they were always badly provided. TEX goes a good half way. By separating the diacritical from the letter to be modified TEX permits any combination of diacritical and letter. Thus we can have ṃ, or ́k, and so on, besides the more usual combinations. TEX can also support other non-Latin based languages, such as Cyrillic, Japanese, Hebrew and Arabic.

So in TEX we have a reasonably extensive academic tool, suitable for many disciplines. Is this enough?

3.3   TEX in the world

The nearest thing to organisation in the TEX world comes from TUG, the TEX Users Group. This was originally nurtured under the wing of the AMS (the American Mathematical Society), but more recently has become sufficiently secure to stand on its own. Besides organising TEX courses at various levels, TUG organises an annual conference, and publishes a 2–3 times yearly newsletter. What proportion of TEX users subscribe to TUG? This is unknowable, but we would suggest that it is neither universal, nor even universally known. If your only contact with TEX is through The TEXbook, then you will only know about TUG through Appendix J, the last printed page in the book (after even the index). This very short account of TUG's activities does not make it clear just how useful joining the Group could be. The problem is even more acute for LATEX users. Lamport insists that individuals are themselves responsible for maintaining awareness of LATEX bugs and problems (although nowhere in the LATEX manual is TUG mentioned, really the only place you could reasonably expect to find such information). However, TUG only employs two or three full time staff. The point here is that with such a limited personnel (who in any case are there for the membership), there is little scope (or budget) for the type of marketing which we have come to associate with the desktop world.

Marketing of TEX does go on however. When this paper was originally prepared, in late 1987, the following was true: Addison Wesley were promoting TEX generally, in order to sell Knuth's books, as well as two implementations of TEX, MicroTEX for the IBM-pc, and *Textures* for the Apple Macintosh. Similarly, two German firms, Tools GmbH, and Kettler EDV-Consulting, were promoting their respective Atari ST implementations; FTL systems in Canada their Macintosh version, PC TEX of the US, its IBM-pc version; TextSet had a very wide catalogue of TEX products, and were advertising actively, and so on. This does have the effect of throwing choice at the prospective purchaser, choice he or she is often ill-able to handle. When trying to decide which 'publishing' package to select, it is little help to be offered several different implementations of ostensibly the same package. Since each has slightly different features (although the central core is identical), the prospective purchaser could end up feeling that none of them is ideal. Even more confusion is at hand. Of the half dozen or so firms mentioned above, only two have survived unscathed: Tools GmbH and Personal TEX Inc. Addison Wesley 'divested' its software interests – i.e. TEX. They continue to sell the books. It was not until autumn 1988 that MicroTEX found a new home (with ArborText). *Textures* was marketed by the company which had ported it to the Mac, Kellerman and Smith. Hardly had the dust settled when Kellerman and Smith parted company, to be replaced by Blue Sky Research (Barry Smith), and Northlake Software (David Kellerman). Both of these firms continue to deal in TEX products. FTL systems *seem* to have disappeared, but no-one is very sure; Kettler-EDV certainly has disappeared. TextSet, perhaps the longest surviving vendor of TEX software, changed its name to ArborText. None of these changes has damaged the underlying products, but they are confusing, both to prospective and existing purchasers of the commercial software. People do not feel confident when the software vendor disappears, either entirely, or to reappear under a new guise.

3.4 TEX and the new world of DTP

Desktop publishing covers a multitude of sins. To believe some of the advertising which has been prepared, it would seem that all you require is a simple micro and a dot matrix printer – and lo, you are a desktop publisher! Desktop publishing, or dtp, really stems from two origins: from enhanced word processors (which are themselves typewriter improvements); and from more powerful micros allowing traditional publishing to be accomplished from those micros. There are several publishing programs, like MagnaType and JustText which place the capabilities of typesetters within the framework of a micro. At the enhanced word processor end, automatic, continuous justification is normal, and has given rise to '*wysiwyg*' systems, where there is considerable correspondence between what can be seen on the screen, and what the final 'hard copy' will look like.

Desktop publishing is not new, and certainly existed before the Apple Macintosh. The Interleaf WPS system is still one of the most sophisticated and pleasurable *wysiwyg* publishing systems, and predates the Mac. But Apple marketed the concept. And it took them by surprise too. And eventually everyone else jumped on the band-wagon.

There is a real difference between a system targetted as an extension to a typewriter (although probably not called that any more), and one designed to manipulate type. Those chained to typewriters have always seen what they get, as they create it. Printers never have until a galley or proof is run off. The worlds are different, and the current fusion is not perfect.

This has been written as if mainframes no longer exist. They do, and shared software on a mainframe must account for a large proportion of the document preparation software around. It will take some time before mainframes accommodate *wysiwyg*, if they last that long. The mainframe manufacturers with some interest in office automation have moved in this direction, but rather inadequately. Take Digital for example. They recently unveiled 'VAX integrated publishing solutions': a three and a half pronged attack on 'corporate electronic publishing'. The first prong is DECpage, an enhancement to their existing WPS+ word processing software; the intermediate prong and a half are PageMaker on a Vaxmate, together with Interleaf IWPS running on a Vaxstation or micro-Vax; while the remaining leg of the stool was their old batch typesetting package DECset, now renamed Pager – hardly an inspiring approach, especially when the DDIF (Digital's Document Interchange Format) software to integrate the prongs has yet to appear. What makes this even more galling is the existence of several Vax VMS versions of TEX. In 1979, Gordon Bell, then Digital's Vice President of Engineering wrote 'At Digital, we hope to use TEX immediately.' Digital went on to produce the VMS version 4 manuals using TEX. They also use TEX as the formatting engine of 'VAX Document', a carefully concealed product. And more recently the mathematical part of TEX has surfaced in DecWrite. Why does TEX play such a small part in Digital's corporate strategy? What went wrong?

But is a *wysiwyg* program all that easy to use? We confess that Page-Maker seems bewilderingly fiddly – but this is as much a reflection of unfamiliarity with the contents of all the menus and the options available (and rather non-iconographic minds). In the hands of an adept remarkable results follow. In the hands of the merely mediocre, the end product is less exciting. Ventura too has some peculiarities. Since (in some versions of the package at least) kerning is manual, it turns out that a running headline which requires kerning, but has a different type face from the rest of the text, may be kerned incorrectly. Of course this is trivial, but it helps to point out an aspect of these packages. They are all fairly new, and had limited exposure before marketing.

3.5   Talk to me

Almost every publishing package is capable of importing files from word processors. The same is true of TEX. But two important distinctions arise. The first is that these convertors are usually add-ons. They are not part of TEX, and information on their availability is rather limited. Since they are add-ons, they tend to be available for given systems: this is not an extreme liability. Converting from Digital Runoff to TEX is something you would want to do on a Vax under VMS, not an IBM under CMS or DOS. There are few word processors which are available over a range of machines. Of course, once the text was in a form suitable for TEX, you could run it on any machine you wished. The second distinction is a reflection of TEX's markup nature. The embedded (implicit) control sequences in the word processor text are converted to explicit control sequences understood by TEX. Since word processors rarely understand the notion of macros, such features cannot readily be present in the converted text for TEX.

To take a specific example, MacTEX (an implementation of TEX running on the Apple Macintosh) has two convertors, one from Microsoft Word, and one from MacWrite. In this case, they are not add-ons, but are part of the overall Macintosh application. When the particular sequence which MacWrite uses to represent 'TEX' is encountered, it is turned into the sequence T\subscript{E}X. What this actually gives is TEX rather than TEX. Which is not what we wanted. Similarly, an itemised list is signified by preceding each item by

```
\nointerlineskip\null\vskip 2\li
\fulljustify \singlespace
```

Straight TEX would simply have said something like

```
\item{}
```

We have managed to throw away all of TEX's conciseness in order to achieve this supposed 'ease of entry'. The problem is of course deeper. Markup languages can be structural. They can help to guide and control the nature of the end product, without much consideration being given at the time of data entry to the form of the end product. *Wysiwyg* systems encourage continuous assessment of the form. For a short document, this may be fine: for a longer one, it is less attractive.

We would contend that there are two major problems with convertors. The first problem is that they are not comprehensive: they fail to emulate every feature of their parent. In other words, there are some things that a typewriter does which a typesetter does not, and certainly much that a typesetter can do beyond any word processor facilities. And secondly, convertors produce poor TEX. Why should this be an issue? It is an issue if you want to exploit the power of TEX in your document, and not go back to the word processed version. By starting from MacWrite or Microsoft Word, you are hamstrung, the possibilities are curtailed. But there is clearly a place for convertors. An office with hundreds of documents prepared with WordPerfect or whatever would probably not be pleased to have to rewrite them with TEX from scratch. On the other hand, whoever gets the task of polishing the converted text to working TEX will not be pleased with the inefficient use of TEX, and will find it awkward and unwieldy.

Such deficiences of convertors are not confined to the TEX world. Anyone who has tried importing a Microsoft Word file into Ventura using the convertor provided, will find a great deal to be desired in the final unenhanced output. Although a wide range of convertors are provided with Ventura to import files from various word processors, Ventura really works best if you use it from scratch, reading in plain, standard ASCII text files.

3.6 Using TEX is good for you

One of the major advantages of TEX is that it is complete. No new features are about to be added. Everything which is there, works. It is almost bug-free. There are one or two known bugs, but they are rather obscure and unlikely to cause any real problems. It is remarkably well tested. This final release of TEX has been available for some years, over a wide range of equipment, and has been exposed to the TEX-hacker as well as the TEX-user. It emerges unscathed from their ravages. It is solid.

It has been targeted for a vast range of devices – both computing engines and output devices. Perhaps no other piece of software is available so widely. In order to accommodate a wide variety of potential output devices, TEX generates a device independent (DVI) file: the device it is independent of is an output device such as a laser printer or typesetter. All this file contains is information on the placement of characters on the page. An 'output driver' then interrogates this dvi file to produce commands specific to a given printer – whether that printer is a matrix printer, a laser printer or a phototypesetter (or even a high resolution screen). Unlike TEX itself, these printer drivers are (with one or two notable exceptions) seldom public domain, and vary in capability and price, although pricing still tends to be cheap – another reflection of the public domain status of their parent. The tables indicate the major computer systems now running TeX, with associated output devices. The full range is even wider, but it is impossible to illustrate concisely. The aim here is to provide a 'flavour' of TeX's availability and range.

Since TeX is a published program, it is not surprising that its algorithms crop up elsewhere. What is most surprising is that they don't crop up everywhere. It is difficult to imagine anyone designing a dtp system who did not know about TeX, troff, *Scribe* and so on, but this does seem to happen (or perhaps they do take them into account and then ignore them, or worse still, fail to acknowledge them). But of the systems which do acknowledge TeX, we can mention the widespread use of the hyphenation algorithm (due to Liang; Knuth, 1986a), which is employed by Interleaf (Morris, 1985a) and JustText (Youngs, *pers. comm.*), and perhaps by SUSI (Daube, 1985). An advantage of this algorithm is the relative ease with which other languages can be accommodated (including European, with all those accents). Unlike a dictionary approach, the basic structure is easily transported (Désarménien, 1985; Appelt, 1985; Buckle, 1984).

Other elements of TeX that have found favour with developers of alternative document preparation systems include the 'box' structure – fundamental to TeX – which appears again in Interleaf (Morris, 1985a) and in Edimath (Quint, 1984). In the world of page description languages, Impress, Imagen's page description language, was heavily influenced by TeX's page model (Morris, 1985b).

TeX is also used in conjunction with SGML (ISO, 1986), to provide the formatter, and also specialised mathematical setting (Smith, 1987; Lee van Huu, 1985).

That TeX has failed to penetrate the majority of dtp packages is evident from the cumbersome way such packages tend to handle kerning. Again this reflects the distinction between the 'typewriter enhancement' class of package (where kerning is an unknown quantity), and a typesetting tool (where it would be expected).

3.7   Talking TeX's language

One of TeX's mixed blessings are its macros. To be honest TeX is really a programming language for typesetting, and it contains many of the attributes of a 'normal' programming language (scoping rules, local and global variables, loops, conditionals and branching, procedures, recursion) – you can even do calculation in TeX.

There are hundreds of TeX commands, to control aspects of formatting ranging from simple paragraph indentation to complex tabular layouts. Most TeX commands are in fact 'built up' from combinations of other TeX commands – such combinations are called macros. TeX supplies many pre-defined macros as standard. Essentially the aim of a macro definition is to simplify

	MULTI-USER SYSTEMS									
	Amdahl	CDC	DG	DEC	HP	IBM	Prime	Symb	UNIX	VAX
PREVIEWERS										
Video Display			•		•					•
LASER PRINTERS										
Agfa P400						•			•	•
Canon				•	•				•	•
DEC LN01									•	•
HP LaserJet Plus				•	•				•	•
IBM 38/4250, Sherpa						•				
Imagen	•		•	•	•	•		•	•	•
Océ 6750										•
PostScript devices				•	•	•	•	•	•	•
QMS Lasergrafix	•	•	•		•	•	•		•	•
Symbolics				•					•	•
Talaris						•			•	•
Xerox Dover				•					•	
Xerox 2700II		•		•		•			•	
Xerox 3700/4045				•					•	
Xerox 9700	•					•			•	•
TYPESETTERS										
Lasercomp						•			•	
Linotype CRT										•
Linotype 100,300	•				•				•	•
Linotype 202										•
Alphatype CRS				•						
Autologic	•			•		•			•	•
Compugraphic 8400										•
Compugraphic 8600		•				•				•
Harris 7500									•	
Hell Digiset						•				

Table 1. Multi-user mainframe systems running TEX, and supported output devices (excluding dot matrix printers and certain other low resolution hardcopy devices). Source: Hosek (1988), and additions.

the use of TEX, such that the user does not have to keep resorting to fundamentals. Do-it-yourself macros can be built up by users to help tailor the use of TEX to their individual requirements. They can ease the creation of

	MICROS/WORKSTATIONS									
	Amiga	Apollo	Mac	Atari	HP	IBMpc	IntSol	Sun	Texas	VAX
PREVIEWERS										
Video Display	•	•	•	•	•	•	•	•	•	•
LASER PRINTERS										
Canon				•		•	•	•		
Cordata						•				
HP LaserJet Plus	•	•		•	•	•	•	•	•	•
Imagen		•	•			•	•	•		
Kyocera				•		•				
PostScript devices	•	•	•		•	•	•	•	•	•
QMS Lasergrafix		•				•		•		
Talaris						•		•		
Xerox 9700	•							•		•
TYPESETTERS										
Linotype 100,300		•	•			•		•		
Linotype 202						•				
Autologic	•				•	•				•
Compugraphic 8400					•	•				
Compugraphic 8600						•				

Table 2. Single-user and workstations running TEX, and supported output devices (excluding dot matrix printers and certain other low resolution hardcopy devices). Source: Hosek (1988), and additions.

an index or a bibliography, or build a table of contents as well as other more elaborate tasks. Macros can be used to add structure, or impose consistent style to a series of documents.

TEX's capabilities mean that it is possible to build convenient 'macro packages'. These can sit on top, or alongside, TEX itself, and are generally 'tailored' to specific types of application. LaTEX (Lamport, 1985) and AMS-TEX (Spivak, 1986) are well known. LaTEX typifies the 'on top' approach, tackling document structuring for the mainly non-technical user.

Just as AMS-TEX was written to simplify and extend document preparation for the American Mathematical Society, INRSTEX (Ferguson, 1986) is an extension to the basic TEX style, while P$_{s}$izzl was written at Stanford Linear Accelerator Center for physicists (Ogawa, 1985). Ray Cowan's TABLES.TEX (Cowan, 1985) was written to make table construction more straightforward, while more recently, Michael Spivak's 'T2D4' (Spivak, 1987) addresses a much wider range of tabular formats. There are many other macro packages around, and if we extend this to cover LaTeX 'style-files' – instructions to emulate particular document requirements, from a journal's instructions to authors, through to a particular institution's thesis requirements – the scope is even wider. But amongst this rosy picture, a word of warning, not unrelated to TEX's public domain status.

Excluding LaTeX and AMS-TEX, the novice user about to tackle a document may not have heard about the macros available. Most of the macro packages were written at particular institutions, and only slowly percolate to the outside world. It is only through the good nature and cooperation of their originators that they escape at all. Many TEXies are too modest, or if they are not, they are unwilling to spend the time and effort to document their creations to the extent that they could be used by novices. It is probably easier to write software (TEX macros included) than to document it adequately. Even LaTeX suffers here – additional LaTeX style files are widely available, but over electronic networks. This is not without its problems: again the novices are handicapped, particularly if they cannot fall back on computing expertise available within a large institution. For those using TEX from a micro, or commercial users, these style files may as well not exist. Some effort is now being made towards providing these files on floppy disk – but first the user must know that they exist.

TEX users at large institutions such as universities have access, directly or indirectly, to various sources of TEX information. But what about the situation down among the micro users? They are on their own, with no friendly local TEX advisor. Reviewing the manuals which accompany PC TEX (Spivak, 1985), *Textures* (Kellerman and Smith, 1987) and MacTEX (FTL systems inc., 1987), not one mention is given to TUG. Spivak (1986) mentions TUG on page 5, and also devotes an appendix to it, but no reference at all appears in the LaTeX manual (Lamport, 1985).

TEX was designed for technical text, and it is difficult to look at any other system which purports to handle maths (in particular) without seeing their flaws. Systems like VuWriter, T^3, Expression, MacAuthor (Laser Author in the US) or MacΣqn do not produce output of the quality of TEX. Even when they can be coerced into giving something reasonable, editing is a nightmare. Again, we are talking in part about the distinction to be made between *wysiwyg* (with hidden control sequences) and markup. But we are also talking about the difference between a system which is geometric and one which is structural. *Wysiwyg* equation handlers place 'that squiggly thing there' over 'this squiggly thing here'; TEX places a gamma over an epsilon. Many exceptionally able technical typists work by pattern matching: essentially they do not know what it is they are doing, but they usually get things in the right place. But since TEX 'knows about' equations, it also knows about spacing. It can distinguish between + used as a dyadic and monadic operator, for example. These things are built in, so that even a novice can produce very attractive equations.

Is it difficult to use T_EX for equations? Yes and no. If you have a smattering of mathematics, no; if you don't, then yes (maybe). Essentially T_EX linearises mathematics. If you imagine yourself talking to someone, without benefit of pencil and paper (or blackboard and chalk), and trying to verbalise an equation, then what you and T_EX would do are fundamentally the same. This is sufficiently true that T_EX has been used as the vehicle by which mathematics has been taught to blind students. The structure is sufficiently clear and unambiguous. Perhaps the biggest difficulty lies in the way that T_EX is approached. Often it is used when all else has failed: in other words, when we are trying to do something which *is* very tricksy. It should come as no surprise that doing difficult things is often not easy. Jumping into T_EX (or any other software) without bothering to learn any of its basics is asking for trouble.

The need to provide equations for *wysiwyg* users has been combined with the excellence of T_EX, and has led to some interesting developments. There are several vendors now offering '*wysiwyg* equation to T_EX' programs – among them ArborText, with Publisher (ArborText, 1986), Te Co Graf, with easyT_EX (Crisanti, Formigoni and La Bruna, 1986), Cooke Publications, who provide MW2TeX to convert their MathWriter to T_EX, and Icon Technology's Formulator.

3.8 A price to pay

T_EX's versatility comes packaged with the inevitable drawback or two. In order to achieve its standardisation, T_EX standardised its fonts. Instead of adopting whichever fonts were available on the output device, a common family, Computer Modern (CM) was created. T_EX works best with Computer Modern. Not all output devices support Computer Modern, and few, if any, other packages use it. The CM family is large – it encompasses serif and sans serif faces, as well as maths symbols and a few 'fancy' fonts. Naturally it has attracted criticism. After all, it was not introduced in the 16th century by a master typographer, as all the best fonts were.

You can also use the fonts available at the output device, although this does rather defeat the objective of the metafile (or DVI file) which T_EX produces. Nevertheless, it does mean that T_EX can be directed to machines as diverse as the Compugraphic 8600 and Autologic APS–5 typesetters, as the earlier table shows (whether with the CM or 'native' fonts is another matter). Although the DVI file is described as device independent, it is not font independent.

Many implementations of T_EX (particularly on mainframes) come with a wide range of T_EX's own fonts (and sizes), but for others there may be something of a distribution problem. Micro versions tend to have a 'cut down' range, although additions to the fonts are starting to be made available.

Despite the availability of T_EX on many devices, screen preview is poorly supported. Really only a few implementations can be said to have adequate preview – chiefly the micro versions. It is rare on mainframe implementations. People who have never had preview often feel they can live without it. Those who have seen it once know better.

The lack of preview with TEX has prompted some interesting developments, as cited earlier in relation to *wysiwyg* equation handling. In addition, attempts to combine TEX with some form of instantaneous output are in progress: ArborText's Publisher is altogether the most sophisticated of these, giving interactive page-by-page processing. There have been consistent rumours of 'incremental TEX' for some time: essentially this seems to be an incremental TEX compiler. Put another way, TEX output is created as text is input. TEX's line breaking, hyphenation, and page breaking would be continuously updated. Given sufficient processing power, this seems attainable, although the 'ripple-back' might be disconcerting (Morris, 1985a). To some extent the VORTEX project (Chen *et al.*, 1987), which targets a version of TEX for the Sun seems to be aiming for this objective. Maths would still be a little tricky, since it tends to occur in discrete chunks which do not make sense outside their context, although Agostini *et al.* (1985), Appelt (1986) and Quint, Vatton and Bedor (1986) also discuss 'interactive' approaches to equation creation through TEX.

At first glance, graphics are poorly served with TEX. Especially when compared to conventional dtp packages which take it as axiomatic that you will wish to incorporate graphics. Nevertheless, the hooks are there. If there had been a common graphics standard when TEX was developed (one common across many output devices), it is likely that graphics handling would have been much better. But almost every TEX laser printer driver has a way in which graphics can be included, whether from QUIC, PCL, Impress or POST-SCRIPT. And work is progressing to translate the dumber page description languages into the smarter ones, like POSTSCRIPT.

Despite TEX's uncomfortable handling of graphics, it is actually closer to generality than any other system. But there is extensive variation in the way in which individual device drivers handle POSTSCRIPT (say), and the opportunities they provide. This is likely to be organised better in the future, since it is currently an area of active debate among the users and writers of device drivers.

Mention must be made of TEX's error handling. TEX does have an integral help system, which illuminates the problem in many instances, often with a dash of humour. It is comforting to be told 'Such booboos are generally harmless, I should carry on if I were you'. But other errors may throw up 'help' messages bearing no apparent relation to the fault – they obscure rather than clarify. This is partly due to TEX's approach to processing – as a compiler of text. The cause of an error can pass unnoticed, only to create confusion later. The misleading 'TeX capacity exceeded, sorry' is a case in point – most frequently this merely means a forgotten closing brace to an earlier command. In time one gets used to these idiosyncracies, but they are daunting for the novice user.

3.9   How the world sees TEX

No software, however thorough in concept and painstaking in execution, will be without flaws, real as well as imagined. The nature of TEX's fonts, and vagaries in the provision of screen preview and graphics, may pose some difficulties, and error messages may be entertaining, if not always informative. There are other *perceived* problems however, which should be distinguished and addressed. The following quotes may help to illustrate them:

> 'notoriously difficult to learn. To get the best out of them [JustText and *Textures*] takes many hours of thumbing through manuals and simply testing programs to see if they produce what you want.'
> 'unfriendly product'
> Computer News, July 23rd, 1987.

> 'although programs like troff or TEX might look very appealing, people still have to go through a very cumbersome learning process.'
> Kircz, 1985.

> '...a very difficult typesetting language to learn.'
> O'Connell and McCartney, 1984.

> 'If you delight in constructing IBM or ICL Job Control macro commands, then probably TEX is the typesetting program for you...
> 'TEX and Lasercheck have some good features in this area [mathematical typesetting], but they are not ideal.'
> Browning, 1984.

> '...learning to use TEX requires hard work.'
> '...software that in itself is not that easy to use.'
> Johnson, 1985.

But let us try to put some kind of context here. Is there an easy typesetting language to learn? If there is, we don't yet know about it. For this is what TEX is, a typesetting language.

In a recent MacUser, Gregory Wasson (1987) discusses 'professional' desktop publishing, based on his use of JustText, and suggests, among other things, that anyone planning to take this path should 'learn the rudimentary facts and conventions of proofreading marks and typesetting terms', and notes that 'typesetting is an art and a tradition', warning the unwary to ignore this at their peril. In a similar vein, McCague (1984), considers that 'the interpretation of the Author's original manuscript should be left to the professional (I have no objection to the Author carrying out this task, but he or she must be *professional* as a Typesetter)'; Johnson (1983) suggests that 'Printing a book of the "finest quality" is a very difficult task. It demands attention to many interacting details. This type of problem is certainly beyond the capability of most computer software.'

Reluctantly we must also discuss *The TEXbook* (Knuth, 1986a). Reluctantly, since we believe that it is the root of much of the resistance to TEX. Reluctantly because any criticism of *The TEXbook* is usually seen as a criticism of Don Knuth. For Computer Scientists, for mathematicians, for physicists, *The TEXbook* poses no problem. Johnson (1983), in his review of *The TEXbook* says, 'I wish every piece of software came with a manual as good as this.' It is a well written book; it is exciting; it almost has a plot – as an introduction to TEX, for the occasional user, for the person who does not see document preparation as a form of 'Dungeons and Dragons', it *is* a problem. Some vendors have recognised this. PC TEX do not supply *The TEXbook* with their software, instead issuing a '*PC TEX Manual*' written by Michael Spivak. With the exception of a short '*First Grade TEX*' (Samuel, 1983), there is no other introductory TEX material available (we are excluding the manuals by Lamport and Spivak here, since strictly they do not discuss TEX, but an add-on).

3.10 Conclusion

We began this paper as an exercise to explain to ourselves the strengths and deficiencies of TEX, especially in the face of so many apparently successful dtp packages. Our basic fear was that TEX was losing the battle. Our conclusion now would be that while TEX is not perfect, it is very healthy, and is successful in the areas which it set out to address. It never was intended as a 'corporate electronic publishing' tool, or for 'in-plant' publishing. It is indeed intended for publishing – an inherently non-trivial and potentially tricky area – and in that context it can survive. The growing number of books published using TEX attests to that. In its handling of graphics we feel it offers the potential for greater standardisation than any other package; if we must point to deficiencies, it must be to the limitations of screen preview, narrowly for TEX itself, but more generally for page description languages as a whole.

Availability must be one of the key phrases in any discussion of TEX. Where else is there such widespread availability? Availability both of systems running the software, and output devices which can be supported. If we must make an analogy, it might be to compare TEX to mediæval Latin, as a *lingua franca* – universally understood, but not necessarily understood by everyone.

The documentation problem will improve. Several books, addressing different levels and aspects of TEX, are known to be in preparation and should at least broaden the choice for potential TEX users. The distribution and dissemination of macros, fonts and general information is improving. Besides the TEX Users Group, with its newsletter and annual conference, there are other forms of contact, like *email* distributions in the USA and the UK (at least), relatively informal publications, like *TEXline* and the electronic magazine, TEXMAG, local users groups (e.g., in France, the Netherlands, Scandinavia Germany and Japan) and an almost annual European conference. Nevertheless we suspect that this 'visible' TEX is only a small proportion of 'used' TEX, and that there are far more people out there getting on with the job of typesetting books, theses and papers (amongst other things), than there are worrying about its future.

In the longer term however, we consider that TEX may harbour the seeds of its own destruction. Since its algorithms are completely open to all, we believe they may become absorbed into other software, until at some point all its capabilities are contained within these other software packages, together with other software and hardware advances which will have occurred. This is not a bad thing. Far better that it survives within (even) *wysiwyg* software of the future, improving it, than it is abandoned and forgotten. Of course, until the power of micros supercedes mainframe capabilities, TEX will still admirably serve its purpose on such multi-user machines – continuing the link with its origins.

Bibliography

M. Agostini, V. Matano, M. Schaerf & M. Vascotto, 1985, *An interactive user-friendly TEX in the VM/CMS environment*, pp.121–136, *in* D. Lucarella, *ed.*, TEX for Scientific Documentation, Addison Wesley.

Wolfgang Appelt, 1985, *The hyphenation of non-English words with TEX*, pp.65–70, *in* D. Lucarella, *ed.*, TEX for Scientific Documentation, Addison Wesley.

Wolfgang Appelt, 1986, *Running TEX in an interactive text processing environment*, pp.1–8, *in* J. Désarménien, *ed.*, TEX for Scientific Documentation, Springer-Verlag.

ArborText, 1987, *User Manual: The Publisher*, unnumbered.

G. K. S. Browning, 1984, *Automatic typesetting*, University Computing, pp.95–98.

N. Buckle, 1984, *Word hyphenation in French*, pp.108–113, *in* J. J. H. Miller, *ed.*, PROTEXT I, Boole Press, Dublin.

Ray F. Cowan, 1985, *Making tables with macros*, unpublished, 5pp.

P. Chen, J. Coker, M. A. Harrison, J. W. McCarrell & S. Procter, 1987, *The VORTEX document preparation environment*, pp.45–54, *in* J. Désarménien, *ed.*, TEX for Scientific Documentation, Springer-Verlag.

E. Crisanti, A. Formigoni & P. La Bruna, 1986, *EasyTEX, Towards interactive input for scientific documents input with TEX*, pp.55–64, *in* J. Désarménien, *ed.*, TEX for Scientific Documentation, Springer-Verlag.

Klaus Daube, 1985, *SUSI – Just another text formatter?* pp.17–28, *in* J. J. H. Miller, *ed.*, PROTEXT II, Boole Press, Dublin.

Jacques Désarménien, 1985, *The use of TEX in French: hyphenation and typography*, pp.45–64, *in* D. Lucarella, *ed.*, TEX for Scientific Documentation, Addison Wesley.

Michael Ferguson, 1986, *INRSTEX: a document preparation system for multiple languages*, pp74–88, *in* J. Désarménien, *ed.*, TEX for Scientific Documentation, Springer-Verlag.

FTL systems inc., 1987, *The MacTEX user's guide*, 157pp.

Don Hosek, 1988, *TEX Output Devices*, TUGBOAT, vol.9(1), pp.25–33.

ISO, 1986, *Information Processing – Text and office systems – Standard Generalized Markup Language (SGML)*, ISO/DIS 8879.

Guy Johnson, 1985, *(book review) The TEXbook*, IEEE Software, vol.2(2), pp.108–109.

David Kellerman & Barry Smith, 1987, *A User's guide to Textures*, 113pp.

Joost Kircz, 1985, *Will physics publishing survive the electronic challenge?* pp.22–22, *in* J. J. H. Miller, *ed.*, PROTEXT II, Boole Press, Dublin.

Donald E. Knuth, 1979, *TEX and METAFONT, New Directions in Typesetting*, American Mathematical Society and Digital Press:
Part 1, *Mathematical Typography*, 45pp;
Part 2, *TEX, a system for technical text*, 201pp;
Part 3, *METAFONT*, 105 pp.

Donald E. Knuth, 1986a, *The TEXbook*, Addison Wesley Publishing Company, Reading, Mass., 483pp.

Donald E. Knuth, 1986b, *TEX the program*, Addison Wesley Publishing Company, Reading, Mass., 484pp.

Leslie Lamport, 1985, *The LATEX Document Preparation System*, Addison Wesley Publishing Company, Reading, Mass., 175pp.

Lee van Huu, 1985, *SGML: A standard language for text description*, pp.198–212, *in* J. Désarménien, *ed.*, TEX for Scientific Documentation, Springer-Verlag.

Séamus McCague, 1984, *Phototypesetting – an art*, pp.34–54, *in* J. J. H. Miller, *ed.*, PROTEXT I, Boole Press, Dublin.

Robert A. Morris, 1985a, *Is what you see enough to get? A description of the Interleaf publishing system*, pp.55–81. *in* J. J. H. Miller, *ed.*, An introduction to text processing systems, Boole Press, Dublin.

Robert A. Morris, 1985b, *Page description languages*, pp.67–85, *in* J. J. H. Miller, *ed.*, An introduction to text processing systems, Boole Press, Dublin.

Art Ogawa, 1985, *Pizzj user's guide: how to create documents using TEX with the aid of a high level language*, Stanford Linear Accelerator Center, SLAC-REP-268, 186pp.

John A. O'Connell & W. G. McCartney, 1984, *Text processing – a shared resource*, pp.203–206, *in* J. J. H. Miller, *ed.*, PROTEXT I, Boole Press, Dublin.

Vincent Quint, 1984, *Interactive editing of mathematics*, pp.55–68, *in* J. J. H. Miller, *ed.*, PROTEXT I, Boole Press, Dublin.

Sebastian P. Q. Rahtz, 1987, *The processing of words*, pp.69–89; *in* Rahtz, *ed.*, Information Technology in the Humanities, Ellis Horwood, Chichester.

Vincent Quint, Irène Vatton & Hassan Bedor, 1986, *GRIF: An interactive environment for TEX*, pp.145–158, *in* J. Désarménien, *ed.*, TEX for Scientific Documentation, Springer-Verlag.

Arthur Samuel, 1983, *First grade TEX, a beginner's TEX manual*, 34pp.

Craig Smith, 1987, *DAPHNE – an implementation based on the Standard Generalized Markup Language (SGML)*, SGML User's Group Bulletin, vol.1(2), pp.75–82.

Michael Spivak, 1985, *PC TEX Manual*, Personal TEX, Inc., Mill Valley, CA.

Michael D. Spivak, 1986, *The Joy of TEX*, Addison Wesley Publishing, 290pp.

Michael D. Spivak, 1987, *T2D4, Tables to die for*, 81pp.

Gregory Wasson, 1987, *Typecasting*, MacUser (US), vol.3(7) supp., pp.18–22.

Malcolm Clark
Imperial Cancer Research Fund
Research Computer Unit
PO Box 123, 44 Lincoln's Inn Fields
London WC2A 3PX
UK

Cathy Booth
University of Exeter Computer Unit
North Park Road
Exeter EX4 4QE
UK

Chapter 4
TeX Device Drivers Today

Lance Carnes & William S Kaster

We discuss the state of TeX device drivers today, focusing on the capabilities that are available in Personal TeX, Inc.'s range of products. Opinions regarding new features to be added will be entertained, as well as opinions regarding old features that are unusable and should be modified or deleted.

Emphasis will be placed on TeX screen previewers, towards determining an absolute minimal set of core features.

Lance Carnes & William S Kaster
Personal TeX Inc
12 Madrona Street
Mill Valley
CA 94941
USA

Chapter 5
Quality Printing of TEX DVI Files

Jan van Knippenberg

Océ has developed a laser printer, the Océ 6750, based on the wellknown and proven engine of the 1900 copier family. The laser printer has a resolution of 508 dpi (20 dots/mm). The printspeed is 23 pages per minute.

The heavy duty engine guarantees a target load of 150,000 pages per month. Paper input and output are as usual for the Océ copiers. Input is via two trays $(1600 + 600)$ and output is to 20 selectable bins of 100 sheets each.

ODA is the first Open Systems standard to provide an information architecture. ODA is a framework for products which communicate and interwork using OSI standards like X-400 electronic mail standards. The Océ 6750 is an ODA-printer.

Océ has developed software to connect the Océ 6750 laser printer to a wide range of VAX/VMS computers. The TEX DVI output files are converted to the ECMA/ODA protocol of the Océ 6750 printer. The software furthermore contains a print symbiont. The symbiont controls the printer controller and the conversion program. Also available are a series of font tools for generating TEX pxl and tfm files with the METAFONT package and converting TEX pxl files into the format for the Océ 6750 laser printer.

5.1 Introduction

Developed and manufactured by Océ in The Netherlands, the Océ 6750 laser printer is a medium volume, high resolution A-4 document printing system with wide operational flexibility. It is based on Océ's electro photographic process whose proven technology has been implemented and further complemented with solid state laser techniques. The 6750 includes high reliability features such as a fault-free belt transport and an extremely short paper path and offers an exceptionally high print-quality that can easily be compared with that of printed matter.

The 6750 is a productive printer, offering a print speed of 23 pages per minute with volume printing of up to 150,000 prints per month. The two separate paper-input compartments contain a comfortable 2,200 sheets. High resolution of 508 dots per inch gives sharply defined characters and graphics with high edge acuity. Because of the one-component dry toner and the method of image transfer, the print quality is consistently high, giving clean prints with excellent contrast form the first to the last print. A 20-bin sorter has a capacity of 2,000 (20×100) sheets and features an addressing mode which offers additional convenience of personalized printing.

The Océ 6750 laser print allows unattended and fault-free operation.

Océ has developed modular software that can run on any VMS-based VAX or MicroVAX system. It offers a number of unique opportunities to the community of DEC/VMS users. There are two major software modules.

5.1.1 Scientific publishing

Because of the high resolution and offset print quality, the Océ 6750 is well suited for the printing of scientific and technical documents that would normally require (photo) typesetting. TEX, a trademark of the American Mathematical Society, is a popular and public domain typesetting software package, especially designed and developed for complex scientific and technical documents. TEX supports the use of a virtually unlimited number of fonts and character sets. It generates output data that is DeVice Independent (DVI) formatted. Océ has developed software that is able to convert these DVI-formatted files to be printed on the Océ 6750 laser printer. Any DVI-formatted file can thus be printed on the 6750. As a result, Océ offers the best of two worlds.

To facilitate the variety of paper-in and paper-out handling, the software includes a user interface based on standard DCL-commands.

TEX applications are typically technical reports, scientific documents, mathematical papers, theses, book typesetting and manuals. TEX is largely used in scientific typesetting environments.

5.1.2 Electronic forms overlay

The combination of offset print quality, print speed and volume load of the 6750 allows for mass production oriented, on-demand printing, making stock and storage, as well as separate copy runs in many cases redundant. Moreover, the 6750 also fits in Data Processing environments because of its reliable printing performance, unattended operation and cost effective production. Essential elements in mass forms printing jobs like invoicing and direct mailing.

For this type of applications, Océ has developed a software package called 'Forms Overlay Language'. FOL is a simple, yet powerful tool to design and create electronic forms, use forms, control 6750 paper handling facilities and augment documents with typographic components. FOL easily allows forthe merging of electronic forms with variable data, typographic fonts, company logo's and halftones. FOL can be used for printing almost any data that has been generated in a VAX/VMS environment.

The 6750 offers swift and quiet operation and can therefore be installed in any office environment without creating disturbance. Extensive and automated sorting capabilities (personal, setwise, sortwise, interrupt, confidential) overcome time consuming print queues and avoid messing up documents from different originators.

5.2 DEC-Océ 6750

The interface of the Océ 6750 laser printer is based on the ODA (Office Document Architecture), a standard defined by ECMA, the European Computer Manufacturers Association, to interchange complex (data, text, graphics and images) documents between dissimilar computer systems and printers.

Océ offers interfacces for Q-bus, Uni-bus and Bl-bus. VMS 4.4 and upwards is supported on any (Micro) VAX. The Océ 6750 is capable of emulating DEC's LN03 Plus and most lineprinters.

Jan van Knippenberg
Océ-Nederland BV
St Urbansweg 43
PO Box 101
5900 MA Venlo
The Netherlands

Chapter 6
High Quality DVI Drivers

Klaus Guntermann & Joachim Schrod

Document preparation with TeX is done in two steps – first TeX formats the document, afterwards a DVI driver creates the final output. While TeX is reliable and produces the same results in each implementation, DVI drivers remain the critical part of the document preparation process. To specify a high-quality DVI driver the circumstances of its usage must be analysed. We identify four groups of persons concerned with the handling of a driver: users, (TeX) system administrators, distributors, and developers/maintainers.

The demands on a DVI driver are mainly high reliability (the device must remain in a consistent state), a uniform user interface (previews and printer drivers should behave similarly), and a standardized treatment of extensions (e.g., handling of graphics inclusion). Other matters of interest are available features, accuracy of output, throughput, font handling, portability, and maintainability. This analysis yields in criteria for the judgement of a DVI driver's quality – furthermore these criteria constitute a contribution to the standardization process.

6.1 Introduction

We will not discuss the latest high resolution output devices and the drivers
that can be used to make them print the most beautiful documents. Instead
we will stress drivers for any output device and describe their usage and
features, to see whether they can be considered high quality. This will not
lead to 'the ideal driver', but result in better drivers that become as reliable
as TEX is.

Of course the requirements for a driver are different for all the people
who come in touch with it. We will start with an investigation of the life of
a driver, then we will go into details of user interfaces, output creation, and
implementation issues. Finally we will propose standards for extensions via
the \special command.

6.2 Who is involved?

To identify the groups of persons who get in contact with a driver we look
at the 'life' of a driver. It must be taken into account that these groups are
distinguished by the functionality they have during the driver's life, not by
the identity of subjects. Of course, this covers the widespread situation that
the persons who implement a driver write the user manuals, too, and are
therefore also users of the driver. As with every software product the life of
a driver is not a straightforward sequence of actions. Nevertheless stages can
be characterized with the model of the *software life cycle* (Peters and Trip,
1978).

- The driver must be documented, implemented, and tested, afterwards
  (or in parallel) a user manual must be written. We call this phase the
  development and documentation phase and the persons concerned the
  developers.
- Then the driver must be sent to its user by a *distributor.* There is
  neither a big difference whether this distributor is a commercial one or
  not, nor is there a big difference what kind of media is used for the
  distribution – the principal work of sharing all files that resembles a
  driver is the same. In this context we want to call your attention to the
  assumption that the driver is distributed as a system ready to use, i.e.
  in executable form including a set of fonts, without any sources. If the
  sources shall also be distributed, arrangements must be made for the
  automatic creation of a consistent, running system.
- The next step is the receipt of the driver by those who want to use it.
  This driver must now be installed; if the user is a single person this will
  be done by himself. But in many cases a (TEX) system administrator
  will have to do it. These system administrators most often want to
  adapt the driver to local requirements, too. Therefore we distinguish
  the installation phase and call the persons concerned *installers.*

- After the driver has been installed it can be run by *users*. During this phase errors will be detected (no software system is free of errors) and hints for changes or extensions will evolve.
- The feedback of the users will be treated by the *maintenance group*. If they change the driver due to this feedback the cycle is entered at the point where the test and the documentation has been done.

During the stages of the software life cycle different people work on the driver. All those people have different requirements – these can even be contradictory. But because the system is made for usage the requirements of the users must have a strong preference over the other ones, our study will start with the user's point of view. In the rest of this paper we will distinguish from whom the specific requirement will come. Only if all groups have the same requirements or if the context clarifies the persons concerned we omit the distinction.

6.3   User interface

The most interesting part of a driver is of course a list of its capabilities. These make it more or less usable. Looking around in the scientific community most people have to deal with heterogeneous computing environments. Documents are often enough moved from one computer to another in the different stages of document preparation. In this case it is mandatory for satisfactory results that drivers in the different environments behave similarly. This user requirement splits into several conditions:

- The drivers must offer the same set of options with a uniform command language interface – as far as reasonable interpretation is possible; see the list below. Additionally there may be alternate command language interfaces that are compatible to the computing environment in question: e.g. a menu and buttons for systems with a graphical shell or any other command language specific option method with prompts for mandatory options etc. These site specific additions make usage easier for people who are restricted to one environment and help them to become familiar with the driver. This may also hold for support staff that has to maintain command scripts for all programs and prepare additional user documentation.
- The drivers must create the same visual output on all devices – with respect to resolutions. This condition is extremely important to make previewing reasonable.
- The drivers must handle exceptions the same way. Of course it is the responsibility of the people who install a driver to make the same set of fonts available for all drivers and output devices.
- Activation of any extensions through the \special command must be standardized, otherwise misinterpretations of commands will lead to

unexpected results. Extensions that are not handled must have no effect other than creating a warning message.

Printer drivers must be able to run unattended (in 'batchmode'). Requiring interaction in exceptional cases is not tolerable when drivers are processing output files in a spool queue.

Now we list a number of options that is to be included. We start with those options that are considered to be a minimal set:

- Partial output of a DVI file. The selection must allow to give at least the:
  - starting page number, referring not only to TEX's \count0, which designates the printed 'page number' in most macro packages, but also with respect to the order of pages in the DVI file. This distinction is necessary because some macro packages use the same counter values in several parts of a document. Thus a selection using \count0 does not lead to the desired page in all cases.
  - a maximum number of pages to print (not reasonable for preview drivers) or
  - an end page number, also either referring to \count0 or with respect to the order of pages,
  - an increment used to step through the document (with the reasonable default value 1, but not required for preview drivers, see below)

  For printer drivers multiple ranges in one run of a driver are required, otherwise the initial overhead of a driver run can accumulate.
- Override the magnification for the document to obtain a zoomed output. Of course this will also affect all 'true' dimensions.
- Specification of the number of copies – selectable as the number of copies of each page or the number of times the selected page ranges are repeated.
- Placement of the output on the page: values for top and left margin. The default margins must depend on the paper format. In the US the standard margins are 1 in for legal paper. For the European A4 paper size, 2 cm margins have proved reasonable.

Additionally the following options can enhance the versatility of a driver:

- Selection of pages with respect to the other counters, namely \count1 to \count9. (These counters are seldomly used by macro packages because they usually allocate their counters dynamically.)
- Processing of multiple files in one activation. This reduces the overhead for initialization in printer drivers and allows switches from one document to another without leaving in preview drivers.
- Selection of orientation – portrait or landscape.

Printer drivers have additional features which should be part of a high quality driver:

- Selection of processing order for the pages to override default. Default must be the reading order when the pages are taken from the output stacker, i.e. reverse for face up output, forward for face down or sorter output.

- For devices that allow multiple input stacks or sorter output these must be controllable by driver options. In a multiuser environment operating procedures may require that some of these features can be disabled for the normal user. Otherwise an output job might block the queue waiting for insertion of a sheet in a single sheet feeder.
- Selection of paper format.
- Placement of multiple pages on larger sheets is a requirement for professional output.

Preview drivers require another degree of interactivity. Thus some of the options from above show up again as dynamic selections in the following list:

- For small screens allow reduction of the output to see a whole page on the fly (and switch back again), even if the text is not readable any more.
- Show information about the current page including page number (it may not be written on the page), relative position of the page and the total number of pages in the document.
- For small screens allow the user to select the displayed part freely.
- Let the user scan a page with simple commands if it does not fit on the screen. Where these commands move the displayed part in discrete steps across the page, there must be an overlap between the actual and the next page notch.
- Let the user select the next page to be seen interactively but make the default easy without tedious interactions for
  −moving to the next or the previous page,
  −skipping to any page by page number,
  −skipping to any page by relative distance (forward or backward),
  −skipping to a page relative to start or end of document.
- If the host operating system supports a multi-tasking window system, the driver must be able to use it.

Again there are some options that are not required in each case but make things easier under many circumstances:

- Let the user select the size of a virtual output sheet and handle offset parameters like the printer drivers. Thus positioning of output can be checked completely on the screen.
- Allow display of a ruler to measure distances in the document. The labeling must be user selectable using all the units provided by TEX.
- Override the magnification during the session for closer inspection.
- Let the user scan the page in a natural way, if it does not fit on the screen. The same command goes right as long as there is something not seen and then returns to the left base for the next slice; skip to the next page when the bottom right part was seen.

- Let the user interactively specify the home position on the screen, i.e. the position in the page which will be shown first for a new page.
- Let the user select foregound and background colour if the display is not monochrome.

The principles of operation, any drawbacks or limitations, and the user interface must be described in a manual. It must contain:

- the environment requirements of the driver (main memory, disk space, special hardware or interfaces),
- precise specifications for all options and their default settings,
- any other way to change the behaviour, e.g. environment controls,
- a reference to all error messages and suggestions for user reaction,
- a description of installation procedures in a separate section, and
- an index.

To help casual users either online documentation through help or online manual features of the host should be available. These must include all possible options with short explanations. If no help system or online manual is available, the driver must give the necessary information when asked. A cryptic list of option switches without explanation is not sufficient.

Developers become users of their drivers when they prepare their documentation. For driver families it is rather straightforward to create one document and select the host specific sections through conditional parts included in TEX's \if and \fi.

6.4   Expected characteristics

Beyond all bells and whistles there are a few overall characteristics a driver is expected to have. The most important one is its reliability. A driver must not crash nor must it leave the computer system or the device in an inconsistent state.

- Printers must be reset to a usable state, a following job must be able to use it without difficulties. If font management, independent of application software, does not exist, the driver must delete all fonts it has downloaded.
- Previews must leave a usable terminal which accepts user input.

The other side of reliability is a good error recovery. The driver should try to output as much as possible – and the output should be the best approximation to the DVI document which can be made. If the device storage is not large enough to hold the contents of one page, if a font or a character is missing, or if some components cannot be output due to hardware drawbacks: in each case the driver should try to discard the page component which leads to the error and should leave the space for it if this is possible.

The error messages should be precise and include information for the user (or the maintainer) to identify the source of the problem. All error messages should be written to a log file, too – the user does not want to copy it to paper by pencil.

These points are much more important than every feature of the driver and even more important than performance. A very fast driver with a bunch of features which does not produce correct output and crashes leaving the system in an inconsistent state (and supplying cryptic error messages) is of no use for realistic productive document preparation.

Nevertheless performance is an important *feature*, too. A high quality driver should not be the 'bottleneck' of the printing process – devices and communication lines are usually very slow. Under some circumstances it can be prefered to discard the support of some features of the user interface while featuring performance issues, e.g. for a production driver for high resolution devices where only final printing is done.

6.5   Output

The essential task of a driver is to create the most satisfying output which is possible using the intended device. This output is described in the DVI file (Anon., 1982). As the name expresses the representation of the document is device independent, which is achieved by the following characteristics:

- The characters are not regarded as elements of (device-specific) fonts but as elements of a type in a specified magnification. The assignment to fonts (and then to font files) must be done by the DVI driver.
- The positions of these characters (and rules) are given in scaled point (sp), with 2^{16} sp in 1 point and 72.27 points in 1 inch. Because there is no device available which may resolve to a scaled point (and surely will not be in the future) a driver has to transform the position details in minute raster into the coarser meshed raster of the device.

The consequences of these items for a DVI driver are discussed in this section.

6.5.1   Fonts

Fonts (that is, collections of character images for a specific output device) are one of the main resources a driver must handle. For each group of persons different views of the font handling can be stated. The primary interest of the developers who must implement, document and maintain a couple of drivers is a uniform handling of these fonts, i.e., a uniform naming scheme. System administrators have to install the driver – they want to adapt the naming scheme to the existing system environment. The user of the DVI driver wants to have a complete set of fonts so that he can create documents with the usual TeX macro packages and does not have to be concerned with the availability of fonts.

The format of a font

Fonts are stored in font files. Currently, three different 'official' formats of these font files have been published:

- The GF (generic font file) format (Anon, 1985) is output by METAFONT.
- In the older PXL format (Fuchs, 1981) each character is represented as a bitmap with each bitrow padded to 32 bits. This format has the drawback that an important oiece of information (the device dependent width) is not included.
- The PK (packed font file) format (Rokicki, 1985) was introduced to achieve savings in the demands for disk space. With this PK format the needed disk space is reduced to about 40% of the demands of fonts stored in the PXL format.

A driver must at least be able to process fonts in the PK format, and the support of the GF format is highly recommended. The PXL format is – due to its space requirements and its lack of device dependent widths – not as important as the other two formats, but a high quality driver should also support it because many old drivers use it and their fonts can be used in this way. If one of the two formats GF or PXL cannot be used, then conversion programs to the PK format should be part of the driver delivery. High quality DVI drivers may add another capability: the usage of fonts which reside in the device itself.

The name of a font file

It can be assumed that every operating system where a DVI driver can run allows files to be organized hierarchically. We can regard such a hierarchy as a directed graph with filled nodes. A node contains files and other nodes that are at a hierarchically lower level.

The full name of a font file consists of the name of the node in which the file is stored and the file name itself. Most often, these parts are concatenated with a delimiter in between. It is very usual that file names are treated as a composition of two parts, connected by a dot: the name and the extension. These syntactical elements must be restricted in their length to achieve exchangeability between many systems; the names of the nodes and the name part of the file name must have at most eight characters, file extensions must be limited to three characters (Beebe, 1987).

These restrictions – which are necessary for a uniform naming convention on many different computer systems – have a major impact on the organization of the whole collection of font files. The fonts come in different magnifications and magnified fonts are often used as a (bad) replacement for nonexisting sizes of the requested type.

- The name of the font file must contain its type name. Its extension can indicate the font file format. But this indication should only be of relevance for the human, DVI drivers must look at the magic numbers inside the font file to decide if this file represents a font and to determine the format of the font representation. Since the extension must not exceed three characters it is not possible to include the coding of an arbitrary magnification in it.

- The fonts with the same magnification should be collected in one node at the lowest level of the font file hierarchy. The name of this node must represent the magnification since it cannot be included in the file names.
- All fonts in all magnifcations for one output device should be clustered in one node at the next higher level in the font file hierarchy. If the fonts are generated by METAFONT the node that represents all fonts for one device should be named with the identifier of the *mode* parameter (shortened to eight characters).

This proposed structure of the font file allows the developers to handle different fonts for different devices on different computer systems in the same way.

System administrators have to install the driver – during this installation process the most time will be spent by copying the fonts. An estimation of this time and a specification of the needed disk space must be found in the documentation to allow scheduling the administrator's work. The font file names will be fixed but the other parts of the full file name can be subject to change.

- At the least it must be allowed to specify the placement of the node that represents all fonts for one device, e.g. by prefixing it or by locating it in a directory structure.
- The names of nodes containing all fonts with the same magnification must contain the magnification of these fonts but high quality drivers should allow to adapt the naming conventions to local circumstances. We propose allowing two alternatives:
  - it should be possible to influence the digit representation of the font magnification; at least two representations are widely spread, the scale factor in per mille relative to 200 dpi and the font resolution which can be associated with this magnification;
  - it should be possible to insert the representation of the magnification as above in an arbitrary string to form the node name.

With these provisions it is easy to embed a DVI driver into an existing environment.

Another important point for the system administrator is the ability to share the font files between computers in a network, which results in reduced consumptions of computer resources and a reduced handling time. A high quality driver should support the file access over networks.

Additional fonts

The set of fonts delivered with a driver is subject to a future step of standard-ization. In any case there will be documents which require additional fonts, be it complete new fonts or unusual magnifications of fonts. If TEX is used in a multiuser environment an author seldom has the opportunity to install these fonts at the place where the complete font set is located. But even if he could he often wishes to distinguish the delivered 'standard' fonts from the document specific ones, i.e., he wants to store them in a different place.

Every driver must allow document specific fonts to be held 'near' the written document, i.e., to install the magnification nodes of these fonts in the same node where the document is placed. Furthermore high quality drivers will accept a list of nodes in the file hierarchy where fonts are searched. The user should be able to define this node-list either in the command line or via the host system in which the list is associated with a name if the host system supports that kind of string mapping (e.g. the environment variables of UNIX or the logicals of VMS). The name of this list must be device specific because each device will have a different search list. With this capability it is possible to install fonts that are used by a team or only by one person and to have enough flexibility for the management of documents.

Missing fonts

But, what if a font file cannot be found? First it must be guaranteed that a correct magnification value has been used; incorrect magnifications can be introduced due to the fact that they are partly represented as integers in per mille. If this can be assured replacement fonts should be looked for.

Every driver must replace nonexistent fonts at least with an unmagnified font of the device – of course, the same type should be used. High quality drivers will also look for other magnifications to choose a font which comes closest to that the user has wanted. If still no font can be found the TFM files (normally used by TEX only) may serve as a source for informaton about the dimensions of these font's characters, so that an appropriate space can be left. All this should be done in the spirit of 'don't cancel the output – an author wants to see as much as is available.'

We strongly recommend not to scale bitimage characters to the desired size within the driver. Either the document is important, when the desired font should be created by METAFONT, or it is a document for which this small work is still too much, and another font can be chosen.

6.5.2   Typesetting is at least setting type

The quality of the output must not be determined by the driver. The user of a driver expects that the output is as accurate as the device can do it and that equivalent results are received on other computer systems and other devices (with respect to different resolutions and deficiencies in the printing engines). The program DVItype (Fuchs, 1986) claims to create *the* correct output and that every DVI driver must not differ in its positioning results. Therefore DVItype shall be a kind of 'prototype' for each DVI driver and the developer can check his implementation.

To produce satisfying results a font designer can decide to choose another device dependent width for a character other than the equivalent of the device independent width, e.g., the device dependent width of 'm' in the unmagnified font cmr10 made for the printing engine imagen is one pixel wider than the equivalent of the device independent width in pixels. Therefore the DVI driver must not ignore the device dependent width. The *only* exception of this fact comes along with the usage of substituted fonts: the device dependent widths are wrong (because it is another magnification) but the device independent widths can be scaled to the desired magnification and can be used as *the* width of the respective character. Please note, that this implies a necessary change in DVItype because the usage of fonts in the GF or PK format must be supported that include this information.

The differences which exist between device dependent and device independent widths result in different positions in the 'device raster' and the 'device independent (DVI) raster.' Furthermore differences are established due to rounding errors, as explained in DVItype. These differences must be adjusted at defined places and must not be allowed to diverge beyond a given limit. Both situations are covered in DVItype – and the treatment of both is not completely satisfying.

- The adjustment of the horizontal difference should only occur between words, so that the distances between characters in one word are not altered. A similar policy should be used for the adjustment of the vertical differences, they should disappear only between lines. This will lead to the same vertical position of the character's baselines in one line even if a fraction is inserted in it. Therefore we have to identify the place where a word ends and we have to distinguish the dividing space between two lines from a vertical movement within a line.

  – It is a typesetting standard that words are divided by approximately $1/3$ quad. This may vary usually by $1/9$ quad, but bigger differences are seldom used. Therefore a right movement of 0.2 quad or above can be considered as the dividing space between two words.

  The same amount must not be taken for left movements, because TEX does relatively wide left movements to position accents above characters. The relevant characters are the small ones, capitals are only used at the beginning of a word. An acceptable limit is 0.9 quad, since no non-capitals are beyond this limit.

  – As baselines are approximately 1.2 quad apart, 0.8 quad seems to be a suitable limit for leaving the line area.

The difference to DVItype is not the method but the values. In particular the limit for the left movement is too small in DVItype, since it does not cover all non-capitals.

- Version 2.6 of DVItype introduces the concept of a 'maximal drift' to limit the difference between the device position and the DVI position: if a maximal difference is exceeded the device position is corrected. The problem with the realization of this concept is twofold:

  - The maximal difference *max_drift* is expressed as a fixed dimension, i.e. its current value is two pixels (for a standard device with 300 dpi, originally 200 dpi). If the same value will be used for another device with a different resolution the correction of the device positions will be done at different DVI positions – resulting in a different output that is gone beyond the difference caused by the different rasters. Therefore we propose to choose a value in a device dependent unit, e.g. one percent of the resolution's dpi-value. This value will still be used as a dimension in pixel.

  - If the device position must be corrected, DVItype does this by a movement of *max_drift* pixels towards the DVI position. This always results in a device position one pixel next to the pixel equivalent of the DVI position, regardless of the resolution. This movement (and also a direct movement to the DVI position) is not satisfactory because it will eventually get too large and will disturb the eye of the reader. We propose to position half-way between the device and the DVI position, i.e. to move $\lceil max\_drift/2 \rceil$ pixels towards the DVI position. For the current value of *max_drift* (two pixels) this does not change the behaviour of DVItype.

6.6   Implementation

The requirement of similar behaviour is achieved best by drivers derived from the same source. The best known example of such a set of drivers is the driver family by Beebe (1987). Furthermore this simplifies the implementation of a driver for a new device, if the device can be handled similar to one already in the set of supported devices.

In the following section we will distinguish between the host computer and the output device itself. Usually they will be connected by a communication channel. The bandwidth may range from a serial line with rather poor throughput to a very closely coupled system where the device has access to the internal bus of the host and transfers can be made via direct memory access (DMA).

In general one has to distinguish two different types of hardcopy output devices:

- Some need the output as a complete bitmapped page image. In this case a huge amount of data (increasing very rapidly with growing resolution) must be transferred from the controlling host to the output device. This leads in general to serious performance restrictions unless there is a high bandwidth communication channel between the host and the device.

  To reduce the size of the bitmap that has to be stored and transmitted one wishes to reduce the size of the buffer used. Unfortunately it is not possible to use the size from the DVI file postamble, which is supposed to give the dimensions for the largest page of the document. The values do not reflect any parts added when TEX composed the page image and included the head and footlines, nor does it contain all overfull lines.

  Into this category we also take devices that need the printing information not as a dot matrix, but as a list of vectors that must be painted.

- Other devices can use local memory to store downloaded font sets. This can lead to reasonable throughput e.g. in a workstation environment even when the device is linked to the host by a serial line. This holds only for the current desk top printers with resolutions of 300 dpi. Higher resolutions again require higher throughput unless the patterns of the characters are sent encoded instead of indicating the bit patterns.

  There may be differences whether the download of a character may occur at any time, only between pages or only at the very beginning of an output job. Furthermore often the size of downloadable characters is limited and larger characters must be inserted as bitmaps anyway. Also the number of downloadable characters may be limited on a per page or per job base, and these limits may vary when the description of a page grows large, or large graphics images are included.

  The movement of the virtual output cursor may be limited, such that output for a page must be sorted in either vertical or also horizontal order. This holds especially for devices that can move their output medium only in one direction and are not capable of storing the contents for a full page in local memory.

For screen previewers another categorization must be made. Vector displays are of limited usability, when single bit addressing capabilities are required to display dot matrices. In current workstations or personal computers the screen image is composed of bitmapped memory regions, even multiple bitplanes are used for colour output or greyscale displays. These bit planes are usually addressable by the controling host, at least at the system level. The main difference in system throughput is, whether there exist special purpose processors ('blitters') that can move rectangles of these bit planes with high efficiency. This is due to the fact that the character images must be moved to arbitrary bit positions on the screen, but the master processor can address the memory only in 8 bit quantities, or even larger chunks, and thus image lines for each character must be shifted to the proper position before they can be inserted. The blitter processors are designed to handle these shifts internally and can change arbitrary regions.

When the display is not connected to the host's bus, but through a slow terminal line, one needs local intelligence in the 'terminal' to emulate a downloadable device to achieve reasonable throughput if bit images shall be displayed. If this intelligence is absent or not programmable, one has to live with output that cannot show accurate positions, because the proper fonts cannot be used. Such output can only be considered as a preliminary solution and does by no means lead to high quality output.

6.6.1 Language issues

The main problems for implementation of a driver family are caused by the need to implement drivers for different devices in a variety of computer architectures and operating systems. To make such a family manageable it is necessary that the 'base' implementation language allows modularization. Without software modules the resulting software system becomes too large to maintain or even to compile on small computers.

An implementation for a new device can require basic changes in strategy for some parts of the driver. These can be handled best by replacing certain modules with versions specific to devices or device families. Of course the interface of the module in question must be clearly defined and obeyed by all implementations.

To make it easy to port the driver to a variety of computer systems the language must be available with a reasonable amount of standardization. From the developer's point of view it is important that the language has a literate programming extension. This will, by the way, make the developer a user of the driver even during implementation and maintenance.

Changes required by different operating systems or architectures can be made using a change file mechanism, as Knuth introduced with WEB. This mechanism was first only available for all the 'literate programming' language extensions; but it has been implemented recently by a small tool (Guntermann and Rülling, 1986) for any base language.

6.6.2 Host requirements

Due to hardware drawbacks it may be necessary to be able to limit the amount of main memory required for the driver or parts of its internal tables in certain environments (e.g., in the Intel processor line with their 64 KByte addressing limitation). Also the number of files usable in parallel may be limited, or the output channel to the device might be of low throughput. On the other hand it may be useful to provide features for operation of the driver in a networking environment, where the font files reside on file servers and the output may be spooled to print servers. At least the driver should be able to access the files over a network when the operating system allows this.

6.6.3   Device features

Device 'hardware' features

Another Pandora's box opens when you ask for the variety of special features of hardcopy output devices. There exist lots of different concepts for paper handling:

- multiple input stacks,
- single sheet feeders,
- output in different bins or through sorters,
- both sides printing,
- changes of paper sizes and output placement.

And even with dot matrix printers it is almost impossible to find two models using the same single sheet processing commands.

Not all of these features can be reasonable in each environment, e.g., it is not wise to allow single sheet insertion for an unattended device that is connected to a spool queue. Such features must be disabled for spool operation.

For printer drivers, but even more for preview drivers, it is necessary that the driver program clips any parts of the output page that do not fit onto the current page to fit into the current output window or the whole screen, if the device does not support clipping by itself.

A time consuming part of device customization is the selection of parameters for the creation of fonts with METAFONT. This problem cannot be neglected, because especially for new output devices it seems to be very hard to find out how to create satisfactory fonts. Unfortunately it is not sufficient to feed the device resolution into METAFONT. Other parameters that reflect the appearance of output created by the device must be determined. This becomes even more complicated when a device has a knob to change its printing parameters (e.g. darkness). In this case different software packages might require different positions of the knob to produce optimal results and thus different parameters for METAFONT are necessary. Similar problems occur if the appearance of output depends on the quality of paper inserted.

Device 'software' features

The situation is in no case better for the software features. The feature most requested by users is the possibility to integrate graphics into documents. The following formats for graphics are currently found:

- Most printers can handle graphics in bitmap format. But the encoding of the bit image to the printer formats is more or less obscure and by no means generalized. Also the rapidly growing size of bitmap images with increasing resolution makes the usage of this kind of graphic inclusion not very attractive.
- For diagrams etc. the use of vector graphics may be more appropriate.
- The most flexible solution can be achieved by use of a page description language such as POSTSCRIPT. This offers a broad range of applications.

But one must be aware, that all these extensions lead to non-portable documents. One of the main advantages of the TEX DVI output is lost.

For devices with the same font parameters but different bitmap encodings it is possible to integrate a uniform raster image support. This format can be driver family dependent (unless standardized) but allow at least a limited portability of graphics. The format must include the dimensions of the graphic anyway and even preview drivers that use a different resolution can display a frame in the size of the graphic insert to allow checking of correct positions. Additionally the raster can be stored in a compressed format, like the one used in the PK format and thus at least the disk's storage requirements can be reduced. If the device requires the full bitmap no savings can be achieved for the transfer. But if it supports a special encoding with reduced amount of data the graphic data can be transformed to achieve best throughput.

6.7   Support of extensions by \special

A driver may allow activation of device specific features through the \special command provided by TEX's DVI output.

When such extensions are supported by a driver, it is necessary that they are clearly tagged such that other drivers will not attempt to interpret them inadvertedly. The following form for the \special string is recommended:

    <tag>: <action>

The <tag> is supposed to indicate the type of extension. This can resemble driver specific or device specific tags. Each driver may handle more than one tag. Special strings starting with tags that are unknown to the driver must be ignored. A warning message should be issued. To get a uniform handling among different drivers all tags must be registered – the appropriate place for this seems to be TUG. TUG can control that new tags are mnemonic and that their meaning is properly specified.

The <action> entry defines the action that shall be performed. Its recommended form is

    <function> [:<parameters>]

where all legal functions must be specified with the registration of the tag. The entries <tag> and <function> must not be case sensitive. The optional

<parameters> section specifies additional information for the function (the delimiting colon is needed to allow parameter lists that start with white space).

To include a picture file myfile.pic in the format described above one may write, for example:

\special{picfile: include: myfile.pic}

Often \specials are demanded that activate any directive for the driver and document it in the DVI file. For example

- page orientation and placement,
- horizontal and vertical offset,
- number of copies,
- sheet feeder input,
- output stacker or sorter selection,
- processing order, and
- colour selection (where appropriate).

But the current DVI file format does not allow \specials to appear outside of pages – they are only allowed between *bop* and *eop*. If one of the above directives is within a page then parts of this page can already be output. Furthermore other pages can be output before, therefore an implementable specification of this \special will be rather difficult.

For documentation purposes an additional **comment** tag should be included. This allows adding information about the source and status of the DVI file, which is tied to the file, but not printed in the document.

Device specific functions can also be made available. If a device offers a 'local' command language (e.g. POSTSCRIPT or PreScribe), escapes can be made through the \special mechanism. They must be tagged by the name of the local command language or the device name to avoid misinterpretation by other devices. The required functions may be **command** for the execution of an immediate local command given in <parameters> or **include** for copying a local command sequence from a file.

The user should not have to write these \special commands by himself. In most cases it is more appropriate to offer additional command definition files with macros that map logically structured functions to the proper \special sequences, e.g., in the case of graphics inclusion the macro should also take parameters for the desired space for the picture and add all the necessary positioning commands to make the placement of the picture correct.

6.8 Installation

During the installation of a driver the following actions must be undertaken:

- check the completeness of the distribution,
- setup the programs and customize search paths for the files used,
- enable or disable selectable features, and

- finally, contain a test run to make sure that at least the easy things work properly; this test should exercise all extensions of the driver.

The installation procedure must be described in the manual. If the host computer is a multi user system, the installation part of the manual must be separable. For update versions a replacement installation must be supplied.

6.9 Conclusion

We have listed the main issues for reliable drivers of high quality. Currently most existing drivers do not meet all points. The distinction between a minimal subset of functions and additional features may serve as a measure of quality. It is intended that discussion of this article will carry on the standardization process (McGaffey, 1987), leading finally to more conforming drivers which make life easier for everyone who creates, maintains or uses them.

Bibliography

Anon., 1982, *Device independent file format*, TUGBOAT, 3(2) pp.14–19.

Anon., 1985, *Generic font file format*, TUGBOAT, 6(1), pp.8–11.

Nelson H. F. Beebe, 1987, *A TEX DVI driver family*, pp.71–113, *in* TUG VIII Conference Proceedings, *ed.* Dean Guenther, TEX Users Group, Providence.

David R. Fuchs, 1981, *The format of PXL files*, TUGBOAT, 2(3), pp.8–12.

David R. Fuchs, 1986, *The DVItype Processor (Version 2.7)*, WEB Program, Stanford University, August 1984.

Klaus Guntermann & Wolfgang Rülling. *Another approach to multiple change-files*, TUGBOAT, 7(3), p.134.

Robert W. McGaffey, 1987, *Developing TEX DVI driver standards*, pp.69–70, *in* TUG VIII Conference Proceedings, *ed.* Dean Guenther, TEX Users Group, Providence.

J. L. Peters & L. L. Trip, 1978, *A model of software engineering*, pp.63–70, *in* Proc. 3rd International Conference on Software Engineering, Institute of Electrical and Electronics Engineers, New York.

Tomas Rokicki, 1985. *Packed (PK) font file format*, TUGBOAT, 6(3), pp.115–120.

Klaus Guntermann
Institut für Theoretische Informatik
Technische Hochschule Darmstadt
Alexanderstraße 10
D-6100 Darmstadt
FRG

Joachim Schrod
Detig·Schrod TEXsys
Kranichweg 1
D-6074 Rödermark-Urberach
FRG

Chapter 7
An Environment for TEX-Output with Original Monotype Fonts

Thomas Stadler & Tibor Tscheke

The paper will show what has to be done to use the original Monotype fonts when working with TEX. What kinds of incompatibilities turn up when TEX output is to be processed on the Lasercomp, and in where do the standard macro packages have to be changed?

Integrating the *Monotype Times* in TEX involved the problem that the results can only be viewed after processing on the Lasercomp. Visual control that late makes it considerably more difficult to use TEX as an interactive means of typesetting. For this reason we made METAFONT produce typefaces with the width table of the *Times font*, but of course, using the *Computer Modern* sources. The resulting PK-files are public domain. With these you can anticipate the exact positions of line make-up and page make-up of the Lasercomp on both screen and laserprinter: thus it is possible to simulate Lasercomp output. In addition we are planning to make characters and fonts available that are missing in the TEX character pool, such as phonetics, gothic fonts and special characters for various university faculties.

We have put together font, TFM-files, macro packages and special characters into a package wich is easy to install and which enables an author to switch from the *Computer Modern* environment to the *Monotype Times* and back.

Thomas Stadler & Tibor Tscheke
Stürtz AG
Beethovenstraße 5
D-8700 Würzburg
FRG

61

Chapter 8
The Cambridge TeX-to-Type Service

Rod Mulvey

Cambridge University Press has integrated TeX into its production of books and journals. This integration has addressed all aspects of text preparation that relate to writing, design, editing, typesetting and generation of camera-ready copy. The Press has had to examine the way that TeX redefines the roles of author, editor, designer and typesetter. This has resulted in a new role for the DTP specialist working alongside the designer and typesetter.

Several benefits can result from authors having a direct hand in the production of typeset pages leading to reduced costs and faster turnaround, without a corresponding drop in quality. Widespread experience demonstrates that these benefits do not necessarily follow just from a willingness to adopt DTP methods and we have analysed why this is so within the context of the large printer-publisher. This analysis and the resulting TeX-to-Type service will be described.

Rod Mulvey
CUP
Printing House
Shaftesbury Road
Cambridge CB2 2BS
UK

Chapter 9
LinoTEX: Professional Electronic Publishing

Gerlinde Petersen

GESYCOM has developped a TEX-driver for the Linotype type set-
ter LTC 300/500, which allows professional publishing with high
quality laser technology and a resolution of 2540 dpi. The basis of
the driver development was to avoid any restriction in the available exposure device functions and technology. Moreover, all the
exposure functions should be supplied to the user with special commands, (e.g. tint and pattern, transposed and arbitrarily rotated or
electronically modified blocks). The driver is available for MSDOS-
PC's. The PC is directly coupled to the Linotype Laser exposure
device, LTC 300/500, (without a PostScript raster image processor). Formatting via TEX is achieved by means of the Linotype font
metric data for approximately 2000 fonts. The TEX mathematical
fonts were newly digitised from Linotype in the required TEX font
structure. Preview is available on a number of graphic cards using
TEX reference fonts and Linotype metrics. Proof printing is carried
out in the same way on HP-Laserjet+ (compatible) laserprinters.
This driver offers users new possibilities of high quality output together with additional exposure functions. The typesetting industry, as the place of production, can take particular advantage of
the TEX-typical formula composition. As a service industry a typesetting firm can secure an almost undeveloped sector of market for
itself.

9.1   Who or what is GESYCOM and what does it do?

GESYCOM GmbH was founded in 1982 as a consultancy firm dealing in the application of modern communications technology to the EDP and typesetting industries. GESYCOM has been a system house since 1984. Our main emphasis in development lies in complete solutions for document-processing systems in which various hardware and software components can be employed, according to the intended application and quality requirements, and to the available or deployable equipment technology. The necessary developments included:

- a universal driver concept for text and picture graphics on differing screens and printers;
- the implementation of convenient user-interfaces;
- the integration of modern EDP-technology in closed systems of the typesetting industry;
- user packages for document processing and production.

Thus originated, for example, PC-workstations with PC TEX as the formatting core, which permit the integrated and professional processing of documents with text, pictures and graphics. Knowledge of the available equipment technology in the typesetting industry on the one hand, and constantly rising quality requirements in the processing and production of documents on the other, have led to the development of the product presented here.

9.2   Professional publishing

High demands are made on computer aids in the field of professional publishing. High quality is also a presupposition of the formatting process as is the best possible output quality of the end product.

9.2.1   From the user's point of view

The user demands that productions tools should be as transparent as possible with regard to the quality of the end product. A better quality output, for example on phototypesetting exposure devices, must be achieved by a maximum in computer aids, for example, preview and proof print using matrix or laser printers, and automatic integration of additional kerning values in the ligature tables without manual intervention.

9.2.2   From the printing industry's point of view

The printing industry demands that document processing and production systems show no limitations in the functional extent of the typesetting program used. For example, there may be no limitations in either the use of *all* available font varieties and type sizes of any exposure device, or the use of *all* the properties of the exposure device – grid and pattern, transposed and arbitrarily rotated or electronically modified block.

9.3   Components in the field of phototypesetting

9.3.1   Historical development

From the time of Gutenberg, and therefore from the beginning of the printing industry, the document production process,has been characterised by the equipment technology available at the time and the quality consciousness of the customer.

Each new development phase in the printing industry, from lead type through hand setting to photo-typesetting, has resulted in simplified and more elegant methods of production. The technological standards of present-day exposure devices make manual assembly processes almost superfluous. GESYCOM has fulfilled the requirement that the typesetting programs used must support all exposure device functions, by developing a TEX driver.

9.3.2   The configuration for professional electronic publishing

The GESYCOM-TEX driver runs at the present time under MS-DOS. The PC is directly coupled to the Linotype laser exposure device LTC 300/500 (without a POSTSCRIPT RIP). Previewing is achieved on various screens with the GESYCOM product *LinoView*. Proof printing (*LinoProof*) occurs on a laser or matrix printer coupled to the PC. Proof printing with orginal Linotype fonts can take place on a Linotype laser printer which is directly connected to the exposure device.

9.3.3   Input

For the input GESYCOM has developed a TEX-orientated editor, which, amongst other things, can convert a series of ASCII codes directly into TEX typesetting commands.

9.3.4   Formatting

Formatting via TEX is achieved by means of the Linotype font metric data. GESYCOM make available the metric data for all (approximately 2000) Linotype 300/500 fonts.

9.3.5   Preview

Previewing is carried out for a number of graphic cards using TEX reference fonts and Linotype metrics. By means of a software tool the user can undertake as many substitutions of the reference fonts as he wishes.

9.3.6   Proof print

As in the case of the preview, the proof print on non-POSTSCRIPT printers is carried out by means of TEX reference fonts and Linotype metrics. The substitution procedure is the same as that of the preview. On POSTSCRIPT-capable printers the proof print is achieved by means of the Adobe fonts.

9.3.7   Output

Type and mathematical fonts

In TEX the Linotype fonts are called up by their original type designations during font allocation. As the maximum type size is approximately 300 points, block lettering can also be exposed by means of TEX. The TEX mathematical fonts were newly digitised from Linotype with the assistance of GESYCOM. We also provide the metric files with orginal Linotype kerning values for approximately 500 of the most commonly used fonts.

Special exposure-device functions used in operation

A series of exposure-device functions which are not includeded in the range of TEX functions are made available by GESYCOM in the form of special commands,for example:

- definition and call-up of grids and patterns;
- transposed lines, text blocks and;
- electronic cursive or modified type.

Special exposure-device functions used in output technology

All the special functions for the output technology of the exposure device can also be called up via macros or drive options, for example:

- positive/negative exposure;
- side-reversed exposure;
- arbitrarily reduced exposure (reduction in size);
- landscape exposure; and
- exposure with general x-, y-offset.

Direct-to-plate

In addition to the familiar exposure techniques on film or paper, the Linotype laser printer also permits direct exposure on offset-foil. This 'direct-to-plate' exposure presents a priceworthy alternative for small but nonetheless high-quality production.

9.4   Advantages

9.4.1   For the user

The TₑX operator is provided with output possibilities which were previously not available to him:

- highest quality output via photocomposition (2540 lines per inch);
- extensive font choice (approximately 2000 Linotype orginal fonts), partially provided with aesthetic values (kerning);
- additional typesetting functions;
- large type sizes;
- alteration of the output format without renewed formatting;
- previewing and proofprinting on standard EDP hardware;
- priceworthy production via direct-to-plate.

9.4.2   At the place of production

The place of production can, on the one hand, be itself the user, and on the other hand, can also be a service operation. As user the typesetter industry can take particular advantage of the elegant TₑX-typical formula composition. In the function of a service industry a typesetting firm can, with the necessary technical equipment, secure for itself an almost undeveloped sector of the market, as TₑX output in photocomposition quality with the increased function range for the Linotype exposure device has not previously been offered.

9.5   Further developments round and about TₑX

GESYCOM is working on the following TₑX-related further developments:

- TₑX-compatible implementation under UNIX with enlarged typographic model;
- driver developments for new high-definition screens and printers;
- integration of grey-tone exposure devices, logos and graphics in TₑX exposures;
- exposures for colour output;
- macro packages for non-academic users.

These further developments were made necessary simply by fact that TEX, as the most professional typesetting program, must also be accompanied at all stages of production by the best equipment technology that is available now or in the future.

Gerlinde Petersen
GESYCOM GmbH
Eupener Strasse 22
5100 Aachen
FRG

Chapter 10
The Notation and Structure of Mathematical Texts and their Representation within Electronic Documentation Systems

Francis J Cave

The development of mathematical notation is inextricably entwined with the development of mathematics as a whole, viewed both as an area of scholarly study in its own right and as a toolkit for scholars working in other disciplines. It can be argued that advances in human knowledge are impossible without suitable language for articulating such knowledge, and the abstract concepts of mathematics provide extreme examples of this. The paper discusses the impact that electronic methods of communications have on the use and development of mathematical notation, which could have a significant impact on future developments in mathematics as well as in other fields. It considers how currently-available systems for electronic document description perform in recording and conveying the concepts that scholars wish to share through the medium of the electronic document.

Francis J Cave
Pindar Infotek
2 Grosvenor Road
Wallington
SM6 0ER
UK

Chapter 11
TeX Fonts in Image Generation Software

Jörg Winckler

One problem in pseudorealistic computer graphics is the provision of letters in two and three dimensions which are both detailed and smooth. METAFONT is a source of two dimensional letters. The internal representation of letters in METAFONT uses Bézier splines. The great advantage of splines is their independence of the image resolution. We use the splines of METAFONT to triangulate the letters, while transforming their shapes into *design patches*. These patches have abilities to describe their own border curves. Design patches have been implemented in the VERA-raytracing software for use in CAD-systems. (VERA is a software product of the Department of Computer Science, University of Karlsruhe) The design patches allow the generation of highly smoothed free form surfaces without increasing the rendering time for raytracing algorithms. We built three dimensional letters with these design patches. In the image generation, the design patch is refined into usual triangles, which are scene adapted: letters which are 'far away' are refined into a small set of triangles, and letters 'close' to the eye point are refined into a larger set of triangles guaranteeing smooth border curves for the letter.

11.1 Motivation

In pseudorealistic computer graphics three-dimensional letters are needed. For example in the area of architecture the designer wants to use letters at building entrances, etc.

There exist a lot of methods for designing and creating 3D-letters. I want to show three of them:

- **3D-design:** The single letters are constructed by joining basic geometric objects like triangles, cylinders, spheres, rotational objects and patches into a letter.
- **Digitising:** The method mostly used to obtain three-dimensional letters in pseudorealistic computer graphics is the following one: if you want to use the logo of a company you have to zoom the logo on a photostatic copy and then digitise it from a sheet of paper with a tablet into the computer. Afterwards the polygon will be divided into triangles. These triangles will be copied while the new ones get a new z-coordinate. Now we have two front surfaces of the letter. The side surfaces are constructed by connecting the two surfaces with quadrangles. These quadrangles are again constructed out of two triangles. These operations are done by hand and are very expensive.
- **Pixel based:** Another possibility to get fonts in 3D is to zoom normal (2D) letters. If you change every pixel into two triangles you get too many triangles to deal with. It is possible to gather a bunch of triangles together to one big triangle but there will be at least much more triangles as if you would triangulate by hand. Libraries with fine divided letters will need very much disk space.

In each case these three methods have a big disadvantage. The approximation of the border curves is constant, no matter if the letter is very near or very far from the eye point in the scene. If the eye point is too near the letter the viewer can see the single objects (especially triangles) and the border curves are no longer smooth. If the eye point is very far away from the letter the resources for memory and CPU are wasted for a lot of triangles which can not be seen by the viewer.

Our approach to this problem is the definition of letters with resolution independent graphic objects. These objects are triangles which describe their own border curves with Bézier Splines. We call them *Design Patches*. This approach gives us the possibility to use a big source of two dimensional letters, the program METAFONT.

11.2 Bézier splines

A Bézier spline is a curve, which has a start point and an end point and several control points which describe, how the curve bends between its ends. The number of control points determines the complexity of the polynomial, which is the mathematical background of this sort of curves. These polynomials are called *Bernstein-polynomials*. The common formula for Bernstein-polynomials is:

$$z(t) = B(z_0, z_1, z_2, \ldots, z_n; t) = \sum_{i=0}^{n} \binom{n}{k} (1-t)^{n-i}(t)^i z_i$$

In our case we have only two control points. So we deal with *cubic* Bézier splines. The resulting polynomial is:

$$z(t) = B(z_0, z_1, z_2, z_3; t)$$
$$= \binom{3}{0}(1-t)^3(t)^0 z_0 + \binom{3}{1}(1-t)^2(t)^1 z_1$$
$$+ \binom{3}{2}(1-t)^1(t)^2 z_2 + \binom{3}{3}(1-t)^0(t)^3 z_3$$
$$= (1-t)^3 z_0 + 3(1-t)^2(t)^1 z_1 + 3(1-t)^1(t)^2 z_2 + (t)^3 z_3$$

This polynomial is easy to handle. Bézier splines have several properties. One of them is the *convex hull property*. It means that the curve lies always in the area which is determined by the convex hull of $z_0, \ldots, z_3$.

The gradient of the end points of the curve is equal to the gradient of the straight line between the control point and the end point. The connection of two Bézier splines is smooth if the two control points near the connection point and the connection point itself lie on a straight line. With this property it is possible to connect several splines to a smooth border curve. A connection of splines will be called *contour*. If the start point of the first spline in a contour is the same as the last point of the last spline, then the contour is called *closed*.

Probably for these reasons Donald Knuth chose Bézier splines for the internal representation of letters in his program METAFONT (Knuth, 1986).

11.3   Getting splines

As we know METAFONT is a font compiler. It transforms the description of a letter, given in textual form by an user into letters for raster displays. A raster display has a fixed resolution. But METAFONT wants to be independent from resolutions. So the internal representation of the letter shape uses Bézier splines.

While describing a letter shape the user gives a path of two-dimensional points on which the virtual pencil is drawing. The procedure *make_choices* transforms this path (and additional informations) into *cubic Bézier Splines*. In the same part of the memory where we find the splines METAFONT stores also other informations. After METAFONT executes *make_choices* we can be sure, that the part of the memory, which is referenced by the value of the parameter of *make_choices* will only hold splines. We extract all these splines and write them into a new METAFONT-file named `myfile.spl`. In this file we write only closed contours because the other contours in the memory are parts of closed contours.

11.4   Design patches

Design patches are triangles with curves instead of line segments between the edges. So the patch needs additional information about the curves. This information lies in three normal vectors, one in each edge, and in six tangent vectors, two in each edge. These tangent vectors lie in the plane perpendicular to the normal in the edge.

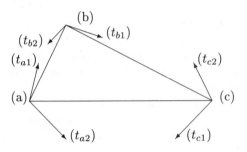

Design patches are useful not only for plane objects but especially for free form surfaces. For example it is possible to design a sphere with eight design patches.

The design patch will be refined at run time, what allows scene adapted refinement. If the letter is far away in the scene then we need only a few standard triangles to represent the letter. In the other case if the letter is very big, we define the possible error of fitting, which controls the refinement to very small triangles and we receive enough triangles which guarantee a smooth border line. This error limit can be chosen automatically in relation to the eye point and the size of a pixel.

The design patch follows three criteria of refinement:

- **minimum length:** if a edge gets too short the edge will not refined any more.
- **fitting error:** the error of fitting will be calculated by measuring the difference between border curve and edge at three different points of the

edge. The result can be expressed in a relative value (e.g. 20% error). If the value is lower than a certain limit, the edge will not be refined.

- **recursion:** for each edge, the number of splits are counted. If the number of splits is greater then a certain amount, the edge will split no more.

A second version of the design patch has four edges which allows the modelling of the 3D part of the letter. Tangent vectors are not all we require for curve specification, in addition we need the normal vectors for normal interpolation. This again has a smoothing effect.

11.5   Triangulation

The problem of triangulation can be solved by the user (in dialogue with a graphic program) or automatically by a triangulation algorithm. The output is in both cases a set of design patches. First we implemented a graphic program for our SUN-workstations which allows to triangulate the letter by clicking the vertices and the control points with the mouse.

The triangulation by the computer is much more complicated. The input of the triangulation algorithm is a set of splines. This set of splines fits together to a closed contour. The triangulation of a single contour is no problem. Much more difficult is the triangulation of two contours, one enclosing the other. We must detect such inclusions and then arrange the spline points of the inner contour towards clockwise order. The points of the outer contour will be in clockwise order. This allows a triangulation algorithm to triangulate contours with holes. The basic algorithm deals with polygons. Working with splines is not the same. The polygon algorithm inserts new points into the polygon. This is impossible for splines. So we have to modify the algorithm to work with splitting splines. This algorithm is in development.

11.6   The third dimension

Not all characters should have the same depth (in this case the sense of *depth* is not the same as in METAFONT. We use it for the third dimension). We wanted to keep all dimensions variable. This means that the single letter can be scaled in all dimensions. The scaling is done by the image generation system.

Our main problem was the sides of the tree-dimensional letter. It was impossible to use normal triangles or patches or even design patch with three edges for modelling the side surfaces. Fortunately there exists a version of design patches with four edges. With these patches we are able to create the side surfaces in the same manner as the front surfaces. Only the normal vectors, which are needed for the calculation of the reflection of light, were different from the normal vectors of the front surface. They can be calculated with the tangent vectors in the start and end points of the border curve.

11.7 Further possibilities

Now it is possible to use METAFONT-logos in 3D computer graphics. Other software products will have a great variety of fonts to choose.

Another application is the possibility of the design of three dimensional objects with METAFONT. So, with our transformation we gained a new design tool.

With the 3D fonts it is possible to built a 3D-TEX. This sort of text is very useful in the presentation of informations, statistics, movies or in commercials.

Bibliography

Donald E. Knuth, 1986, *The METAFONTbook*, Addison-Wesley Publishers, Reading, USA, 361pp.

Jörg Winckler
Universität Karlsruhe
Institut für Betriebs- und Dialogsysteme
Postfach 6980
D-7500 Karlsruhe 1
FRG

Chapter 12
METAFONT versus PostScript

Victor Ostromoukhov

The problem of the inter-relationship between METAFONT and PostScript should be discussed in the context of wider problem of communication between TEX-based software and PostScript-based printing equipment.

In the present study, we examine the basic constraints which should be imposed on METAFONT sources in order to translate them into proper PostScript outline font descriptions. These constraints are:

- to inhibit use of the 'unfill' and 'undraw' primitives in the METAFONT sources
- to avoid excessively long and complicated constructions in the METAFONT sources
- to forsee and avoid curves that may be ambiguously interpreted on the pixel grid by the PostScript interpreter.

The latter constraint, the most crucial one, is related to the famous 'one-dot problem' which very difficult to resolve inside PostScript.

The mechanism of translation of METAFONT sources into PostScript outline font descriptions will be illustrated using Mac-METAFONT, the author's implementation of METAFONT, and applied to the *Computer Modern* family.

Victor Ostromoukhov
EPFL/LSP
IN-F Ecublens
1015 Lausanne
Switzerland

Chapter 13
Using Menudriven TeX under MVS

Rainer Rupprecht

In this article, written for the 1988 European TeX Users Conference at Exeter it will be shown how to use a full screen environment which makes the use of TeX easier; how to write it, and what the task of the TeX system maintainer will be. Within this article some other facilities developed at the Computing Center, will be mentioned. The help of those who have contributed to the installation and running of TeX on the current system must be acknowledged, especially:

- Dietmar Heinrich: Menus development and LATeX Styles
- Martin Kerner: TeX implementation, CLISTS and Menus
- Harald Meyer: Device driver, Graphics in TeX and Menus.

All the menus, helps etc., are made in the German language, but there should not be any problems to translate them in foreign languages. All the menus and their programming are created with the operating system BS3000 (nearly compatible to MVS) using the PFD facilities (like ISPF). In January 1989 it will be completely changed to MVS and the ISPF facilities.

13.1   Introduction

A TₑX user knows that there is not any system, without cost, which makes typography as perfect as TₑX does. Of course, it is not easy to learn, but if you know it, it is perfect. Using Lamport's LATₑX it is very easy to get a perfectly styled document in a relatively short time. While *wysiwyg* (what you see is what you get) systems (especially on the PC's and without the qualities of TₑX) allow text input (editing), text processing, storing and output within one program, the TₑX formatter is very uncomfortable and you have to do many things by your own:

- text input and editing outside of TₑX;
- running TₑX (interactively or in batch) – getting a device independent file (DVI) (LATₑX users have to do this part two or three times);
- perhaps using utilities (like BIBTₑX ...) outside the normal TₑX run;
- looking/printing the the log file (error message);
- running the device driver for getting an output; perhaps using a screen preview.

In recognition of these problems it has been the goal to provide the user with an aid to use TₑX. (Using TₑX now on mainframe and also on PC, without the guides described later, you know what a fight against the computer it can be to run TₑX.)

13.2   The idea

In running TₑX (especially LATₑX) there are a lot of datasets to be combined with the TₑX formatter. These are for example under MVS, datasets like `prefix.myname.tex` as the TₑX input file or `prefix.mysteyle.sty` as a LATₑX style file. Other datasets are created by TₑX itself (LOG, DVI, AUX, ...). For beginners (in TₑX and perhaps the operating system) its easy to become confused, wishing to run TₑX never again.

To satisfy these users, the minimum of knowledge must be enough for obtaining the best styled layout; but for the experienced users it must be possible to do things like writing macros, including graphics, creating their own style files...

The interactive help and the documentation should be added quickly. New things (releases, macros, TUG news) should be included as soon as possible.

13.3   The primary (main) menu

The program is called by typing `tex`. If any parameters of the logon are not right (e.g., region size) a warning appears on the screen, including a message how to do it correctly. Then the TₑX main menu appears on the screen.

```
-------------------------< TeX - Auswahlmenue >----------------------------
Option ===>
---------------------------------------------------------------------------
  H    Hilfe      F   Fonts    N   News (Stand:  10.06.88 )    Userid - RZ32
                                                              Time   - 10:15
  1    TeX        - Tex-Formatierer aufrufen                  Date   - 11.06.88
  1B   TeX        - TeX-Formatierer im Background starten
  2    Edit       - Schreiben bzw.  Korrigieren von TeX-Eingabetexten
  3    Log        - Log-Datei ansehen
  3P   Log        - Log-Datei drucken
  PFD  PFD        - PFD-Utilities benuetzen
  B    BibTeX     - Aufruf von BibTeX
  D    Drucker    - verschiedene Ausgabegeraete ansprechen
  K    Konversion - Wandlung von DVI-Dateien in das hier benoetigte Format
---------------------------------------------------------------------------
  TeX input          :LATEXJOB
  Source LIB(s)      :RUP.SAS.SCRIPT                               (optional)
                     :                                             (optional)
  UserStyles(LaTeX)  :                                             (optional)
  TeX Format         :LATEX      (PLAIN, EPLAIN, LATEX, ELATEX, GELATEX, AMSTEX)
  Log Datei          :
  DVI Datei          :RUP.DVI
---------------------------------------------------------------------------
Ende:  END KEY druecken
```

In this menu options can be choosen by typing the code. The possible options are:

H displays the primary help menu. The 'Help' key also can be used (see also section about the help menus).

F lists the available fonts – names and description.

N this options shows the NEWS file. Any changes (perhaps in style files, new devices ...) are listed. The date in brackets shows the last change.

1 runs TEX interactive with the paramenters specified in the lower part of the menu. (The dataset rz.rup.sas.script(latexjob) is TEXed in this example, using LATEX with German hyphenations as format.)

1B creates the JCL (Job Control Language) for a TEX batch job and submits it. Job parameters are requested in a menu.

2 invokes the PFD (ISPF) editor, used for the editing of datasets (it must not be TEX.)

3 invokes the PFD (ISPF) browse, used for examining the log dataset.

3P prints the log dataset on a system- or local printer.

PFD invokes PFD (ISPF) facilities (creating datasets, deleting members, ...).

B runs BIBTEX interactively. The parameters used to run BIBTEX are to be filled in in the BIBTEX menu.

D displays the printer menu (see section about printer).

K conversion of standard TEX DVI files to datasets with specified parameters.

The lower part is used for the information about datasets and the format. TeX input means a dataset named **prefix.xxxx.tex** (sequentially organized)

while no Source LIB is specified. If Source LIB(s) are specified the formatter
looks for a partitioned dataset sourcelib (TSO conventions) with member
texinput. More than one source library can be concatenated, this may be
useful if macros are used. Datasets with user defined L^AT_EX style files may
be included. The T_EX format is selected by inserting plain, latex, etc. in
the TeX Format field. The two lines at the bottom are used to specify the
datasets for saving the T_EX produced LOG and DVI. Advice about the DCB
parameters are given in the help menus.

13.4   Examples of the menus of the next generation

13.4.1   The help menu

Using the option H or the PF key for help in the primary menu shows the
primary help menu. The primary help looks like the following:

```
---------------------------<  TeX Hilfe Menue  >----------------------------


    Waehlen Sie das Hilfethema aus :_


    1    TeX        - Tex-Formatierer aufrufen
    1B   TeX        - TeX-Formatierer im Background starten
    2    Edit       - Schreiben bzw.  Korrigieren von TeX-Eingabetexten
    3    Log        - Log-Datei ansehen
    3P   Log        - Log-Datei drucken
    PFD  PFD        - PFD-Utilities benuetzen
    B    BibTeX     - Aufruf von BibTeX
    D    Drucker    - verschiedene Ausgabegeraete ansprechen
    K    Konversion - Wandlung von DVI-Dateien in das hier benoetigte Format
    DOK  Doku       - Dokumentationen und Informationen zu TeX / LaTeX

    Fuer weitere Informationen wenden Sie sich an :

    Rainer Rupprecht, RZ Zi.  207, Tel.  4031,  RZ32 an DKAUNI48



    ------------------------------------------------------------------------
    Ende:  END KEY druecken
```

As you see, the options are closely related to those in the primary T_EX
menu. If someone chooses a help option, detailed information concerning T_EX
or the menus are given. The DOK option shows DVI files with information
prepared for output.

13.4.2   The printer menu

After the completion of formatting the user starts a DVI_to_printer_driver.
By choosing option D in the main menu the printer menu (shown below) is
invoked.

```
----------------------< Drucker - Auswahl - Menue >------------------------
Option ===>_
---------------------------------------------------------------------------


   Am Rechenzentrum stehen Treiber-Programme fuer folgende
   Ausgabegeraete fuer TeX zur Verfuegung:



   1   Benson     - Benson-Treiber DVIF77BE / DVIF77A1 starten
   2   HP Laser   - HP-LaserJet-Treiber DVIF77LJ starten
   3   GDDM       - Ansehen der Ausgabe am Memorex-Bildschirm
   4   Xerox      - Ausgabe am Xerox 4050-Laserdrucker (Testbetrieb)
   5   Kyocera    - Ausgabe am Kyocera (HP-Laserjet-II-Emulation)




---------------------------------------------------------------------------
Ende:  END KEY druecken
```

At present there is support for five output devices on the mainframe. By
choosing the option (1 through 5) new menus are displayed. Then a batch job
creates a device specific file and transfers it to the printer (plotter). Printers
used are:

- BENSON electrostatic plotter model 9424 (254 dpi):
- HP Laserjet (300 dpi); the Laserjet dataset then must be transferred to
  a PC with a Laserjet+:
- KYOCERA 2200 (300 dpi) using a Laserjet II emulation, joined to the
  mainframe as a 'Local Printer' using a COAX Interface: and
- the XEROX 4050 Laser Printer (300 dpi) with a capacity of 50 pages
  per minute.

The GDDM is a driver for previewing TₑX output on IBM3279 terminals,
compatible MEMOREX 2079 and PCs with 3279 emulation.

When selecting a DVI driver a new menu is displayed on the screen. As
an example the XEROX menu (option 4) is shown. Users knowing the system
can type D.4 in the primary TₑX menu option line and will get directly to
the XEROX menu

```
----------< DVIF77XG -- Ausgabe am Laserdrucker Xerox 4050 im  RZ  >----------

Der DVIF77XG-Treiber fuer den Laserdrucker Xerox 4050 wird im Background auf-
gerufen.  Bitte geben Sie hier die fuer den Backgroundjob  benoetigten Parame-
ter ein:

     Account-Nummer           :_          (z.B. AB005)
     Jobname-Zeichen          :XER          CPU-Zeit-Vorgabe in Min.  :  1


     DVI-File                 :RUP.DVI

     Startseite lt.  TeX      :_
     Max.Seitenzahl           :_
     Neue Vergroesserung      :_
     H Offset in mm           :_
     V Offset in mm           :_               Orientierung P/L :_


     Namelist CTLIST (Teil A) :_
     (fuer Son-      (Teil B) :_
       derzwecke)    (Teil C) :_

--------------------------------------------------------------------------------
ENTER    druecken um SUBMIT durchzufuehren
Ende:  END KEY druecken
```

Within this menu parameters concerning JCL and the document are requested. There are three JCL parameters: accounting information, jobname
and maximum CPU time. The other parameters are used as follows:

DVI File	The DVI file which should be printed
Startseite lt. TeX	The first TEX page to be printed
Max. Seitenzahl	Number of pages to be printed (maximum)
Neue Vergroesserung	field for the magnification
H offset in mm	the horizontal offset (unit=mm)
V offset in mm	the vertical offset (unit=mm)
Orientierung P/L	orientation P=portrait, L=landscape; also possible (test) is P2 using both sides of the page
Namelist CLIST ...	used for driver options (copies ...)

The other menus look similar.

13.5   Conclusion

This examples of TEX menus should be enough to introduce the use of TEX
on the Siemens 7881 mainframe at the University of Karlsruhe. Maybe those
responsible for other TEX systems will try to do something similar. The
experiences at Karlsruhe are very good, and even students who have simple
text to write are now using TEX on the mainframe! Of course this has not
been the goal of our efforts (simple text should be processed on PCs), but it
shows that the usage is very easy and comfortable.

Appendix: Menu programming examples

1   TEX primary option menu

```
%-------------------------< TeX - Auswahlmenue >-----------------------------
%Option ===>_OPT        +
+---------------------------------------------------------------------------
%  H  +Hilfe      %F  +Fonts    %N  +News (&STAND        +)   +Userid - &ZUSER
%                                                             +Time   - &ZTIME
%  1  +TeX        - Tex-Formatierer aufrufen                  +Date   - &ZDATE
%  1B +TeX        - TeX-Formatierer im Background starten
%  2  +Edit       - Schreiben bzw. Korrigieren von TeX-Eingabetexten
%  3  +Log        - Log-Datei ansehen
%  3P +Log        - Log-Datei drucken
%  PFD+PFD        - PFD-Utilities benuetzen
%  B  +BibTeX     - Aufruf von BibTeX
%  D  +Drucker    - verschiedene Ausgabegeraete ansprechen
%  K  +Konversion - Wandlung von DVI-Dateien in das hier benoetigte Format
+---------------------------------------------------------------------------
+  TeX input         :_SRC                                                  +
+  Source LIB(s)     :_LIB1                                   +(optional)
+                    :_LIB2                                   +(optional)
+  UserStyles(LaTeX) :_STY                                    +(optional)
+  TeX Format        :_FMT      +           Formate: | PLAIN   LATEX    AMSTEX
+  Log Datei         :_LOG                          +| EPLAIN  ELATEX
+  DVI Datei         :_DVI                          +| GEPLAIN GELATEX
+---------------------------------------------------------------------------
+Ende:%END KEY+druecken+
)INIT
  .HELP = TEXH
  IF (&FMT=' ')
    &FMT = 'PLAIN   '
)PROC
 VER (&FMT,LIST,PLAIN,EPLAIN,LATEX,ELATEX,AMSTEX,LATEXT,GEPLAIN,GELATEX)
 &SEL = TRANS( TRUNC (&OPT,'.')
             PFD,'PANEL(JRR#POM) NEWAPPL'
              H,'PGM(JRRHELP) PARM(TEXH)'
              F,'CMD(%TEXM3 ''RZ.TEXFONTS.DESCR'')'
              N,'CMD(%TEXM3 ''RZ.TEXNEWS.TEXT'')'
              1,'CMD(%TEX2PFD &SRC FORMAT(&FMT) PFD)'
              1B,'CMD(%TEX2BG)'
              2,'PGM(JRREDIT)'
              3,'CMD(%TEXM3 &LOG)'   /* BROWSE */
              2D,'CMD(%TEXM2D &LIB1 &SRC)'   /* EDIT TEST */
              3P,'CMD(%TEXM3P)'  /*print */
              B,'CMD(%TEXMBIB)'
              D,'PANEL(TEXD)'
              K,'CMD(%TEXKONV)'
              ' ',' '
              X,'EXIT'
              *,'?'  )
)END
```

2 Primary help menu

```
%--------------------------< TeX-Hilfe-Menue >--------------------------
%
%
% Waehlen Sie das Hilfethema aus :_OPT +
%
%
% 1  +TeX        - Tex-Formatierer aufrufen
% 1B +TeX        - TeX-Formatierer im Background starten
% 2  +Edit       - Schreiben bzw.  Korrigieren von TeX-Eingabetexten
% 3  +Log        - Log-Datei ansehen
% 3P +Log        - Log-Datei drucken
% PFD+PFD        - PFD-Utilities benuetzen
% B  +BibTeX     - Aufruf von BibTeX
% D  +Drucker    - verschiedene Ausgabegeraete ansprechen
% K  +Konversion - Wandlung von DVI-Dateien in das hier benoetigte Format
% DOK+Doku       - Dokumentationen und Informationen zu TeX / LaTeX
%
% Fuer weitere Informationen wenden Sie sich an :
%
% Rainer Rupprecht, RZ Zi.  207, Tel.  4031,  RZ32 an DKAUNI48
%
%
+------------------------------------------------------------------------
+Ende:%END KEY+druecken+
)PROC
  &SEL = TRANS( &OPT
               1,TEXH1
               1B,TEXH1BG
               2,TEXH2
               3,TEXH3
               3P,TEXH3P
               PFD,TEXHPFD
               B,TEXHB
               D,TEXHD
               K,TEXHKONV
               DOK,TEXDOKU
               ' ',' '
               X,'EXIT'
               *,'?'  )
)END
```

3 XEROX printer menu

```
%----------< DVIF77XG -- Ausgabe am Laserdrucker Xerox 4050 im  RZ >----------
%
+ Der DVIF77XG-Treiber fuer den Laserdrucker Xerox 4050 wird im Background auf
+ gerufen.  Bitte geben Sie hier die fuer den Backgroundjob  benoetigten Parame
+ ter ein:
%
+ Account-Nummer          :_ACCNT+    (z.B. AB005)
+ Jobname-Zeichen         :_JCH +        CPU-Zeit-Vorgabe in Min.  :_TIME+
%
+ DVI-File                :_DVI                                       +
```

```
%
+  Startseite lt.  TeX       :_SPAG                                    +
+  Max.Seitenzahl            :_MPAG                                    +
+  Neue Vergroesserung       :_SCAL+
+  H Offset in mm            :_HOFS    +  Optimierung    :_OPTI   +
+  V Offset in mm            :_VOFS    +  Orientierung P/L :_ORIE    +
%
+  Namelist CTLIST (Teil A) :_CTLSTA                                 +
+  (fuer Son-      (Teil B) :_CTLSTB                                 +
+   derzwecke)     (Teil C) :_CTLSTC                                 +
%
+-------------------------------------------------------------------------------
%ENTER  +druecken um SUBMIT durchzufuehren+
+Ende:%END KEY+druecken+
)INIT
  .HELP = TEXHD4
  IF (&TIME='')
     &TIME = '1'
  IF (&JCH='')
     &JCH = 'XER'
  IF (&SPAG='')
     &SPAG = ' '
  IF (&MPAG='')
     &MPAG = '1000000'
  IF (&SCAL='')
     &SCAL = ' '
  IF (&HOFS='')
     &HOFS = '21'
  IF (&VOFS='')
     &VOFS = '21'
  IF (&ORIE='')
     &ORIE = 'P'
  IF (&OPTI='')
     &OPTI = '3'
  IF (&CTLSTA='')
     &CTLSTA = ' '
  IF (&CTLSTB='')
     &CTLSTB = ' '
  IF (&CTLSTC='')
     &CTLSTC = ' '
)PROC
  VER (&JCH,NONBLANK)
  VER (&ACCNT,NONBLANK)
  VER (&TIME,NUM)
  VER (&MPAG,NUM)
  VER (&ORIE,LIST,P,P2,L)
  VER (&OPTI,LIST,1,2,3,4)
  &SEL = EXIT
)END
```

Rainer Rupprecht
Universität Karlsruhe Rechenzentrum
Postfach 6980
Zirkel 2
7500 Karlsruhe 1
FRG

Chapter 14
Type & Set: TeX as the Engine of a Friendly Publishing System

Graham Asher

The front end to Type & Set has two parts: a style sheet editor which automatically writes out a large and intricate macro package embodying the design of a document; and a file conversion program which takes documents created on a user's favourite word processor and converts them into standard TeX format.

The back end is possibly the most interesting part of the system, and was certainly the most difficult to write. It is a page make up system called PAGE which takes the galley DVI files produced at the TeX stage, reads the style sheet associated with the document, and pastes up the material into pages, adding running headers, running footers, folios and footnotes, and positioning spaces left for figures. The document is globally optimised using a system resembling the TeX counting algorithm: TeX itself cannot optimise over an entire document, which is one of the reasons PAGE was preferred to an output routine written in TeX.

Tables are created on the screen in semi-*wysiwyg* form and converted into suitable Type & Set format by Table.

14.1   Introduction

Journal publishing needs reliable and automatic conversion of typewritten
text to a form which can be conveniently edited, previewed and typeset. The
format of the input text must be simple and compatible with the typist's
preferred word processor; but this information must be capable of carrying
enough information to specify all the detail needed by the typesetting process.
Some form of style sheet system is needed in order to store the particular format of a given publication. A style sheet, once created, will very rarely change;
but must nevertheless be easy to create, examine and modify. Editors need
to preview the typeset output on the screen and mark it up on paper. This
means that any typesetting system must handle at least three types of output
devices: screen, phototypesetter and some type of intermediate-quality device
such as a laser printer. The typesetting system must handle high volumes of
input with little intervention from the user, once the style sheets have been
created. The output must be in the form of fully made up pages which can
be realised on all three kinds of output device. Finally, as an auxiliary part
of the system there should be some convenient method of typesetting tables
and integrating them into the page makeup process.

14.2   The old system

The previous typesetting system used CORA V, the native language of the
Linotype series of phototypesetters. It comprised the following phases:

- conversion of the input from word processor text containing embedded
  markup codes;
- counting paragraphs into lines;
- page make-up;
- previewing on a screen or laser printer; and
- typesetting on the Linotron 101.

This system, running on a network of Apricot computers, was used to typeset
all the publications of Gower Academic Journals for about three years.

   In early 1987 I conducted a full examination of the system and concluded
that while many parts of the design were sound, the system could not be
marketed unless it was replaced by one which used a more flexible and device-
independent language to CORA V. T_EX was chosen as the engine of the new
system.

14.3   The new system

The new system, Type & Set uses T_EX as its counting engine. In order to be
able to produce output using non-T_EX fonts on devices such as the Linotron
101 and laser printers we had to create programs to produce appropriate T_EX
font metric or TFM files. Since these TFM files have no associated screen pixel
files a screen preview program was written using a universal 'stick-font'.

Type & Set relies on style sheets for all the information about the formatting of documents: one style sheet is needed for each different document style. A program called Style was written which allows the user to create and edit style sheets, and write out macro files embodying this information.

14.4   Using Type & Set

Type & Set was devised for a journal publishing house, so let us imagine that you are now in charge of the typesetting of a new journal. You have Type & Set running on all your in-house microcomputers, and on the micros used by your home typists. It takes up a couple of megabytes on the hard disk of each computer, and is happy running on any machine with a version of TₑX.

The first task that concerns us is the design of the journal. Traditionally, a designer would produce a list of fonts, point sizes, leading and a choice of justification for each sort of text in the journal, and a page design incorporating running headers, footers and folios. Under Type & Set he or she runs the Style program from the main menu. This allows the designer to work in much the same way as a traditional designer, but on a screen rather than a word processor. Style is a tree-structured menu-driven program which works by a very simple form-filling process. It creates a *style sheet* which is used by the rest of Type & Set to make up the finished document.

The different types of text in the document, such as headings and body text, are called *modes*. To create a new mode the designer simply types the name of the mode on a grid. The mode is now a menu item, which, when selected, gives access to further menus allowing selection of fonts, leading, point sizes and about twenty other pieces of information.

The designer will rarely fill in more than five or six of the fields on any one menu. All fields are preset to contain sensible default values: for example, the justification field contains the value full by default. As far as possible the Style program uses all the terminology and measuring units with which the designer is already familiar. You can type dimensions in the same range of units as TₑX, with two changes: scaled points are not supported – designers do not need units smaller than the wavelength of visible light – and a new unit called pp (for 'points and picas') has been added, so that a distance of twenty-one picas and three points can be entered as 21.03pp. The modes that the designer creates, the bundles of attributes to be used for each functionally different type of text, belong to *blocks*, which are one level further up in the hierarchy than modes. The block information includes the measure (that is, the width of the text between margins), the number of columns and the *category* of the text: whether it is body text which flows from the text area of one page to the next, or repeating material such as headers, footers and folios. The highest level in the Style hierarchy is the page design, which is very simple. All you need to think about is the size and shape of the text area and where it is placed in the left hand and right hand pages.

Once the design is complete, or at least at a stage worth looking at, you can display it on the screen using high-resolution graphics, giving a representation of the double-page spread with the positions of all its various components. If you need a printed record another Style command prints out a formatted English description of the style sheet.

So the design is done, and the first issue of the journal must be typeset. One of the papers contains a table and another a figure, but the rest is ordinary text. This is typed using Wordstar by your regular typists, who each have a list of the modes created by the designer of the journal. When the typist needs to invoke a mode, he or she types a backslash, followed by the name of the mode – for a mode is nothing more than an automatically-written T_EX macro output by the Style program. The typist need not learn T_EX. The whole system is designed so that the only macro names ever typed by the typist act as, and in fact are, a customised markup language consisting of single words with no parameters. Happiness is never having to type a curly bracket. There are a few rare exceptions to this principle, but only where it is absolutely necessary to mark a section of text for special treatment.

How you can select bold-face, or italics, or subscript or superscript, without using \bf and the like? The answer is that Type & Set accepts input from Wordstar in Wordstar's own format, using its native control characters to select special effects. To get bold face the Wordstar typist just types the standard Wordstar bold-face control sequence (<control>-P B), and the text appears in bold on the screen. The style sheet defines a \bf control sequence locally within each mode, and this in turn invokes the font that the designer specified as the bold font for this mode.

Earlier I mentioned tables and figures. This imaginary issue has to leave a space for a figure two inches high spanning both columns of a two-column body text block. There is also a table which spans just one column of the same block. The figure is no problem. The typist types \figure 2, meaning '2-column figure', at the ideal position for the figure (that is, just after the first reference to the figure in the text), then any caption which should go above the figure, then indicates the space for the figure itself by typing \figurespace 2in, then types any caption needed below the figure, then closes the figure environment using the control sequence \endfigure. The page make-up system will float the figure to a decent position, making sure that it appears after the reference to it. The table is created using an editor which is more at home with various graphic characters than Wordstar. This is so the table can be typed in a *wysiwyg* format, which is then converted to T_EX by the Table program. After conversion he table is embedded in the text using the normal \input primitive. That is, if the table is called mytable, Table writes a file which is called mytable.tex to be placed in the main text of the journal by the command \input mytable.

The running material – text that has to be repeated on every page – is only typed once at the end of the document. The typist knows which mode to use for the running headers and folios: thieir special treatment stems from the blocks they belong to, which have been given *category codes* by the designer. For example, the category code for a folio which should appear on left hand pages is `pl`, an abbreviation for 'page-number left'. The typist types `\folio` where the page number is to be typeset: the page make-up program will fill in the correct digits.

Most of the human work is now over. The typist sends the disk to you containing the text of the journal issue. You copy the file on to your machine and select the 'make pages' option from the Type & Set menu. Four or five minutes later you are looking at a screen preview of the final result. Normally few changes will be needed: Type & Set has produced the best possible page make-up conforming to the rules and constraints laid down in the style sheet. You now have a device-independent file that looks exactly as if it was produced using raw TEX. If it is likely that further editorial work is needed on the hard copy you can laser print the issue so that it can be marked up; or if you are satisfied with the result you can send it straight to a phototypesetter such as the Linotronic.

After you have created the style sheet – which admittedly is a job needing a lot of care and attention – producing an issue of the journal is a quick and routine job that varies little from month to month. TEX does its usual immaculate job of breaking paragraphs into lines, and the galleys are made up into pages using criteria you have chosen regarding the relative undesirability of orphans, widows, excessive white space and unbalanced columns.

14.5   Fonts

Good intentions about device-independence can often founder on the rock of font layout: yet any professional publishing system must promote device-independence.

By 'font layout' I mean a scheme for arranging the letters, digits and punctuation marks – the 'ordinary characters' – together with the more unusual characters which the traditional typesetting community refers to as 'pi characters'. Knuth (1986) extablished a set of font layouts for use with plainTEX of which four are adequate for normal publishing: text, math italic, math symbol, and math extension. I decided that everything in Type & Set should be as compatible as possible with the plainTEX macros, which meant somehow emulating the TEX font layouts. Difficulties arose immediately. TEX has no distinction between ordinary font characters and pi characters – a TEX character of whatever status, whether it is the letter A, or the most arcane mathematical symbol, is simply one of 128 characters within a font. On the Linotron typesetter, on the other hand, an ordinary character such as A is available in any one of many fonts (sixty-four in our installation) such as Garamond Book, or Optima Bold Italic. However a mathematical symbol is available in only one font, the 'pi font', which consists of a few hundred special characters.

The way the problem was eventually solved, or at least converted into smaller difficulties which could be overlooked or postponed, was to pretend that the Linotron organized its fonts in the same way as T_EX. We created ordinary TFM files for the Linotron fonts using downloaded width tables. The math italic, symbol and math extension fonts were created out of a mixture of Linotron 'ordinary' characters and pi characters, and given TFM files of their own; and an extra TFM file called xx.tfm was created as a rag-bag for characters generally desirable but not catered for by the T_EX layouts, such as Å as a single character (not a character-plus-accent combination). This allows Type & Set to invoke T_EX in the normal way, and for users to employ any of the three hundred or so plainT_EX macros described in the *T_EXbook*. When the dvicora program converts the resultant DVI file into CORA V (the Linotron typesetting language), it reads a series of data files mapping T_EX characters onto ordinary or pi characters as required.

One major feature remains incomplete because of the inadequacy of the pi font installed at our site: full mathematical setting. This lacks only time and manpower, since all we need to do is specify and order a customised pi font including all the mathematical characters, and encode the necessary ligatures and extensible character recipes into the TFM files. This has taken second place to the completion of the page make-up system.

The other font problem is the combinatorial explosion. T_EX has an intimate relationship with the plainT_EX font family system. For the plainT_EX macros for roman, bold and italic styles, and the plethora of mathematical macros to work at all, a series of font families must be set up and mapped onto the actual TFM file names. plainT_EX handles the math font problem by assuming that you need mathematics in just one style and – which is much more of a restriction – in one point size. If you have no more than the plainT_EX macros math mode is the only way to get superscripts and subscripts. In Type & Set a mode called 'text' has a macro of the same name associated with it. This macro must do all the work of making the standard font macros – \rm, \it, \bf and \bi (bold italic) – invoke the fonts that the user has decided (via the style sheet) to call 'roman', 'italic' and 'bold face' in this mode. As it must create text, script and scriptscript fonts in the four families needed for mathematics and also for the the Type & Set 'xx' font described above, it must set up the \xx macro to invoke this at the three sizes needed. So one mode needs fonts from eight families – roman, bold, italic, bold italic, math italic, math symbol, math extension and 'xx' – at three sizes – text, script (for superscripts and subscripts) and scriptscript (for second-order superscripts and subscripts), making twenty-four fonts in all.

Standard implementations of T_EX aloow a maximum of seventy-six fonts to be loaded. Since Type & Set allows up to forty modes to coexist within a style sheet, each with a possible twenty-four different fonts, in theory nine hundred and sixty different fonts might be needed; but in practice most of the modes will share the same fonts, which eases the problem somewhat. What did cause most distress, however, during the development of Type & Set was T_EX's habit of running out of string space during the processing of a long document. Every font change meant a new set of twenty-four \font statements, each of which would use a string such as **un45 at 11pt** (that is, Univers 45 at 11 points) to specify the TFM file and point size. TEX would not load the TFM file unnecessarily if it was already in residence, but it would persist in making another copy of the string.

I decided that **Style**, the program which creates the style sheet would create three macros for each unique font: one to load the font, one to invoke it, and a third (boolean) macro to check whether it was loaded, and so avoid storing the string twice (or more). **Style** gives the fonts arbitrary names starting with \Fa...\Fz and going on to \Faa...\Fzz, and so on. The mode macro then uses \let to 'point to' the unique font macros it requires. But what about superscripts and subscripts? I wrote new macros which work outside mathematical mode and so allow any ordinary text to be superscript or subscript material. The math mode system still works in the way described in the *TEXbook* – but now, of course, it works in the point size of the current mode.

14.6   Page make-up

The problem with TEX output routines is that they are too difficult to write, or at least a general-purpose one is. Knuth's example output routines for the *TEXbook* work very well for the specific styles for which they are intended, but are exceedingly difficult to modify. Since TEX holds everything it needs in memory it cannot optimise the page layout over an entire document; some amount of text between nothing and one and a half pages is in memory at any one time.

At the start of the **Type & Set** project I experimented with output routines to switch between one, two and three column format. The results were so full of bugs and anomalies as to render them unusable. TEX is handy for the development of small macros – up to thirty lines of code or so – but as a tool for creating more complicated systems it is disasterous, for me at least. I simply cannot work with a language which has over three hundred primitives, no data structures, and no way of doing anything non-trivial without writing code that dynamically redefines macros. On the other hand, the output of TEX is very easy to work with, consisting as it does of an elegant low-level code running on an imaginary 'DVI machine'. I had already discovered the pleasures of DVI interpretation while writing the screen driver and the driver for the Linotron typesetter.

The design of **PAGE** started with the following premises, assumptions and axioms:

- it is very easy to interpret DVI files;
- we can put any extra information we like into DVI files my means of TEX's \special command;
- somehow we shall be able to extract the original lines of text from a DVI file; and

- with all this information, and the original style sheet, also encoded in some sort of easy-to-read way, we can convert a galley typeset by TeX into a fully paginated document, globally optimised using a similar algorithm to Knuth's method of dividing paragraphs into lines.

All these assumptions were true, but two of them required hard work. The easier of the two was extracting the original lines from a DVI file. When TeX writes to the DVI file it uses two mutually recursive procedures, *vlist_out* and *hlist_out*. These write vertical and horizontal lists respectively: if either of them comes to an embedded list it simply calls either itself or the other routine, reflecting the nested structure of the data in the program's flow of control. Here is the useful fact arising from this knowledge: both routines embed the material they write between DVI *push* and *pop* commands to save the DVI registers, principally the coordinates h and v. While parsing the DVI file PAGE can identify a line by first finding something which ought to belong in a line, such as a command to set a character of text, and then assuming the line to include all the material between the innermost enclosing *push pop* pair. In fact this approach works remarkably well, with the proviso that it has to be modified when the first character turns out to be something that is superscript or subscript or part of a mathematical formula.

Having read the DVI file, PAGE writes out another file detailing the start and end of every line and which mode it belongs to, together with the mass of flags, pointers, indices and structures needed to determine the leading, glue, penalties and everything else needed for good page breaks. The reason it writes a file rather than keeping the information in memory is so that it can deal with documents of unrestricted length: the *line file* is accessed using a virtual memory system originally developed for the screen previewer. In practice the length of the document is limited by the stack size: at present we have PAGE with a 16 Kbyte stack which allows documents of about a hundred pages to be globally optimised.

The difficult bit is pasting up the pages and optimising over the whole document. PAGE builds up a directed graph in which each node represents a feasible break between two pages, and simultaneously traverses the graph, pruning branches which lead to solutions worse than the best so far. A directed graph is like a tree of possible routes, with the difference that the branches can converge as well as diverge, and indeed all do eventually converge together to the node representing the end of the document. The best route is defined as that which minimises the sum of a *badness function* applied to every page on the route. Type & Set's page make-up system uses the same general method as TeX's paragraph breaking method (Knuth and Plass, 1981), with some simplifications.

There are some major difficulties with page make-up as opposed to paragraph breaking. While paragraph breaking involves traversing a single list comprising alternating words and spaces, in page make-up three lists are woven together to produce the final page: the text list, the footnote list and the figure list. The footnotes and figures are cited in the text; and ideally all footnotes and figures should appear on the same page as their citations, with their order preserved. By special dispensation figures are allowed to appear one page after their citations. Another problem is breaking galleys into columns. At first sight this looks as if it is isomorphic with paragraph-breaking, but in fact it is not. In paragraph breaking the measure or width of all lines except the last one is known before the operation starts. The equivalent of the measure, applied to column-breaking, is the length of all the columns except the rightmost; and this is initially unknown, since the available material might not be enough to reach the foot of the page. The balancing process must arrive at the best possible split producing balanced columns with the minimum glue stretch or shrinkage, and only after this has been done can the glue be stretched or shrunk to even up the column lengths – yet the *potential* length of the columns has to be monitored during balancing to ensure that the current breaks are feasible: in other words, that it is possible to stretch or shrink them so that each column is as long or longer than the one to its right.

When PAGE has found the ideal document it writes out a new DVI file. This part is relatively easy. The document at this point is represented as a linked list of nodes: a page is an arc connecting two successive nodes. Each node contains three numbers, indicating points within the text list, footnote list and figure list. PAGE builds up a tree structure similar to TEX's iut-put list, containing pointers to ranges of lines, their x and y coordinates on the page, and their glue set ratio (how much to stretch or shrink any glue that may be present), PAGE then traverses the list, writing a DVI file that precisely reflects its structure. Every time a line is written out its DVI op-codes are copied directly from the source (galley) DVI file that TEX produced, and enclosed in a *push pop* pair to preserve the coordinates. One interesting wrinkle here is that PAGE has to perform register tracking on the four DVI registers w, x, y and z. These are set by various DVI move commands, and used by others; if the setting command has become separated from the commands which depend on it, the moves generated on output will be the wrong size unless the appropriate register is reset.

The new DVI file can now be rendered on your favourite output device using a standard DVI driver.

14.7   Tables

TEX has a powerful table-making system that is extremely hard to use. While ordinary text in a TEX document looks relatively similar to the final result – in fact has a small degree of *wysiwyg*-ness – the average \halign is baffling in its opacity. We knew from the start that we could not expect our users to construct \halign preambles, but at the same time we did not wish to give up the power of TEX in typesetting the text within tables. Type & Set's table system gives us and our users the best of both worlds. To create a table you type it straight onto the display of a full-screen word processor in a semi-*wysiwyg* format. You need not worry about the width of the columns, as long as they are lined up one above the other. In short, all you have to do is type in a very poor 'typewritten' version of the table, as you might do while hurriedly typing a letter, and use a few simple graphics characters to represent the edges of columns and any vertical and horizontal rules you need.

The fonts and rule weights come from a 'table mode' in the style sheet, which is similar to an ordinary text mode, but allows you to give information specific to tables. The Table program translates your topological *wysiwyg* version into standard T_EX code that can be \input into the main document. When the page make-up program analyses the DVI file the table will be recognised as such and dealt with in the same way as a figure.

14.8   Tytpe & Set: use and availability

Type & Set is used at Current Science Ltd to typeset the *Current Opinion* series of journals and a few others – about twenty journals in all. This makes Current Science probably the largest commercial T_EX user in the United Kingdom in terms of the number of published pages per month.

Current Science employs typists working at home on Amstrad computers to type the copy. The Wordstar files are then taken to the office where they are loaded on a network of Dell computers. Here operators create any tables that are needed, run the files through Type & Set and print proofs on laser printers for the editorial staff to check and mark up. After editing on the network, files are re-run through Type & Set and typeset on a Chelgraph IBX phototypesetter at 2000 dpi. This camera ready copy is then checked and if necessary re-edited. When no further changes are required it can be sent to the printers.

Development work now in progress includes a Linotron 202 driver and an enhanced table processor with more capacity and some new features.

Bibliography

Donald E. Knuth and Michael F. Plass, 1981, *Breaking paragraphs into lines*, Software Practice and Experience, vol.11, pp.1119–1184.

Donald E. Knuth, 1986, *The T_EXbook*, Addison Wesley Publishing Company, Reading, Mass., 483pp.

Graham Asher

Informat Computer Communications Ltd

34–42 Cleveland Street

London W1P 5FB

UK

Chapter 15
Sweet-teX, a Report

Frank R Drake, John Derrick & Laurent Siebenmann

Sweet-teX is a TEX pre-processor, intended to make the keyboard inputting of TEX simpler; in particular, easier for a secretary or mathematical typist to use, without first having to learn much about TEX. In effect *some* sort of pre-processor is always going to be used for the keyboard inputing of TEX (be it the crudest of mainframe editors).

Sweet-teX aims to use all the facilities of a good micro (such as the Macintosh), including standard word-processor facilities, together with a range of fonts, to allow the screen display to appear closer to the final intention. As far as possible, each command sequence and each symbol is input by a single keystroke, with as much mnemonic aid as possible, and will look on screen like the intended output. This is of great advantage to beginners, who do not have to learn command sequences, and to poor typists, who do not have to press so many keys; its value to the fluent typist who already knows TEX must be judged by other features.

One of these is that a syntax-checker is provided which checks such things as the balancing of entering and leaving mathematics, TEX-nical braces {, }, and many other details, saving many TEX errors.

Another is that the screen display can be printed in a way which leaves out or modifies the screen symbols representing TEX-nical input (such as enter and leave mathematics, command sequences and TEX-nical braces), giving a pre-print which can be used for proof-reading (or other purposes). A TEX pre-print becomes unnecessary except for particularly awkward material.

There are macro facilities which complement those in TEX. These include 'variant tags' which give very easy treatment of rarely met symbols, in a way which will at least recognizable in the pre-print, and correct in the final output (if TEX has the symbol; the AMS-TEX extra fonts are available). The possibility of resorting to TEX itself is preserved for use in the most difficult cases.

There has been some evolution of Sweet-teX since its public announcement in 1986. Its system of logical formatting using 'road-signs' is more complete, and invisible character trickery is no longer necessary to pass information from *MacWrite* to TEX.

Sweet-teX has been in use in Leeds University Pure Mathematics Department and some account of its use there will be given, in particular the use of a TOPS network to transfer DVI files to an IBM PC clone to print on an HP Laserjet.

Frank R Drake & John Derrick
Department of Pure Mathematics
The University
Leeds
LS2 9JT
UK

Laurent Siebenmann
Mathématique
Bâtiment 425
Université de Paris-Sud
91405 Orsay Cedex
France

Chapter 16
TEX in the Mainframe World
– the Durham Experience

Roger Gawley

The original motivation for installing TEX was curiosity on the part of a couple of Computer Centre staff members, but it became apparent that if we could get TEX working properly, it could displace all other mainframe text processors allowing us to concentrate on one language. As TEX had been installed at the University of Michigan, this was in principle simply a matter of restoring a few files from the distribution tapes to get a version fully customised to MTS. (I have never seen a Stanford distribution tape.) Reality was a little more complicated.

16.1   Introduction

The University of Durham is the third oldest in England. It is a small to medium sized university with 5389 students divided almost equally between the three faculties of Arts, Science and Social Science. Just over one thousand students are postgraduates. This very mixed user population has widely varying needs for text processing facilities.

The mainframe computer system has been used for text processing for nearly twenty years going back to the time when the main input medium was punched cards and the only printer a line printer.

Durham computer users have been very fortunate in being able to use the same operating system for over fifteen years. This stability yields many benefits but it has the drawback that new programs tend to accumulate without any old ones being withdrawn. By 1983, three different text processing programs were in use each with differing abilities to drive output devices and varying ease of use. This situation was very difficult to support particularly when it came to offering an advisory service to users.

In June 1984, representatives from all the MTS sites were in Durham for the annual MTS Workshop meeting. With some help from David Rodgers of the University of Michigan Computing Center we had TEX running on our machine.

It had some problems. The external form of a TEX program assumes an ASCII character set. The Durham mainframe was then an IBM 4341, now an Amdahl V8, both EBCDIC machines although most users use ASCII terminals through a front end network which handles all character mapping. There was no clear agreement on the mapping nor even on the positions of such characters as the square brackets in the EBCDIC character set.

The TEX program itself uses two character arrays, *xord* and *xchr*, as input and output translation tables so that TEX can be made to run on hardware using any character set. At Michigan most terminals are EBCDIC so the distributed version of TEX had the translation arrays set up for the terminals and printers at Michigan. This was not quite so happy for us. The caret symbol (^) did not work either for superscripts or circumflex accents, although the vertical bar (|) could be used instead. Tilde (~) was not accessible from our keyboards at all. Despite these limitations, TEX proved surprisingly usable and our first user course went ahead.

Making TEX work is less than half the story. TEX produces DVI files but users really want printed output. We had a QMS1200 laser printer purchased in January 1984 with the intention of using it for TEX output among other things. This printer understands its own language called QUIC. After some research into our options for producing QUIC code from DVI files, we decided to buy the driver program from Textset Inc. (now Arbortext) of Ann Arbor, Michigan – president David F. Rodgers. Textset agreed to convert their program to run in MTS with the Universities of Durham and British Columbia splitting the conversion costs.

Now the story gets really interesting. QMS made two laser printers: the 1200 based on the Xerox 2700 engine and the 800 based on the Canon. Both use QUIC and are 'compatible'. We learned a lot about compatibility. The driver program as originally supplied was almost useless – it never succeeded in downloading more than one and a half characters and usually left the printer in a state where it had to be power cycled. When it did manage to print one character on a page, the character was rotated by 90°. Although the 1200 and 800 accept more or less the same QUIC language, the Xerox engine in the 1200 scans the page vertically and the Canon engine in the 800 scans horizontally. Downloaded characters must be provided in this form.

Textset had tested their program on a recent model 800 from QMS, but we had an older 1200 purchased from Pragma in the UK. Nobody had told either of us about these differences. Our network links to Michigan were rapidly improving at this time. They were tested by a flurry of messages. Durham had two free changes of ROMs to update our QUIC, and Arbortext sent several patches to their program via electronic mail. After two months we were able to print a page of correctly oriented text. Since then we have printed about 300,000 pages of TEX output. The 1200 is now near the end of its life and will soon be replaced by a POSTSCRIPT printer.

16.2   How to connect a printer

The best way to connect a printer is directly to the machine generating the code for it. The second best way is via a good transparent network, although informal discussions at TEX88 suggest that many networks do not meet that description. A transparent network would be one that delivered to the printer that same character stream that was sent to it.

Probably the worst way, and the way we have done it at Durham, is to connect it through a piece of third-party equipment over which you have limited control. When we bought the QMS1200, we already had two ASCII line printers. These were connected to a Perkin-Elmer 3220 running as a HASP remote batch station. HASP is a spooling package originallay developed by IBM for its 360 series computers. The Perkin-Elmer speaks to HASP on the mainframe using RJE protocols and translates to the codes needed by the line printers. The laser printer was connected as a third line printer to gain speed of throughput and to provide our computer operators with a uniform control interface. The laser printer was used initially to provide high quality line printer emulation, later for graph plotting and last of all for TEX output.

The Perkin-Elmer machine performs a number of transformations on the data sent through it: it deblocks the HASP protocol sent from the mainframe, it translates between EBCDIC and ASCII and it provides some line printer controls automatically. It is not possible to unbundle these functions. We are able to patch the character tranlation table in the Perkin-Elmer but do not have the source code to make more extensive changes.

The Perkin-Elmer adds characters to the stream sent to the printers to produce automatic skipping over perforations at the bottom of a page. This is quite helpful for a genuine line printer but as the 'pages' sent by HASP are unrelated to anything in the TEX input, these extra characters are effectively injected at random.

We get round these problems by introducing another program at the mainframe end. A complete TEX job becomes a three step process. As most users use it through command language macros, they are not explicitly aware of this. This scheme is untidy but workable.

The most interesting of our problems became known as 'the mystery of the missing ψ'. The overtones of Sherlock Holmes are appropriate. One of our mathematicians produced long documents in which the letter ψ occurred frequently except that some of them would be missing. Although this effect was consistent from run to run of the same document, it occurred apparently at random within long documents. Attempts to narrow the problem down produced short documents that printed perfectly. Altering things earlier in the document often caused the missing ψ to appear but another one to vanish.

The clue (obvious with hindsight) is that ψ is \char32 in the maths italic font. The ASCII code for a space is 32 and the Perkin-Elmer software economises by not sending spaces at the end of lines to the printer where they would be invisible if they were genuine spaces. We now ensure that character 32 is not sent at the end of what the Perkin-Elmer thinks is a line.

16.3   Training and documentation

The position of this section does not reflect any view that these topics are unimportant but simply that there is less difference here between the mainframe and microcomputer situations.

The first TEX course at Durham was given by a guest lecturer from London, Malcolm Clark, who indoctrinated 35 potential users over a period of two days. Since then, the Computer Centre have given six courses to a total of over two hundred students. All courses use the mainframe screen editor and command macros sending output to an express queue on the QMS laser printer. We normally manage to return paper to students within half an hour. An on screen preview would provide faster feedback but give poorer retention. The second lecture discusses the appearance of the output from the first practical and paper has advantages for this.

We felt that *The TEXbook* was too expensive for many of our users and contains far more than they want, so we wrote a local guide which includes instructions for running TEX at Durham. This has 8 pages of text and 18 pages of examples. A new guide will be printed shortly with rather more text. We have found example files to be vital to successful teaching. All the examples are available for anyone to copy and adapt. This is very easy to arrange on a mainframe system.

16.4   Other machines

TEX at Durham is not limited to the mainframe system. It is also available on three Sun workstations. These provide full previewing facilities and can print on an Apple LaserWriter attached to them by an Ethernet network.

The Computer Centre has also taken out a site licence for MicroTEX to enable individuals and departments with IBM pc and compatible equipment to run TEX at a reasonable cost.

16.5   Conclusions

The tone of this paper is very negative because it mostly describes problems. The everyday reality of TEX at Durham is happier. We have over 300 TEX users (more than have been on courses) and most of them have never noticed any of the problems described here.

We are convinced that POSTSCRIPT is the way to go in driving laser printers in a university. We have nearly completed the work of implementing Arbortext's DVIPS driver in MTS and hope to have a production service using a POSTSCRIPT printer running before October. This printer will be connected as directly as possible to the machine generating the POSTSCRIPT.

Anyone installing TEX on a new machine would be well advised to obtain a copy of *TEX the Program* (Knuth, 1986). They may never look at most of the pages, but those that they do consult will become well-thumbed.

16.6   Acknowledgements

Many people contributed to this work, including Jackie Bettess, Kari Gluski, David Lee, Ken Middleton, David Rodgers, and Kent Wada.

Bibliography

Donald E. Knuth, 1986, *TEX The Program*, Addison Wesley Publishing, Reading, Mass., USA.

Roger Gawley
Computer Centre
University of Durham
Durham, UK

Chapter 17
UKTeX and the Aston Archive

Peter Abbott

I propose to split my talk into two parts

- UKTeX: I shall discuss its origin, the computing facilities used for this service, give details of the current (June 30 1988) recipients and a suggestion for future developments.
- The Aston Archive: I shall discuss the principles of the archive, the equipment and capacity available, how to extract and contribute material, concluding with a discussion on where to go from here.

17.1   UKT_EX

17.1.1   Origin

Early in 1987 the Vice Chancellor at Aston University expressed an interest in the T_EX processing package. The then Senior Pro-Vice Chancellor purchased copies of the T_EX and L^AT_EX books and sent me copies. (Later on he also purchased the METAFONT book as well).

At that time the University had available Apple Macs (some with Apple Laserwriters), IBM PCs and DEC VAX equipment. My task was to provide text processing facilities to this disparate community. We also have a Linotronic phototypesetter and one of the criteria was that we should be able to use this equipment as well.

As a result of my investigations we acquired PCT_EX from Ewart North of UniT_EX together with drivers for Apple Laserwriter and Epson printers (MS DOS pc based software). An early copy of *Textures* for the Apple Mac was purchased and this has been subsequently replaced by the latest version. For the VAX we obtained a tape from Maria Code. Initially we used drivers with an LN03 but these have been superceded by those for the Apple Laserwriter (from Andrew Trevorrow).

All this activity promoted an awareness of TUGBOAT and eventually we took out an institutional licence to TUG. Eventually, after much experimentation (together with reading of manuals and TUGBOAT) a message to the address `texhax-request@score` was successful and digests started appearing at Aston. Further developments and use of the digest uncovered Piete Brooks and the UK distribution of `texhax` material. This is now the route by which we get all the digests.

Occasionally I get duplicates from the US, usually after the arrival of the UK distributed copy.

As a result of discussions (by which I mean email exchanges) with UK users whose addresses appear in `texhax` it was decided that a UK edition would be helpful and would increase the interchange of ideas and information within the UK. I agreed to act as moderator and the first issue appeared in September 1987.

The first issues were sent out as and when sufficient material had accumulated and in fact the format evolved based on comments received. On one occasion the distribution list was appended to the digest (which was not well received) and there was also some discussion on the length of submissions. The digest has now settled to a weekly issue with the issue number at the top and details of how to submit at the bottom. This ensures that recipients can be certain that the digest is complete.

I also act as the UK contact for T_EXMAG and use the same distribution list to distribute the magazine.

I am pleased to say that since I adopted the approach of a weekly issue there has always been sufficient material.

17.1.2   Equipment

The service is based on a VAX 11/750 with 8 Mbyte memory and 686 Mbyte formatted disc capacity. The operating system VMS with All-in-1 and grey book mail. The distribution list is **not** kept in All-in-1 but the digest is created using All-in-1 facilities. On Friday mornings the prepared digest is exported to a VMS file and a batch job initiated at 17:10 to distribute it.

There are the usual minor hiccups due to systems (or message switching centres) being out of action. The grey book mail system makes a maximum of 30 attempts to send the digest and usually failed ones are reported on Monday mornings so that I can make second (and sometimes more) attempts.

17.1.3   Subscribers to UKTeX as at June 30 1988

You may be interested in where the digest is mailed. It includes commerce in the UK, The Netherlands, Switzerland, France, Austria, New Zealand and back to the US. New subscribers are added at the bottom of the list (but above my own). I always leave myself last so that if errors creep in I can easily spot them. On Mondays I insert the digest into the archive on another system.

17.1.4   Future development

I intend to change the format to correspond more closely with the standards. I have had a comment that it causes problems at one site who split it up. I am awaiting more details of the changes required. Apart from that I am always open to suggestions on how to improve the digest for the community.

Given the time, I intend to locate subscribers at a single site and attempt to persuade one of them to set up redistribution lists or bulletin boards. I consider that because the JANET part of the network is 'free' we have an obligation to make effective use of the resource and to avoid unnecessary duplication.

Having said that I also consider that JANET provides the most effective means of communication in the academic (and non academic) community and is the ideal method of promoting T_EX, which after all is the object of this exercise.

17.2   The Aston archive

17.2.1   Origin

From TUGBOAT I discovered that procedures for creating PXL files for the LN03 had been developed in the US together with additional facilities and 'add ons' to make the life of a TEXie easier. Most of the software was available for 'free'. All I had to do was get hold of it and then it could be implemented.

It was soon apparent that many users in the UK were using FTP (File Transfer Protocol) to ship files across from the US electronically, and even on occasions were sending magnetic tapes at some considerable cost. I also ascertained that sending tapes around the UK was not the most cost effective solution for software exchange. We have JANET (much as it might be maligned by some) which is still the best network available connecting dissimilar systems.

I had been asked for copies of some of the material that I had acquired it seemed more sensible to provide it where possible over JANET. For this initial request the Archive was initiated.

It is continually changing and currently has a number of areas, the latest being a copy of the UNIX distribution dated May 26th 1988. Contributions are always welcome and I am always pleased to receive copies of tapes if one has been requested from the US distribution centres. I am at present hoping that some one will send the latest VMS version for the archive.

17.2.2   Equipment

The archive is based on the VAX 8650 cluster at Aston and occupies almost half of an RA81 some 200 Mbytes of data. To date I have been able to include all material submitted and do not envisage storage being a problem. The cluster runs VMS and the Colour Book software.

I should say at this point that the working version of TEX used at Aston is stored on a different disc to the archive and is *not* currently available to the general user community at Aston

The provision of a central text processing facility as Aston is under discussion and the decision on which system to use has not yet been taken.

17.2.3   Contents of the Archive

The archive is divided into subgroups and these are constantly being revised and improved, usually following suggestions from users of the archive.

APPLE	PL and TFM files for Apple Laserwriter and +
CRUDETYPE	Output on simple devices (Mark Damerell)
CTEX_2_1	Common TEX Version 2.1
DRIVERS	Files for driving laser printers
DRIVERS.UKLN03	Driver from RMCS for LN03
DVITOVDU20	DVItoVDU version 2.0 (Andrew Trevorrow)
FONTS	Two groups of files for QMS and LN03 fonts
LATEXSTYLE	Style files for LATEX
MFFILES	METAFONT files

GFFILES	*GF files in subgroups by printer
PAVEL	Replaced by subgroup UNIX
PICTEX	PiCTeXmacros (thanks to Sebastian Rahtz)
PREVIEW	Programs for previewers
PSFIGTEX	To include POSTSCRIPT figures in TeX
PSPRINT20	Andrew Trevorrow's PSprint 2.0
REPORTS	Reports and other documentation
SAUTER	Files to build PXL for LN03 (John Sauter)
SCORE	Copy of score.stanford.edu
SCORE.BIBTEX	Copy of bibtex directory from score.standford.edu
SCORE.LATEX	Files from score referenced in texhax
TEX.AA_NEWS	Change files to produce TeX2.9
TEX.AMSFONTS	Font files
TEX.DECUS	Format for DECUS proceedings style (Barbara Beeton)
TEX.DVIDIS	Displays DVI files on VAXSTATION running VWS
TEX.MIT	From MIT
TEX.MYERS	Typesetting for technical papers (TechRpt and $P_{S}iz_{Z}l$)
TEX.TEXSIS	Typesetting physics papers
TEXHAX	texhax Digest
TEXMAG	TeXMAG (Don Hosek)
TEXSTATUS	Information on the status of TeX (from Barbara Beeton)
TEXVMS	Items for TeX (VMS orientated)
UKTEX	UKTeX Digests
UNIX	From washington.edu (dated end May 1988)
UTILITIES	Various items for accessing archive (compress, btoa etc.)
UTILITIES.VMSFORMAT	Compress/decompress for VMS systems
VMS	Spell for TeX/LaTeX files under VMS

17.2.4 Access

The archive is available under the user public with the password public. Interactive access to this account is *not* permitted and the major means of extracting material has been FTP. Over the months this has highlighted a number of problems for sites. In particular we have had to update the colour book software on one node (SPOCK) to cater for file in stream_lf format. This problem affected all non-VMS sites.

This did not eliminate all the problems and I advertised in the digest for help in setting up a mail service similar to that provided by Rochester. Both Graham Toal and Adrian Clark responded and currently there is a mail server at Edinburgh (Graham's). This still suffers some problems with some type of file.

The number of successful transfers from Aston ending on May 30 1988 was 33,658.

Adrian has had a number of teething problems with his mail server which is located at Aston but he is attempting to provide 'btoa' (binary to ASCII) and other conversions which will overcome this problem.

17.2.5   Future development

It may be possible to provide 'kermit' type facilities at some point in the future if these are needed. Automatic reply addresses may be possible following various system software updates which are scheduled for the coming months.

17.3   Conclusion

I think that the digest and the archive provide a useful service to the academic community (and beyond) here in the UK. It has helped to foster links and information is now regularly exchanged between Aston and the EEC for our mutual benefit.

I would hope that both continue to develop and would like to invite comment from you as well as take any questions. I shall publish a summary of our discussion in the digest and hopefully leave here with suggestions for improvements to the service.

Peter Abbott
Computing Service
Aston University
Aston Triangle
Birmingham B4 7ET
UK

Chapter 18
Publishing 'Exotic' Documents with ExoTeX

Peter J Olivier

At the end of 1986, I had to look out for some text processing software, in order to prepare about 42 articles of a 'Festschrift' for publication. The contributions to this volume cover a wide range of 'exotic' philologies: Indo-European (comparative) linguistics and related languages, such as Old Indic (Vedic and Sanskrit) and many others, which normally are transliterated by using the Latin alphabet, when either no original character font is available or the citations should also be read by scholars who are not familiar with just these 'exotic' scripts or whatever other reason. Those languages make use of a great variety of diacritical marks and/or even of letters of non-Latin origin. TeX provides a lot of accents, math accents and symbols that are quite useful also for linguistic disciplines, but there are many more characters, which have to be created separately. I tried it my way by writing macros which may eventually be helpful for philologists dealing with 'exotic' languages, to get camera-ready copies of their articles within a very short time, and to avoid painting 'strange' accents and marks by hand. This ExoTeX is still 'under construction', and I would be most grateful for any suggestions by TeXnicians and TeXperts to make ExoTeX more elegant and powerful.

115

18.1   About the needs of 'exotic' philologies

T_EX was originally developed for the typesetting of mathematical texts, containing formulas, diagrams and so on. Some authors wrote additional macro packages like L^AT_EX, A_MS-T_EX or others, to offer different features and to make T_EX easier to use for all who want to write texts in a comfortable way not being interested in 'tuning up' their computers. In fact, with those macro-additions it is very easy to get fine-looking, camera-ready proofs of even the most difficult texts, containing accented words as in French, Spanish, Italian, Portuguese, Polish, other Slavic languages, Dutch, Swedish, Norwegian, Danish, Hungarian, and so on. Now, if we want to write a text in Czech, for instance, we will get along well with *háčeks*, *acutes* or so, but never find the very important long *u*, which looks like *ů*. So what could be done? Shall we forget about this diacritical mark, type a normal *u* and put the circle on top by hand? No, nay, never, because T_EX, besides its function as a highly qualified typesetting program, may also be regarded as a *programming language*, so we can get along a little easier if we *use* that language to *create* whatever we need.

As we have seen from Swedish, Danish and Norwegian, there *is* already a character that has a circle on top, namely *å*. How happy we are, because T_EX shows us the *source code* of that *å*, if we take a look at page 356 of *The T_EXbook* (Knuth, 1986). There we find its definition:

    \def\aa{\accent'27a}

Would it not be an easy way to define that *ů* ourselves in the same way, let's say

    \def\uo{\accent'27u} ... ?

Thus we have written a macro we can use from now on, and continue with our Czech text, having access to our *ů* whenever we need it.

There are many 'exotic' disciplines, that need a lot more accents, than are offered by T_EX or L^AT_EX itself. For example, Indo-European linguistics need diacritical marks to indicate that a vowel might have been long *or* short, as *ă*, *ĕ*, *ĭ*, *ŏ*, *ŭ*, or to indicate that a syllabic consonant represents a vowel quality, as in *r̥*, *l̥*, *m̥*, *n̥* or *R̥*, *L̥*, *M̥*, *N̥*, or in the language of the *Vedas* there are accentuated long vowels, like *ā́*, *ḗ*, *ī́*, *ṓ*, *ū́*, in some other strange language there might be nasalised long vowels as *ā̃*, *ē̃*, *ī̃*, *ō̃*, *ū̃*, and so on. We see, that there are either two accents or marks above one another on top or special symbols beneath a character. All we have to do, is to write a macro that puts two different symbols on top, and one that puts a symbol beneath. As the citations of foreign words normally occur in *italics*, we have to add a little *kerning*, so that the symbol fits correctly above or beneath an italicised character.

18.2   Several accent combinations from one macro

Let us take a look at the macro definition for ă. I named it \brv, to memorize that it puts a *breve* accent on top of any accented or plain character:

```
\def\brv#1{\leavevmode\setbox0=\hbox{#1}\dimen0=\ht0\advance
    \dimen0 by-1ex\rlap{\raise\dimen0\hbox{\char'25}}\box0{}}
```

Now you can put whatever character into the \hbox{#1} to get a *breve* accent on its top. But instead of always writing \brv{\=a}, \brv{\=e}, \brv{\={\i}}... etc. you can simplify your work once more by defining each character with names easy to keep in mind, like

```
\def\loka{\brv{\=a}}
\def\loke{\brv{\=e}}
\def\loki{\brv{\={\i}}}
\def\loko{\brv{\=o}}
```

and so on, and whenever you have to type an Indo-European *ŏlenā 'elbow', you just help yourself with *{\it \loko len\=a\/}. In the place of the *breve* accent there you can put any other diacritical mark, like *acute*, *grave*, *tilde* accents, circles, etc. You just choose a mnemonic code you like – make sure that it isn't defined yet! – and change the above definition in

`\def\lak#1{\leavevmode ...   \hbox{\char'23} ...}`	or
`\def\lgr#1{\leavevmode ...   \hbox{\char'22} ...}`	or
`\def\til#1{\leavevmode ...   \hbox{\char'176}...}`	or
`\def\kri#1{\leavevmode ...   \hbox{\char'27} ...}`	etc.,

then redefine your \lak, \lg, \til, \kri, etc. to \laka, \lake, \laki, \lako, \laku, \lgra, \lgre, \lgri, \lgro, \lgru, etc. as you like, and you will easily get a complete set of á é í ó ú, à è ì ò ù, ã ẽ ĩ õ ũ, å ů, ă ĕ ĭ ŏ ŭ, á́ é́ í́ ó́ ú́, ǎ ě ǐ ǒ ǔ, à̀ è̀ ì̀ ò̀ ǔ̀ and so on. Now you can type any character with two accents one above another.

A different approach was made by Christina Thiele (1985) who wrote a \diatop macro to put a second accent on top of an already accented character. I tested it but it did not show the same results as given in her article. The accent on top was too high, but on the other hand, the *dot-under* command \d works very well here: \d{\~\oe} results in ợ̃ (*not* the given \~{\d\oe})! Her strategy of using \llap and \rlap as well as kerning is the same as mine .

A small change might let the \diatop macro work correctly:

```
\def\diatop[#1#2]{{\leavevmode\setbox1=\hbox{{#1{}}}%
    \setbox2=\hbox{{#2{}}}%
    \dimen0=\ifdim\wd1>\wd2\wd1\else\wd2\fi%
    \dimen1=\ht2\advance\dimen1by-1ex%
    \setbox1=\hbox to1\dimen0{\hss#1\hss}%
    \rlap{\raise1\dimen1\box1}%
    \hbox to1\dimen0{\hss#2\hss}}}%
```

This addition of \leavevmode assures functioning in text mode. We shall now test it with four different examples:

```
\diatop[\d|{\=\oe}]    œ̄
\diatop[\=|{\d\oe}]    œ̄
\diatop[\d|{\~\oe}]    œ̃
\diatop[\~|{\d\oe}]    œ̃
```

From this we see that the \diatop macro really needs the 'above all' accent as first, then the other 'upper' or 'lower' accent as second argument, whereas the \d command has to be placed before another 'above' accent and does not work well when used as the second part of an accented group. The \diatop macro should do its work without any complaint now, when the order of arguments is correct, but I could not test it in *all* cases of occurrence. Nevertheless, I keep on trying.

18.3   Putting things under the line

There are many characters in 'exotic' languages that have diacritical marks beneath, like dots, bars, breves, tildes, cedillas, ogoneks etc., like m s h a s h t q s t a e i o u and so on. Looking up the definition for the *bar under* accent on page 356 of *The TEXbook*, we see that is quite useful for our purpose. (Once I printed some footnotes containing words with the normal *dot under* command, which did not work correctly but put the dot *inside* the character. I changed the *dot under* command according to the *bar under* command, and all dots were at the right place. This fault occurred with a HP Laserjet II, but the driver for a DEC LN03 worked correctly.) As we often use words in *italics*, we add an automatic italic correction. By way of an example, a macro definition for a *tilde* accent beneath a character would look like this:

```
\def\tilu#1{\oalign{#1\crcr\hidewidth
    \vbox to.2ex{\ifnum\fam=\itfam\hbox{\kern-1.8pt\char'176}
    \else\hbox{\char'176}\fi\vss}\hidewidth}}
```

In the same way as indicated above you make this macro available for *dot-under-italics*, *bar-under-italics*, *circle-under-italics*, for *ogonek, breve* accent, for a 'frown' or other symbols whatever by changing the above definition into

```
\def\dotu#1{\oalign{#1 ...\char'56 ...}           or
\def\bui#1{\oalign{#1 ...\char'26 ...}            or
\def\kru#1{\oalign{#1 ...\char'27 ...}            or
\def\og#1{\oalign{#1 ...[math italic 5pt]\char'54 ...}  or
\def\U#1{\oalign{#1 ...\char'25 ...}              or
\def\hvok#1{\oalign{#1 ...[math italic 8pt]\char'177 ...}
```

to get m, h, s, l, r, l, a, i, h, s, u, i and all others you need.

18.4   Other 'exotic' characters

Using and changing the two above macros you can create many other characters with diacritical marks, e.g. $k̄$ $ḡ$ $q̰ᵘ$ $k̰ᵢ$ $m̰$ $m̰ä$ or you can overlap two characters to form a different one, like þ or ŋ by using

```
\def\thorn{p\llap{b}}      \def\ng{{\it r\kern-.25em\j}}
```

you can take symbols from the math set and give them the right point size to fit in the text like ∂ or ∂̄ (which are known as ∂), or in footnotes ∂, ∂̄. For Slavic text in transliteration we need a 'jer' and 'jor' and get it by defining \wz (ь) and \hz (ъ – this nasty looking character will soon be replaced by a new letter generated with METAFONT) as:

```
\font\mitsix=cmmi6
\def\wz{{\mitsix \char'142}}
\font\itsvn=cmti7 \setbox0=\hbox{\mitsix \char'142}
\def\hz{{\itsvn \char'67}{\hbox to 3pt{\kern-.2em{\copy0}}}}
```

for Indic and Tocharian transliteration we often need a *daṇḍa* | and a double *daṇḍa* ‖, to indicate the end of a line in metric texts, or some other punctuation mark ⋄ or its double form, ⅋. We have access to them by defining

```
\def\dan{{$\mid$}      \def\ddan{$\parallel$}
\font\symegt=cmsy8
\def\ip{{\symegt \char'05}}
\newdimen\hx      \newbox\dopp
\setbox\dopp=\hbox{{\symegt \char'05}}
\hx=\ht\dopp      \advance\hx by .1pt
\def\dip{\unhcopy\dopp \kern-\wd\dopp \raise\hx\copy\dopp}
```

Other special symbols like ʾ *aleph* and ʿ *ayin* used in Hebrew, or *alif* and *hamza* in Arabic, can be created in the following way:

```
\font\mitten=cmmi10      \newdimen\hh      \hh=6.9pt
\newbox\alif    \newbox\ayin
\setbox\alif=\hbox{{\mitten \char'055}}
\setbox\ayin=\hbox{{\mitten \char'054}}
\advance\hh by -\ht\alif
\def\){\leavevmode\kern+.1em \raise\hh \copy\alif}
\def\({\leavevmode\kern+.1em \raise\hh \copy\ayin}
```

or you can use a different definition:

```
\mathchardef\lhook="012C   \mathchardef\rhook="012D
\def\alef{\kern+1pt$\rhook$}
\def\ain{\kern+1pt$\lhook$}
```

Those were a few examples of the results you can get when you use macro definitions of your own. I know that my actual definitions still suffer from a lack of elegance, but whenever using them inside the LATEX environment, they worked. Yet I am far away from the 'perfect' EXOTEX, but hope to get along by 'trial and error' and by your highly appreciated comments.

18.5 Using *text Greek* with accents

Reinhard Wonneberger (1986) showed his modifications to get a Greek text font with accents from the Greek symbols of the math italic font. Unfortunately, I had already tried something different, which was inelegant, but working. I can get *acutes, graves, circumflexes* ά ὰ ᾶ, long and short vowel marks ᾱ ᾰ and *tremas* ä above the Greek characters, and a *iota subscriptum* α̨ beneath the vowel. This looks quite fine with exception of η, where it is still too far below. Furthermore, there are no *spiritūs* yet. In the future I shall follow the method of Reinhard Wonneberger; until today there has been no time to add those global definitions.

My way of defining text Greek – a quite unorthodox approach – shows as follows:

```
\def\aaa{$\alpha$}      \def\bbb{$\beta$}
\def\ggg{$\gamma$}      \def\ddd{$\delta$}
\def\eee{$\varepsilon$} \def\zzz{$\zeta$}
\def\hhh{$\eta$}        \def\thh{$\vartheta$}
\def\iii{$\iota$}       \def\kkk{$\kappa$}
\def\lll{$\lambda$}     \def\mmm{$\mu$}
...
\def\ome{$\omega$},
\def\AAA{{\it A\/}}      \def\BBB{{\it B\/}}
\def\GGG{$\Gamma$}      \def\DDD{$\Delta$}
\def\EEE{{\it E\/}}      \def\ZZZ{{\it Z\/}}
\def\HHH{{\it H\/}}      \def\TTH{$\Theta$}
\def\III{{\it I\/}}      \def\KKK{{\it K\/}}
\def\LLL{{\it L\/}}      \def\MMM{{\it M\/}}
...
\def\OME{$\Omega$}.
```

Then I used the math accents to accentuate each character and gave them mnemonic names:

```
\def\agr{$\grave{\alpha}$}
\def\azf{$\tilde{\alpha}$}
\def\atr{$\ddot{\alpha}$}
...
\def\omak{$\acute{\omega}$}
\def\omgr{$\grave{\omega}$}
\def\omzf{$\tilde{\omega}$}
        etc.
```

and so on with all vowels. I defined a *digamma* Ϝ with `\font\sfi=cmssi10 \def\dig{{\sfi \char'106}}`. It saves a lot of time and typing goes quite fluently that way, but alas, no breathing marks!

18.6   Conclusion

While there are lots of mathematicians, physicians and other scholars of the natural sciences, there are comparatively few in the humanities, especially in those 'exotic' domains. But they need useful instruments, too, to typeset their articles. Therefore, they might appreciate a software which enables them to master even the most difficult text passages. ExOTEX could be helpful to achieve this task, even if some important features are still missing. They will be developed and published in a future release.

Though being just a beginner in TEX and LATEX, I followed the advice of Bart Childs (1986) – 'Remember that one of our biggest problems is individual timidity in the submission of papers and ideas to the meetings and TUGBOAT!' – and submitted some ideas. If you do the same, ExOTEX could turn out, in the light of your comments and suggestions, to be a powerful and comfortable macro package.

Bibliography

Bart Childs, 1986, *From the President*, p.129, TUGBOAT, 7(3).

Donald E. Knuth, 1986, *The TEXbook*, Addison Wesley Publishing Company, Reading, Mass., 483pp.

Christina Thiele, 1987, *TEX, Linguistics, and Journal Production*, pp.5–26, *in* TUG VIII Conference Proceedings, *ed.* Dean Guenther, TEX Users Group, Providence.

Reinhard Wonneberger, 1986, *'Verheißung und Versprechen' – A third generation approach to theological typesetting*, pp.180–198, *in* J. Désarménien, *ed.*, TEX for Scientific Documentation, Springer-Verlag.

Peter J Olivier
Institut für Indogermanistik und Indologie
Johann Wolfgang Goethe-Universität
Frankfurt
FRG

Chapter 19
German TEX

Hubert Partl

Although TEX and LATEX have been designed for American standards only, they are being used all over the world and with a lot of different languages. This article is intended to show an example of the problems that arise when modifying TEX or LATEX for easier application with a language other than English. Hints are added, how similar work might be performed for other European languages, with special emphasis on compatibility and portability problems.

19.1   What we need

TₑX, and its most popular macro packages, like IₐTₑX, have been designed by Americans for application in America, and this fact is constantly stressed by Donald Knuth and Leslie Lamport. In spite of this, since they are such excellent products, they are being used all over the world and with a lot of different languages. To make the best out of TₑX and IₐTₑX for a non-English (or, rather, non-American) language, you may need some or all of the following changes and extensions:

- hyphenation patterns for your language,
- support of national keyboards,
- additional TₑX commands to support specific features of your language,
- changes to the texts appearing in the chapter headings, table and figure captions, today's date, etc., as defined in the document style files,
- changes to layout and enumeration conventions, as defined in the document style files,
- changes or extensions to the TₑX software,
- changes or extensions to the Computer Modern fonts.

If you can do *without* any software and font changes, this will save you a lot of trouble, because you would have to maintain these changes for many different computer systems and many different output devices.

In any case, it is vital that users can switch between the modified and original versions of TₑX and IₐTₑX. You *must* maintain compatibility with the rest of the TₑX world. Otherwise, your TₑX version would not be TₑX, and the exchange of TₑX documents and 'macro files' would no longer be possible.

19.2   How to proceed

One of the great advantages of TₑX and IₐTₑX is the portability of document files among all TₑX installations. In order to prevent users from each inventing their own incompatible modifications, which would destroy that portability, the first step should be to standardise the user interface – i.e., the control sequences and commands to be used in the TₑX input files. Together with this standard, a 'quick and dirty' or prototype solution should be provided, so that users can start to apply the new features. Then, usually in several steps, better and more complete and finally even optimised solutions should be developed in such a way, that the users' input files need not be changed, but only the style files, font files, hyphenation patterns and other files that comprise a TₑX implementation are replaced or improved by the installation's TₑX guru.

'German TₑX' is now at the second stage, i.e., the user interface has been defined, and a first realisation is available.

19.3   The user interface

On its 6th meeting in Münster (Germany) in October 1987, the German TEX Users Group has agreed on a standard for a Minimal Subset of German TEX Commands'. These commands shall make it easier to set German texts – both with plainTEX and with the commonly used macro packages like LATEX, $\mathcal{AMS}$-TEX, etc. It is recommended that all TEX installations in the German speaking countries implement at least these commands on all their mainframes and personal computers. Then all TEX and LATEX input files that use these commands can be exchanged freely among all participating sites.

Agreement on this standard was easy, since it was a combination of several ideas that had already been in use in various German TEX installations.

The German TEX commands can be divided into four classes:

- easy-to-use control sequences for constructs that occur very frequently in German texts,
- commands that provide additional features which are needed to typeset German texts,
- changes to the texts appearing in chapter headings, table and figure captions, dates, etc.,
- commands to switch between the German modifications and the original version of TEX and LATEX.

If terminal keyboards or personal computers are available that have special keys assigned to the national characters (umlaut, sharp s, etc.), then these keys shall be used when typing in or editing the TEX input file. In this case, it is recommended that calling TEX shall involve two steps – usually hidden within a procedure: First, a simple conversion programme is called that replaces the national characters by the corresponding TEX control sequences. Then, the resulting file is fed into the original TEX program.

With plainTEX, the German commands are made available by an input command like

`\input german`

With LATEX, they are made available by specifying the document style option german, e.g. with

`\documentstyle[11pt,german]{article}`

In addition, the user should take care that the correct hyphenation patterns for his language are used – usually by specifying the appropriate format file when calling the TEX program. An excellent set of hyphenation patterns for German is available from the University of Bochum.

The German standard does *not* include layout conventions. On the contrary, a variety of document layouts is encouraged. As with conventional typesetting methods, all authors, editors, and institutions should be free to chose their individually preferred document styles and should not be forced to an unnatural uniformity.

19.3.1   Easy-to-use control sequences

TEX supports all sorts of accents and special characters, but in a way that is not very easy to type in or to read. This is no harm for English texts, where they occur very rarely. However, for constructs that appear very frequently in a certain language, easy-to-use control sequences are desirable. For German, the quotes character has been chosen to form such control sequences. The following control sequences are provided:

- "a prints the umlaut a (ä, short for \"a) – also for the other vowels,
- "s prints the sharp s (ß, short for \ss{}),
- "ck prints 'ck' that is to be hyphenated as 'k-k',
- "ff prints 'ff' that is to be hyphenated as 'ff-f' – also for certain other consonants.

19.3.2   Additional features

For typesetting German texts, some additional features are needed that are not part of standard TEX – at least not in a simple way. The following features are provided:

- "' and "' print German quotes („Anführungszeichen", also called „Gänsefüßchen").
- "< and "> print French quotes («guillemets»). These quotes are also used in certain German text styles, sometimes pointing »in« rather than «out».
- In analogy to the TEX commands \lq and \rq, there are also command names \glq, \grq, \glqq, \grqq, \flq, \frq, \flqq, and \frqq for German and French single and double left and right quotes.
- "| disables forbidden ligatures in words which consist of several parts – e.g. to produce 'Auflage' and *not* 'Auflage' for the word meaning 'Auf-Lage'.
- "- marks a hyphenation exception within a long word (like \-, but without disabling automatic hyphenation in the rest of the word).
- "" marks an analogous hyphenation exception, where *no* hyphen sign is added in the case of hyphenation (to be used, e.g., after the hyphen in a word like 'Computer-Gesellschaft').
- The occurrence of an umlauted character or sharp s shall *not* disable the automatic hyphenation for that word.
- \dq prints the quotes character (").

19.3.3   Captions and dates

By selecting the german option in the \input or \documentstyle command, the caption texts and today's date shall automatically be changed to German.

sch"on	$\longrightarrow$	schön
Stra"se	$\longrightarrow$	Straße
"'Ja, bitte!"'	$\longrightarrow$	„Ja, bitte!"
"<Merci bien!">	$\longrightarrow$	«Merci bien!»
Dru"cker	$\longrightarrow$	Drucker or Druk-ker
Schi"ffahrt	$\longrightarrow$	Schiffahrt or Schiff-fahrt
Auf"|lage	$\longrightarrow$	Auflage

Table 1. German TₑX Examples

19.3.4 Switching commands

Commands must be present to switch back to the original versions of TₑX and LATₑX. Two levels of such switches are implemented in German TₑX

- There is a pair of commands that affect the availability of the German modifications listed above.
  - \originalTeX resets all commands and control sequences to their original meanings. This is needed to generate environments that are completely compatible with the rest of the TₑX world.
  - \germanTeX switches on the German TₑX modifications again.
- The command \setlanguage{\xxx} is used to specify the main language of the document. The arguments to this command are to be predefined command names: \german, \austrian, \english, \USenglish, \french, etc. This command switches all text elements to the specified language, e.g. the format of today's date and the texts of the captions used with chapters, tables, figures and the like. In a more complete implementation, this might also include language specific hyphenation patterns and exceptions, special fonts or ligatures, different enumeration conventions and so on. Table 2 shows the effect of \setlanguage on \today for several languages and dialects.

\setlanguage	\today
\german	31. Januar 1988
\austrian	31. Jänner 1988
\english	31st January 1988
\USenglish	January 31, 1988
\french	31 janvier 1988

Table 2. Date Formats

Of course, both commands will be switched to German for mono-lingual German documents. However, there are situations where mixed modes are appropriate. For instance, if, in a German document, I want to use the extended math symbols coming with the AMS Cyrillic fonts, I must switch to \originalTeX before inputting the definition file, because in this file the quotes character is used to denote hexadecimal character codes rather than the German umlaut, and switch back to \germanTeX afterwards. On the other hand, if I use German citations in an English paper (like the one you are reading just now), I use \germanTeX – which enables the German umlaut and Anführungszeichen – and \setlanguage{\USenglish} – which restores the captions and dates to English.

These commands have been designed in such a way that they can be easily extended to other languages in the obvious way. The author expresses his hope that all European T_EX users will adopt the same or at least compatible conventions for their language specific T_EX modifications.

19.4   The present solution

A 'quick and dirty' realisation of these German T_EX commands has been compiled by the author with the help of several other T_EX users in Basle, Bonn, Bochum, Darmstadt, Stuttgart, and Vienna. The file, known as GERMAN.TEX or GERMAN.STY, is public domain. Mainframe installations can obtain it via Electronic Mail from several file servers: Internet users can FTP it from the Clarkson (formerly Rochester) L^AT_EX Style File Collection, and Bitnet users can GET it from NETSERV@AEARN in Linz (Austria) or from LISTSERV@DHDURZ1 in Heidelberg (Germany).

Besides being quick and dirty, this solution has the advantage that it can be used with the original versions of T_EX and L^AT_EX and of the fonts and hyphenation patterns as they are available now. Everything is defined and re-defined using T_EX commands only, and it is just one T_EX input file that can easily be ported to every computer (including personal computers) and is independent of the output devices used.

Care has been taken to make the same file usable both with plainT_EX and with L^AT_EX and other macro packages. This has been accomplished by using plainT_EX commands only, with the only exception of the L^AT_EX command \protect which is defined to \relax within this file if it has not been defined before.

19.4.1   The new features

The umlaut accent is redefined such that with the letters A, a, O, o, U, and u, the dots are positioned a bit lower than in the original version, and the following trick (found by Norbert Schwarz at the university of Bochum) is applied to enable automatic hyphenation in the rest of the word: The command sequence

    \nobreak\hskip\z@skip

is added after the accented character. This makes TEX 'think' that a new
word is started there, but without any space and without the possibility for
a line break.

The same trick is also applied for the sharp s (ß).

The German left double quotes („) are formed by taking the English right
double quotes (") and lowering them by the height difference between quotes
and comma, with some extra kerning. The German right double quotes (")
are the same as the English left double quotes except for the kerning. The
German single quotes are formed in a similar way.

For the French quotes, the appropriate math symbols are used. In the
present version, this works for the normal font size only – we are still looking
for a better solution.

19.4.2   The quotes character

First, the command \dq (short for 'double quotes') is defined to the original
meaning of the quotes character (").

Then, the quotes character is made an active character and is defined as
a control sequence that takes the following character as its parameter and,
depending on the value of this character, does the appropriate actions, i.e., it
prints the corresponding umlaut or sharp s or special quotes, or it performs the
required combination of \discretionary, \nobreak, and \hskip commands.

The quotes character is added to the \dospecials and \@sanitize commands which are used in the verbatim environments.

19.4.3   The captions and dates

The different versions of the chapter and table titles are obtained in the following way: the language changing commands re-define command names like
\contentsname to contain the appropriate texts (e.g. 'Inhalt' for German
texts and 'Contents' for English texts). With plainTEX or other macro packages, this will have the desired effect only if these command names are actually
used to print the respective title lines. With LATEX, it means that the original document style files have to be modified in the following way: the hard
coded English words (like 'Contents') have to be replaced by the corresponding command names (e.g. \contentsname), and these command names have
to be defined to contain the original words, e.g. with

```
\def\contentsname{Contents}
```

Leslie Lamport's comments in the DOC files provide help in finding all places
where such modifications are necessary. Several people in different places have
recently started such modifications, but they all have used different command
names, which will inevitably lead to incompatibility and chaos. The author

	\USenglish	\german
\contentsname	Contents	Inhaltsverzeichnis
\listfigurename	List of Figures	Abbildungsverzeichnis
\listtablename	List of Tables	Tabellenverzeichnis
\abstractname	Abstract	Zusammenfassung
\refname	References	Literatur
\bibname	Bibliography	Literaturverzeichnis
\indexname	Index	Index
\figurename	Figure	Abbildung
\tablename	Table	Tabelle
\partname	Part	Teil
\chaptername	Chapter	Kapitel
\appendixname	Appendix	Anhang

Table 3. Modification of the LaTeX Document Style Files

strongly suggests that all European LaTeX modifiers use the same set of modified document style files and that these files are made available to all LaTeX users in a central place like, e.g., the Clarkson LaTeX style collection.

For two reasons, the author suggests standardisation on the command names introduced by Wolfgang Appelt, and listed in Table 3:

- These names have already been used in a large number of installations throughout Germany and other countries for several years, so they can be viewed as something like a *de facto* standard.
- The names do not contain at-signs. Users can change captions texts to their needs by placing commands like

    \renewcommand{\contentsname}{My Own New Text}

  into the preamble. This may be of interest even in the English speaking countries, e.g. if someone prefers 'Table of Contents' to just 'Contents'.

The different versions of today's date are obtained by re-definitions of the \today command in analogy to the original definition by Leslie Lamport.

19.4.4   The switching commands

The three language switching commands are defined to switch on and off all the appropriate modifications. Finally, the command \germanTeX is executed which switches on everything that is appropriate for typesetting German texts, including \setlanguage{\german}.

19.5   Future work

For the future, a better realisation of the German TEX commands is planned by a team of advanced TEXperts in Germany. This solution shall include the following features:

- The umlaut and special quotes will be designed with METAFONT as separate characters in the text fonts, and they will be accessed as ligatures.
- New hyphenation patterns will be generated that include the umlauted characters, the sharp s, the special ck, and the special double consonants that hyphenate as triple consonants.
- The multi-lingual TEX software will be used to enable the switching of hyphenation patterns for the different languages.

Due to the complexity of this project, it will take some time until this solution will become available for all TEX installations (i.e., all computer types and all fonts for all output devices). However, the user interface (i.e., the TEX commands described above) will remain unchanged with this new solution. Therefore, users who start using them now will not have to change their TEX input files then, and they will still be able to exchange their TEX files with all installations where either the present or the future version of the German TEX commands is installed.

19.6   Other european languages

Several other people have recently started language specific modifications of TEX and LATEX. Two examples were published in TUGboat: first, there is a French TEX called FTEX that works on IBM PCs. It lets the users input the national characters in the extended 256 ASCII character set and maps them into ASCII codes below 128. There is also a Turkish TEX that provides shorthand notations for the various accented characters, using the exclamations sign, number sign, and colon in a similar way as we use the quotes character. Internally, both versions use ligatures that produce the desired characters and that are also included in the hyphenation patterns. This involves modifications (usually extensions) to the TFM and PXL (GF or PK) files for all fonts used.

From my experiences with 'German TEX", here is what I recommend to all language specific modifications of TEX:

- Before you invent your own modifications, talk to other TEX users in your country and agree on a common set of language specific TEX commands and control sequences.
- Do not re-invent the wheel, but collect all the ideas other people in your country and in other countries have already found useful.
- As soon as you have agreed on the user interface, better provide a 'quick and dirty' realisation rather than nothing at all.

- Provide format files with hyphenation patterns for your language in addition to the original ones, or provide the multi-lingual TEX software with hyphenation patterns for English and for your language.
- If national keyboards are in use, provide a conversion routine that replaces the national characters by the corresponding TEX control sequences.
- Provide easy-to-use control sequences for everything that occurs very frequently in your language.
- Provide additional commands or control sequences for everything that is needed to typeset texts in your language.
- Change the LaTeX caption texts and date formats by using the same modified document style files as we did.
- Provide switching commands of the form `\xxxTeX`, `\originalTeX`, and `\setlanguage` with language counters `\xxx` and `\USenglish`, in the same way that we did.
- Take care that your modifications work with plainTEX and with the macro packages LaTeX, *AMS*-TEX, `WEBMAC`, and perhaps others that are in use in your country.
- Make your modifications available for all computer types (mainframes and Personal Computers) and for all output devices.

And, as a final remark: 'Yes, do consider modifying TEX and LaTeX to support your language, and if you have done so, tell other people about it – perhaps at next year's European TEX Conference'.

Bibliography

Alonzo Garpiey, 1988, *French in TEX*, pp.65–69, TUGBOAT, 9(1).

Pierre MacKay, 1988, *Turkish Hyphenations for TEX*, pp.12–14, TUGBOAT, 9(1).

Hubert Partl, 1988, *German TEX*, pp.70–72, TUGBOAT, 9(1).

Hubert Partl
EDP Centre
Technical University Vienna
Wiedner Hauptstraße 8–10
A-1040 Wien
Austria

Chapter 20
With TeX to the Poles

Bogusław Jackowski, Tomasz Hołdys & Marek Ryćko

As rumour says, Poles live somewhere near a Pole. Which one?
– say East... Therefore it may sound odd that they are eager to
use TeX to typeset texts written in their strange language. Believe
it or not – this is true. For strangers an attractive feature of TeX
is its support for languages that use diacritical letters: basic fonts
include a large collection of special symbols (e.g., *cross* '-' to obtain
Polish suppressed 'L' and 'l', i.e., 'Ł' and 'ł', and *long Hungarian
umlaut* '″') and TeX itself provides mechanisms facilitating usage
of these symbols (an \accent primitive, ligatures, implicit kerns,
etc.). In practice, however, TeX turns out to be somewhat foreigner
unfriendly. The obstacles we have met seem to be common to
all TeX users whose native languages contain diacritical letters,
Gariepy (1988) and Partl (1988). This encouraged us to add our
remarks – maybe they will have an impact on further development
of TeX's international standard?

20.1   Cross

Our first disappointment is related to 'Ł' and 'ł', tailored especially for Poles. In plainTeX one obtains them by typing \L and \l, respectively. These macros exploit an implicit kern inserted between the *cross* '‿' (\char32) and a letter:

```
% implicit kern after \char32 causes overlapping
\def\l{\char32l}
\def\L{\leavevmode\setbox0\hbox{L}\hbox to\wd0{\hss\char32L}}
```

As far as 'ł' is concerned everything is all right. Not so with 'Ł'. The problem is that TeX inserts implicit kerns between 'L' and 'T', 'V', 'W', and 'Y', in order to put the letters closer together. The respective values (for Computer Modern Roman ten point font) are: $-5/6$ pt for 'T' and 'Y', and $-10/9$ pt for 'V' and 'W'. The Polish supressed 'L' may precede any of these letters but 'V', which does not belong to the Polish alphabet. Unfortunately, the plainTeX macro \L – as defined – discards any implicit kerns that might have been inserted after 'L'. Since the *cross* '‿' is relatively short, kerns are necessary and when missing, the rhythm of reading is interrupted. Therefore we decided to modify the plainTeX macro as follows:

```
\def\PL{% kerns may occur only to the right of 'L'
\leavevmode{\setbox0\hbox{L}\hbox to\wd0{\hss\char32L}%
\kern-\wd0}L}
```

Since in this definition the letter 'L' is not followed by any of TeX's commands, the implicit kerns are preserved.

20.2   Tails

Another, much more troublesome problem is connected with Polish 'tailed' letters, as they seem not to belong to TeX's standard. These letters are:

    ą Ą   (pronounced like French 'on' in, e.g., *bon*)

and

    ę Ę   (pronounced like French 'in' in, e.g., *vin*).

The question arises: what would Knuth do if Świerczkowski's name (*The TeXbook*, p.53) were Świątkowski? A natural candidate for the tail, i.e., *cedilla* '¸' turns out to be unsuitable for two reasons: first, it serves to mark sibilant letters and second, the Polish tail is rather a mirror image of the *cedilla*. (While preparing this paper we found that the plainTeX *cedilla accent* macro \c yielded characters of 0pt height and depth when used with capital letters – nice, isn't it?) For the purposes of this paper \char19 of five point *math italic* font (Greek *iota*) has been used as the tail. This is, however, not a good solution, since five point fonts can hardly be tailed in this way. Moreover, such tails do not look nice when used with *sans-serif* fonts. Incidentally, a bigger tail should be used for caps, hence, in fact, two tails are needed rather than one. It seems to be a better option either to create a font containing the whole set of necessary tails (or even letters) or to alter some characters of existing fonts. This, however, leads to incompatibility with other TEX installations, unless it is a standard. Knuth is evidently aware of the danger of such incompatibilities, writing in *The TEXbook*: 'The author didn't want to leave any places [in font tables] unfilled, since that would tempt people to create incompatible ways to fill them' (p.430). So, because of two silly tails, the final exhortation of the *The TEXbook*:

'GO FORTH now and create *masterpieces of the publishing art!*'
cannot be followed accurately by Poles. It is a pity, but maybe somebody knows a satisfactory remedy for that 'tail dilemma'? We would gladly appreciate any suggestions.

20.3 Accents

The remaining six Polish diacritical letters, namely: 'ć', 'ń', 'ó', 'ś', 'ź', and 'ż', can be obtained using plainTEX macros \. and \'. These macros are defined simply as:

```
\def\'#1{{\accent19 #1}}
\def\.#1{{\accent95 #1}}
```

They work, hmm – partially, since here once again arises the problem of omnipresent implicit kerns. Wanting to know how often they are inserted, one should look into METAFONT definitions. Just as an example we present here an extract of METAFONT's ligtable definitions that might interfere with Polish diacritical letters:

```
% ligtables for CMR10
% four degrees of kerning:
k#:=-5/18pt#;   u#:=-5/9pt#;
kkk#:=-5/6pt#;  uu#:=-10/9pt#;
ligtable "k": "a" kern -u#, "w": "e" kern k#,
        "a" kern k#, "o" kern k#, "c" kern k#;
ligtable "o": "b": "p": "c" kern -k#, "d" kern -k#,
        "e" kern -k#, "o" kern -k#,
        "a": "j" kern u#, "w" kern k#;
ligtable "A": "R": "C" kern k#, "G" kern k#, "O" kern k#,
        "L": "T" kern kkk#, "W" kern uu#, "Y" kern kkk#;
ligtable "D": "O": "A" kern k#, "W" kern k#;
ligtable "F": "W": "a" kern kkk#, "e" kern kkk#, "o" kern kkk#,
        "A" kern uu#, "K": "C" kern k#, "O" kern k#;
ligtable "P": "a" kern k#, "e" kern k#, "o" kern k#,
        "A" kern kkk#;
ligtable "T": "a" kern kkk#, "e" kern kkk#, "o" kern kkk#,
        "A" kern kkk#;
```

The problem is that an accented letter is no longer regarded by T_EX as the
same letter. In particular, any potential implicit kerns around the accented
letter are discarded. Incidentally, grouping has the same effect, so if the
\accent itself would not discard kerns, grouping used in the accent macros
would do it. Sometimes it is reasonable, e.g., if an accent is wide. Alonzo
Gariepy remarks that French accented letters need special kerning. It would
be less or more acceptable for Poles if the kerns were left untouched. This can
be achieved with the help of a short macro \KK (*keep kerns*) which reads as
follows (a similar trick has been used in French T_EX by Gariepy):

```
\def\KK#1#2{% both left and right kerns will be kept
#2{\setbox0=\hbox{#2}\kern-\wd0#1#2\kern-\wd0}#2}
```

If, using plainT_EX, one types, e.g., w\KK\'owczas instead of w\'owczas, the
kerns between 'ó' and 'w' will be preserved, yielding 'wówczas' instead of
'wówczas'. (This strange word means in English *then*.) Granted, the difference
is not significant, but, after all, what is all that implicit kerning for?

20.4   Hyphenation

The story does not end at this point. The next subject is *hyphenation*. Polish rules of word breaking seem to be simpler than the English ones. T_EX,
however, does not allow to incorporate these rules into the machinery of line
breaking. Even the use of the \hyphenation primitive is limited to words
which do not contain diacritical letters, unless these letters are obtained as
ligatures of characters of category 11 (*letters*) of especially arranged font.
The way round is to make a preprocessor which would insert *discretionary
hyphens* \- into the source text just before compilation. This approach has
some other advantages. One of them is connected with the Polish style of line
breaking. Namely, in Polish printing a single-letter word should not appear at
the right edge of a line. The preprocessor besides *discretionary hyphens* can
insert the *tie* '~' after every single-letter Polish word, such as *a*, *i*, *w*, and *z*
(English *but*, *and*, *in*, and *with*, respectively). The same effect can also be
achieved by turning *<space>*, *<tab>* and *<return>* into active characters,
checking whether they are followed by a single-letter word or not. Such an
approach, however, is less advisable because of its low efficiency. Another advantage of preprocessing is the possibility of avoiding ligatures, which occur
rather rarely in typical Polish fonts of type.

20.5   The Point

This is still not the end of the story, but in order to avoid boring the reader
too much we will not continue the detailed description of pecularities of the
Polish printing style. The point is that the present T_EX's standard is highly

unsatisfactory for the non-English users, since facilities provided for diacritical letters turn out to be not flexible enough. We believe that much can be achieved without changing TEX itself. It seems that adding to basic fonts a few 'accent' fonts, altering some of plainTEX macros and providing some preprocessing facilities would increase significantly the flexibility. But we hope that some day TEX9... will see daylight and from that moment its parochial clones will be no longer necessary. Finally, we would like to emphasize that, to our hearts' content, TEX in Poland finds still more and more fans, and maybe one day Poland will become TEXland, which may God grant us. Amen.

Bibliography

Alonzo Gariepy, 1988, *French in TEX*, pp.65–69, TUGBOAT, 9(1).

Donald E. Knuth, 1986, *The TEXbook*, Addison Wesley Publishing Company, Reading, Mass., 483pp.

Hubert Partl, 1988, *German TEX*, pp.70–72, TUGBOAT, 9(1).

Bogusław Jackowski, Tomasz Hołdys
ANIMA Ltd
ul. Fornalskiej 51
80–289 Gdańsk
Poland

Marek Ryćko
Institute of Computer Science
Polish Academy of Sciences
PO Box 22
00–901 Warsaw PKiN
Poland

Chapter 21
A Survey of Picture-Drawing in LaTeX

Sebastian P Q Rahtz

The plainTEX package does not attempt to provide any tools for drawing, leaving the production of graphics almost entirely to the \special system; the LaTeX package does provide a 'picture' environment, where line drawings are created from characters in special fonts, but the possibilities are quite limited and the commands not easy to use. This paper attempts to outline some of the methods used to get around this problem; examples will be given for LaTeX, but most are also applicable to plainTEX. It describes the different sorts of drawing needed in a typical document – half tones; pure 'art' (bitmaps); vector drawings; and analytical graphics. It also describes solutions, ranging from pasted-in photographs through *MacDraw*-like graphics to LaTeX 'picture'. We will also describe drawing tools in systems like *The Publisher* and *Interleaf*. Nearly all the discussion will assume that a 'large' version of TEX is available and that printing is through a PostScript device: discussion of screen-based drawing tools will be limited to the Macintosh and the Sun workstation.

Sebastian P Q Rahtz
Department of Electronics & Computer Science
Southampton University
Southampton SO9 5NH, UK

Chapter 22
Including Pictures in TEX

Alois Heinz

We describe different methods for including pictures into TEX documents. These methods are applicable on line graphics as well as on raster graphics. We compare these methods under different aspects, such as compatibility with printer drivers, space efficiency and we try to give a complete set of characteristics under which such methods can be compared. We find out that some of the described methods are better than others but, in general, the choice should depend on the requirements of the kind of picture.

22.1   Introduction

Where text and type are concerned, TEX is one of the best systems actually available. But text is only one means to express ideas and imaginations. And more than once one has heard that "a picture can tell more than thousand words". For us who are scientists, immediately the question arises: "Why don't we use more pictures and graphics in our papers?" The answer, until now, was very easy: "With our text processing systems it is easier to create and manipulate text than pictures. And we aren't trained on that job."

Now, with the widespread availability of scanners, CAD systems, and desktop publishing systems, the situation has changed. It has become easier to get digitized pictures into the computer or to create drawings and pictures with the aid of software systems and then to include them into the documents.

But how can we who want use TEX as our favourite text formatter, include pictorial impressions into our documents? TEX itself has very limited capabilities for picture description and formatting. But there are some hooks we can use to get into our TEX documents what we want to go there.

In the next section we will describe how TEX works when it is formatting text, in order to give an impression of where the mentioned hooks are located. Then, in the following sections we will describe one by one all methods we found we could use. In the last section, we will summarize the advantages and disadvantages of all the described methods. And here and there we will make use of a picture to give a better understanding of what we mean or just to give an example.

22.2   How TEX works

This section will not really describe how TEX works. It just tries to give a coarse understanding of what is needed to produce a TEX document and where the hooks for including pictures are located (see Knuth, 1986).

TEX is a batch text formatting system. The main input of TEX is the file with the text that should go into the document and interspearsed commands to rule the formatting process. These commands mostly begin with a backslash character '\' and they can have one or more parameters, sometimes included in curly braces. Additionally, TEX reads a format file that contains precompiled parameter settings, macro definitions, and hyphenation patterns. Besides the main text file, TEX may read further text files containing document style definitions, auxiliary information (e.g. for a table of contents) or even more text. For its job TEX needs some information about each font including the metrics of each character. For this reason it reads TFM (TEX font metric) files.

TEX decides for each character, what its position in the final document should be and puts this position into a so-called DVI file, which is a device-independent description of the formatted document. Besides the `log` files and perhaps some other text files, the `DVI` file is the main output TEX produces.

To see the document described in the `DVI` file, one needs a driver program that interprets the `DVI` commands and produces a visual output using a matrix printer, a laser printer, a screen, or another graphical output device. Additionally, this driver program needs to know the shapes of the characters used. It gets this information from so-called `PXL` files. Sometimes the `DVI` commands are translated into another page description language, which is then interpreted by other software or hardware, e.g. POSTSCRIPT (Adobe, 1987a, 1987b).

The `DVI` file is a byte file which consists of one-byte commands having different numbers of arguments. All commands which belong to one page are surrounded by the commands *bop* (begin of page) and *eop* (end of page), where the *bop* commands are in a linked list with their arguments. Within these surroundings, there are commands to change the current position on the page being set, to change fonts, to set characters from the current font, to push and pop parameter settings, and to set black rectangles of a given height and width. The command '`xxx`' has two arguments, the first giving the length of the second. This command and its arguments are skipped by usual driver programs, that is, it remains uninterpreted. The command is interpretation of TEX's '`\special`' command. Dedicated driver programs may interpret the argument of a '`\special`' command, resulting a picture generated by the output device.

In the following sections we will describe different approaches to combine graphics with text typeset by TEX.

22.3   The simple line-dot approach

The simple line-dot approach is a method used in the times when the favourite output devices were line printers or simple ASCII terminals and TEX wasn't yet born. Tables or simple graphics were composed using the printable characters of the ASCII character set. In LATEX (Lamport, 1986), a special TEX macro package, the definition of such a line-dot graphic can be given within the `verbatim` environment. Figure 1 is given as an example.

Although the generated graphics are very simple, this method has several advantages:

- the graphics can be easily described using standard ASCII editors;
- what you see using the editor is what you get from your document; with regard to the graphics each standard ASCII editor is a *wysiwyg* editor;
- the lettering of graphics (with typewriter font) is possible;
- we are able to import simple line-dot graphics produced by a special purpose ASCII editor.

Besides these plus-points the method has some strong disadvantages:

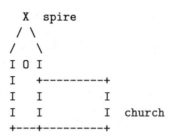

Figure 1. A simple church.

- the graphics are very restricted and primitive;
- the quality of graphics is extremely low when compared with the quality of the typeset text;
- the angles between 'lines' can only be multiples of 45°.

It is easy to realize that it is inadequate to use the simple line-dot approach for pictures together with the typesetting capabilities of TₑX for text. But, as we will see in the next section, an improved version of the line-dot approach will yield better results.

22.4   The improved line-dot approach

The line-dot approach can be improved by using a larger set of picture primitives than only ASCII characters and by allowing to position these primitives freely so that they join each other or even overlap. With TₑX we are able to use nearly as many fonts as we want and to determine the position of each character relative to others. So, if we have designed a basic set of symbol fonts with the accompanying set of macros, it is possible to describe a picture in a logical manner. TₑX has no difficulties in setting these pictures together with the text and DVI driver programs are able to put them out without any modifications.

The LATₑX system has build-in picture making capabilities that make use of the method described above. Inside the so-called `picture` environment there are commands available that place primitive or composed picture elements in a user defined coordinate system. The primitive picture elements are single characters from usual fonts, or from LATₑX symbol fonts, or they are compositions of these and horizontal or vertical lines. Figure 2 gives a very simple example of LATₑX's possibilities.

The picture is given on the left side, the definition on the right side. We could have given a much better example, but the installation where we produced this paper using LATₑX does not contain the LATₑX symbol fonts until now. The given example is in part from Lamport (1986).

The improved line-dot approach is a method that can be used to let the user give an abstract logical description of a picture or of picture elements

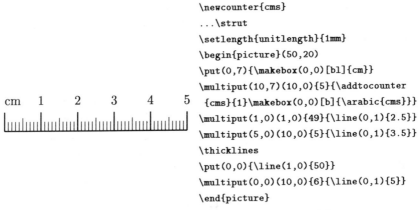

```
\newcounter{cms}
...\strut
\setlength{unitlength}{1mm}
\begin{picture}(50,20)
\put(0,7){\makebox(0,0)[bl]{cm}}
\multiput(10,7)(10,0){5}{\addtocounter
  {cms}{1}\makebox(0,0)[b]{\arabic{cms}}}
\multiput(1,0)(1,0){49}{\line(0,1){2.5}}
\multiput(5,0)(10,0){5}{\line(0,1){3.5}}
\thicklines
\put(0,0){\line(1,0){50}}
\multiput(0,0)(10,0){6}{\line(0,1){5}}
\end{picture}
```

Figure 2. A LATₑX picture without using symbol fonts

and their relationships, while the TₑX macros compute and set the layout of the picture. With the macro package TreeTₑX (Brüggemann-Klein and Wood, 1987) for example, the user defines certain properties of trees and the optimal layout is generated automatically. The benefits of the improved line-dot approach are:

- pictures of high quality are generated;
- the lettering of graphics (with arbitrary fonts) is possible;
- the picture description language can be very powerful and can include repetitions and hierarchical definitions;
- the layout of a picture can be computed automatically and, therefore, it can be optimized.

Some drawbacks are:

- *wysiwyg* editing of pictures is not possible;
- fonts with special symbol characters are needed;
- the slopes of lines and the radii of arcs and circles are restricted to distinct values.

We observed that by the improved line-dot approach we can only include pictures that can be described using a special picture description language. In the next section we describe, how arbitrary pictures can be transformed into a special format and included.

22.5 The line-dot approach with grey fonts

At the lowest level each picture can be considered as a set of rows, each row consisting of an array of grey scale values. And each picture (without colours), whatever source it comes from, can be transformed into this raster form by simply scanning it. This gives us a simple way to get arbitrary pictures into

TEX documents. In a TEX font with 128 characters 128 grey scale values can be encoded using combinations of black and white dots. We can increase the number of available grey scale values by using multiple fonts for each resolution. But it is better to restrict this method to the use of only one grey font because changing fonts is expensive in time and space.

For each picture format of which we want to include pictures, we need a program that scans the picture and generates the description of a TEX *box*, enclosing lines of grey font characters without additional glue between them. These picture descriptions can be given to TEX using the '\input' command. TEX will set a box with many equally spaced characters in it, and the DVI file will contain a *set_char* command for each grey scale value. The main advantages of this method are:

- it is applicable to all picture formats – we can use pictures from arbitrary sources;
- the quality of a picture depends on how fine the sources are scanned and how small the picture elements are.

And this are the main disadvantages:

- for each picture format a special transformation program has to be written;
- if we want to get pictures with a high degree of fineness, the scanning of pictures will produce much data, even if there are not many objects to be displayed (the DVI file will grow large in the same way because even white dots are described using one byte).
- we need special fonts (grey fonts) for different resolutions and scanning degrees.

There is another drawback common to all the line-dot approaches described so far: for each occurrence of the same picture in some document the generating code appears once in a DVI file. The method described in the next section overcomes with this drawback although it is somehow similar to the last method.

22.6   The raster-in-font approach

In the last section we described how a picture can be rastered and decomposed into small pieces. Another possibility is to store the rastered image in a special picture font. The raster image of the picture is included in the PXL file and the metric of the picture is included in the TFM file of a picture font with the aid of a special program. The picture can be inserted into a document by telling TEX to set one character from the picture font. TEX's input would include something like this:

```
\font\gr=graphic
\gr\char0
```

This method has the following advantages:

- it is relatively easy to realize;
- multiple appearances of a picture make use of the same stored raster;
- TEX is not concered in the composing of the picture because the picture is regarded as one character.

Although the raster-in-font approach seems to be an easy solution for the given problem, we discovered that it has strong disadvantages, when we implemented it:

- a rastered image of the picture has to be stored for each supported printer resolution or magnification;
- some DVI drivers make use of font downloading to the printer and have limitations on the number of fonts and magnitude of characters;
- if typeset documents including pictures are sent to other destinations via file transfer or electronic mail, the TFM file and the PXL file have to be included and installed at the new site for each document file.

The last arguments may not count if TEX is used in a closed world environment and if the driver programs compose the typeset pages as raster images that are sent to the output device. In the next section we describe another method that can be used in a closed world environment and that makes use of specialized driver programs.

22.7   Use of '\special' and modified drivers

As we have seen, the standard DVI language has very limited capabilities to describe pictures. But an easy way is provided to extend this standard level. The argument of TEX's '\special' command becomes the second argument of the DVI 'xxx' command, which is not interpreted by standard DVI driver programs. If the source text of these programs is available, routines can be added to interpret the argument of 'xxx', e.g. as commands of a picture description language. The '\special' command in the TEX input could have the picture commands as arguments or it could give a pointer to the file containing these commands.

This method is applicable to all kinds of picture formats. The pictures of Figure 3 are examples.

The raster graphic on the lefthand side was included giving the pointer to the picture file as the argument to the '\special' command, whereas the commands defining the POSTSCRIPT graphic on the righthand side were given directly to the '\special' command. The original output was produced with a *Textures* driver program on an Apple LaserWriter. This method has great advantages:

- the graphics can be very good;
- special graphic systems can be used;
- it is very efficient in disk space because of the use of powerful picture description languages.

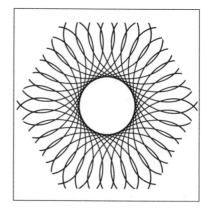

Figure 3. A raster graphic (left) and a POSTSCRIPT picture (right)

There remain some disadvantages:

- standard DVI driver programs have to be modified;
- driver programs not capable of the extensions ignore the pictures;
- it is difficult to include TₑX fonts into the graphics.

In most environments this method will be sufficient and the benefits will predominate the drawbacks. But if compatibility with standard DVI driver programs is required, this method cannot be used. In the next two sections we describe two methods that need neither special driver programs nor special picture fonts.

22.8   Picture rastering in the TₑX input

It is possible to compose a rastered picture with TₑX using its ability to change the reference point on a page and to draw lines of arbitrary width and height. The idea to this method is due to Marc Oswald and his implementation is described in Oswald (1986). He wrote a program that translates GKS (Enderle, Kansy and Pfaff, 1984) pictures into this TₑX-readable form. The TₑX input file looks like the following:

```
\vbox{\offinterlineskip\skip99=.3pt\def\hs#1{\hskip#1pt}
      \def\vr#1{\vrule width#1pt height.3pt depth0pt}
\hbox{\hs{180.0}\vr{0.3}\hs{182.1}}
\vskip\skip99
  .   .
}
```

TₑX interprets the picture and translates its definition into a sequence of the DVI commands *push*, *pop*, *set_rule*, *right* and *down*. The advantages of this method are:

- pictures from arbitrary sources can be included;

- the typeset document is device independent.

But there are some serious shortcommings:

- the pictures have to be typeset by TEX – this takes much time and, even worse, if a picture is too complicated TEX resigns with the message 'capacity exceeded';
- TEX's input and output regarding the pictures is not space efficient;
- it is difficult to include TEX fonts into the pictures.

The main disadvantage of this method is that TEX has to typeset the pictures. The next section describes how this problem can be circled around.

22.9   Use of '\special' and merge

In the last section we described how a rastered picture can be translated into the DVI language by TEX. But there is no reason why this could not be done by the program that scans the original picture. Each picture can be rastered and encoded into a DVI string beginning with a *push* command and ending with a *pop*.

It remains the problem to include this picture string into the text document. This work can be done by a special merge program. This program inserts the DVI strings describing the pictures at the positions of the typeset document marked with '\special' commands and maintains the linked list of *bop* commands. An implementation of this method is described in Blanc (1987). It has the following benefits:

- it is applicable to all picture formats;
- it is device independent;
- standard DVI printers can output the documents including the pictures;
- the merge program has to be written only once.

The following drawbacks can be listed:

- it is not space efficient;
- it is difficult to include TEX fonts.

The advantages of the special-and-merge method could be increased if some advanced commands regarding pictures and picture elements were added to the DVI language. But this extended language could no longer be interpreted by standard DVI driver programs.

22.10   Summary

We have described a set of different ways for including pictures into TEX documents. For each method we have listed the main advantages and disadvantages, where we tried to pay attention to all relevant aspects. We can conclude with the observation that none of the described methods can be said

	Simple-Line-Dot	Improved-Line-Dot	Line-Dot-with-Grey-Fonts	Raster-in-Font	Special-and-Modified-Drivers	Picture-Rastering-in-In...	Special-and-Mer...
High quality graphics	--	+	+	+	+	+	+
Arbitrary sources	-	-	+	+	+	+	+
TEX fonts available	~	+	-	-	-	-	-
Space efficient	+	+	-	--	+	--	-
Use of standard drivers	+	+	+	~	-	+	+
No problem with TEX run	+	+	+	+	+	--	+
Document in one file	+	+	+	-	~	+	+
Independent of resolution	+	+	+	-	~	+	+

Table 1. Comparison of picture inclusion methods

to be the best. Which method is best to be used depends mainly on the kind of pictures and whether compatibility with standard DVI driver programs is desired or not. Table 1 summarizes the results of our examinations.

Bibliography

Adobe Systems Incorporated, 1987a, POSTSCRIPT *Language Reference Manual*, Addison-Wesley Publishing Co.

Adobe Systems Incorporated, 1987b, POSTSCRIPT *Language Tutorial and Cookbook*, Addison-Wesley Publishing Co.

Manuel Blanc, 1987, *DRAW—An Object Oriented Graphic Editor with a TEX-DVI Interface* (in German), Masters Thesis, Institut für Angewandte Informatik und Formale Beschreibungsverfahren, Universität Karlsruhe.

Anne Brüggemann-Klein, Derick Wood, 1987, *Drawing Trees Nicely with TEX*, Research Report CS-87-05, Department of Computer Science, University of Waterloo, Waterloo, Canada.

G. Enderle, K. Kansy, G. Pfaff, 1984, *Computer Grafics Programming*, Springer-Verlag.

Donald E. Knuth, 1986, *The TEXbook (Computers & Typesetting; A)*, Addison Wesley Publishing Co.

Leslie Lamport, 1986, LATₑX: *A Document Preparation System*, Addison Wesley Publishing Co.

Marc Oswald, 1986, *Implementation of a GKS-TₑX Interface* (in German), Masters Thesis, Rechenzentrum, Universität Karlsruhe.

Alois Heinz

Institut für Informatik, Universität Freiburg

Rheinstraße 10–12

D-7800 Freiburg

FRG

Chapter 23
PROTEX: Integration of Text, Graphics and Images

Susanne Lachmann

We – that is GESYCOM GmbH – have been working on and with TEX since 1984. Our environment consists of various IBM compatible PCs with DOS, and our favourite programming language is TURBO Pascal 5.0. We mainly work on software solutions for the typesetting industry, especially the development of connections between different – normally stand alone – systems.

23.1   Introduction

When we first got in contact with TEX, we saw two applications, where a PC-based TEX-workstation really would be effective:

- TEX as a stand-alone author's PC-workstation outside the 'normal' university environment with a TEX-sensitive editor, previewing functions including graphics and images and a 300 dpi laserprinter as the output device;
- TEX as an add-on PC-workstation for special purposes in between a standard typesetting environment with a TEX-sensitive editor, special macro packages, previewing functions, a 300 dpi laserprinter for proof-printing and a high resolution typesetter as the output device.

Therefore we decided to design our own TEX-environment for these two professional applications under the name of PROTEX. What we wanted to reach in the end (and what we have finished now) is a PC-workstation with:

- tools for text, image and graphics editing;
- TEX-macros for the easy and nearly automatic inclusion of graphics and images into the text;
- previewing functions which are able to show not only the TEX-formatted text but also included images and/or graphics;
- printer drivers which are able to work with the connected printer as effectively as possible, especially concerning font downloading and image and graphics inclusion;
- a typesetter driver which is able to work with the original typesetter fonts.

TEX in connection with a typesetter driver is only mentioned here for complete description of our works.

23.2   GESYCOM's driver TEXniques

This paper mainly deals with our efforts to realize an author's system with TEX. At first, we looked for a 300 dpi laserprinter, which would be able to support the TEX-output – including images and graphics – in an effective way. We decided to work with the electronic laserprinter ELSA because this printer had several advantages:

- an internal GKS system, which makes it easy to print vector graphics;
- the possibility to store fonts in EPROMs, which makes downloading unnecessary for these fonts;
- the possibility to have 2 MByte memory inside the printer and with this have a large font download area in addition to the needed bitmap space;
- a printing speed of up to 20 pages per minute.

23.2.1 The font dowloading

We implemented a download algorithm within the ELSA driver which is able
to load single characters and not simply complete fonts into the font download
area of the printer. While printing, the driver saves the already downloaded
characters in a file, from which it is able to decide whether a character to
be printed is already downloaded or has to be downloaded additionally into
the printer. This file also holds the information about EPROM stored fonts
which do not have to be downloaded again. The driver generated download
information file remains active for all following jobs, and only the use of as
yet used characters causes the driver to add new characters to the download
area of the printer.

   This way of handling the character downloading makes TeX-printing very
comfortable for the user. There is no need to download fonts before printing,
all the needed downloading is done by the driver during printing the document.

   Our experience says, that most TeX-users print a document two or more
times and that nearly all commonly known drivers download all fonts and/or
characters every time the job is being printed. After having printed a document once with our driver, the next printings take little time, because only
a few character downloads (if any) are needed then. This way, our download
algorithm saves the user a lot of time.

23.2.2 The graphics inclusion

The works on the inclusion of line-art into TeX-documents started with detailed thinkings about which line-art program could be the best to choose for
the 'normal' TeX-user and – following this – which line-art format had to be
interpreted by our drivers.

   The fact is, that one of the most popular formats is the DXF-format,
created by the graphics program AutoCAD. But we decided not to base our
work on this format because for the 'normal' TeX-user, AutoCAD is much too
expensive. Therefore we looked for a cheaper, but nevertheless good, and for
TeX-users acceptable (in price and functions) line-art program. We decided
to use UniCAD (which is sold under the name ProDesign outside Germany).

   The UniCAD output format PD1 gave us the possibility to design a conversion program for our TeX printer driver an this way to include graphics
into TeX-documents while printing. The line-art inclusion is realized by several special TeX-macros, which allow the user to specify a centered title and
the desired formatting parameters (absolute to the whole page or relative to
the last text line) for the line-art. For the user the handling is very easy:
he does not need to convert the created line-art picture before printing, the
conversion (including zooming to the user specified size) is done automatically
while printing. Presently we are able to include most of the commonly used
line-art formats into all our drivers.

23.2.3 The image inclusion

For the inclusion of pixel-information into TEX documents we made several starts with several different pixel file formats. At first, we decided to work on the internal bitmap-format of the electronic laserprinter ELSA. At this time we worked with a 300 dpi Ricoh-scanner and had already designed a scan-software for this scanner. This software produced an output-file in the internal ELSA format which could be sent to the ELSA printer without conversion.

Because of the need for editing the scanned images, we began to work with the pixel editor PC-Paint, which internally worked on the compressed bitmap format PIC, which is not compatible to the internal ELSA format. Therefore we had to create a pixel-conversion-software to convert the PIC-format into our internal format for printing on the ELSA and vice versa.

After looking for other pixel editors and pixel formats we found out that there was no sort of standard format within the market. Since it made no sense for us to interpret all those different pixel formats in our drivers, we decided to create some kind of standard pixel format. We called this standard format PX0; its most attractive property is that it is simple to understand and interpret – even for inexperienced pixel-freaks.

Last, but not least, we worked on the nowadays most commonly used PCX-format, which is output, for example, from the pixel-editor Publisher's Paintbrush (which has become our favourite). All of our drivers are able to work with this PCX-format and the manner of pixel-inclusion into TEX documents is the same as the line-art inclusion, which means easy to use macros.

23.3 GESYCOM's TEX-products

At the moment we are able to present a variety of TEX drivers and tools, which make the way of TEXing more comfortable and much more fun.

23.3.1 The laserprinter drivers

We developed all our printer drivers with the same functions as our first printer driver for the ELSA (i.e. job-independant character downloading while printing and automatic line-art and pixel-image inclusion). GESYCOM supported printers are:

- ELSA: LISA printing sytem, up to 20 pages per minute, integrated GKS controller;
- GPP8: LED printing system, up to 8 pages per minute, integrated GKS controller;
- GPP15: LED printing system, up to 15 pages per minute, integrated GKS controller;

- GPP30: ionic printing system, up to 30 pages per minute, up to 4 MByte memory, up to 150,000 pages per month, costs less than 0.02 DM per page;
- MultiLaser SP-8: HP-LaserJet compatible, own printer PC card for higher performance
- all other HP-LaserJet compatible printers.

23.3.2 The screen drivers

The development of screen drivers was a natural result of our efforts in developing laserprinter drivers which are able to include graphics and images. Our screen drivers should also be able to show embedded graphics- or pixel-information on the user monitor. Because of the variety of commonly used graphic cards we created several different screen drivers which are able, to show line-art and pixel-images within a TEX document on the screen. In connection with this we have generated own screen fonts, so that out screen drivers are able to show a document at 75 dpi as well as at 150 dpi on the screen. Supported graphic adapters are:

- Hercules compatibles (resolution 720×348);
- EGA compatibles (resolution 640×350);
- CGA compatibles (resolution 640×200);
- MCGA compatibles (resolution 640×400, e.g. 14″ IBM PS-2 Model 30 monitor);
- Princeton compatibles (resolution 1600×1200, e.g. 20″ NCC monitor);
- Wyse 700 with 15″ Wyse monitor (resolution 1280×800);
- Etap with DIN-A-4 Etap Neftis monitor (resolution 720×720);
- Etap with DIN-A-3 Etap Atris monitor (resolution 1440×720, 2 preview pages on one screen).

Most of those screen drivers have been developed in connection with campus licenses, because in a university environment there are various graphic adapters and monitors in use. Any other graphic adapter can be supported within a short time because we based all screen drivers on a unique screen driver concept.

23.3.3 The tools

During GESYCOM's work on and with TEX several tools had been generated which can be really useful for a TEXnician. They can be grouped into two sorts of tools – converting and editing tools:

- converting tools:
  - a tool which converts a TEX-DVI file into a PCX-file, which then can be edited for example with the pixel editor Publisher's Paintbrush. This

gives you the possibility to work on TEX-formatted pages with an pixel editor and to use every function that your pixel editor provides (e.g. underlay text with rasters, rotate parts of the text, draw lines around the text, insert TEX-texts in images etc.).

−a tool which converts each of the four above mentioned pixel-formats (ELSA-internal, PIC, PX0, PCX) into another.

−a tool which converts most of the common line-art formats into some other common line-art or image formats (e.g. DXF into PCX).

• editing tools:

−the editor SEM, which allows the highlighting of special ASCII characters on the screen (e.g. highlighted braces and/or backslashes are very helpful in TEX-sources), to work with nearly the complete IBM character set during editing the text (all TEX-known characters are converted after terminating the editing process) and to work with the word wrap feature during editing (the soft returns are also converted for TEX after terminating the document editing).

SEM is a very useful tool when you have to work on large amounts of text since it formats the text on the screen – a good help to oversee the text's structure.

−the editor FEE, which is a 'terminate and stay resident editor' (i.e. an editor, who stays resident, even if you terminate editing). FEE's main function is, that after TEXing your document, the cursor is positioned on that line where TEX marked an error during formatting and the TEX error message is displayed. Furthermore, FEE provides special key functions for the easy typing of LATEX macro structures.

This editor is very helpful when you are a newcomer to TEX (and therefore produce lots of errors) and/or when you are a LATEXnician.

23.4 GESYCOM's TEX-plans

We are actually working on an own TEX-version, which is supposed to:

• provide another kind of aesthetic model, which uses other and more information to make a TEX document look fine instead of the normally used TEX character kerning pairs;

• provide another kind of hyphenation model, using an external hyphenation program instead of the normal TEX hyphenation patterns.

Susanne Lachmann
GESYCOM GmbH
Eupener Straße 22
D-5100 Aachen
FRG

Chapter 24
Line-Oriented Layout with TeX

Alan Hoenig

We speak of a *line-oriented* layout when the design landmarks in documents are given in terms of lines of the typeset document – lines down from the beginning of a paragraph, lines down from the top of the page, and so on. TeX design specifications are normally made on the basis of units identifiable in the source document file before any typesetting takes place. This paper suggests several techniques for creating TeX design layout on a line-by-line basis. We will discuss three examples: the use of TeX in typesetting 'windows' of space entirely enclosed within paragraphs; the creation of paragraph shapes for an arbitrary sequence of paragraphs; and the creation of a macro to identify the typeset position on the page. These are used to show how to design a page-layout system that might be suitable for a small newspaper or newsletter. This set of page layout macros illustrates the ability to continue stories several pages after they begin and to provide automatic forward and backward page references to the beginning and ending portions.

24.1   Introduction

TEX is great – about 99% of the time. It is easy to increase the interline spacing in a paragraph, for example, because the paragraph is readily identifiable in the TEX source file. It is straightforward to italicize a particular sentence, because a sentence is clearly indicated in the TEX source. It is also reasonably easy to place some marginal notes in the margin of a paper by boxing the comments and \llapping them into the margin. The contents of the box are plain to see in the source file.

But what happens in those cases where we want the layout to depend on landmarks that cannot be known until the typesetting has been completed? Suppose we want to leave room for a picture that will sit at the second line on the second page of a document. Neither the line breaks nor the page break will be known at the time we prepare the source file.

Here is another scenario. We need to place a photo between two columns of text. To accommodate it, the tenth through twentieth lines in both columns must be indented – those in the left column being indented on the right, and those in the right column being indented on the left. We might find such a task problematical for several reasons. plainTEX provides no macros for extending control of paragraph shapes across paragraphs, and it is difficult to see how to instruct TEX to match the right and left profiles of the adjacent columns.

We need *line-oriented* sets of tools for tasks such as these – tools which will use as landmarks the typeset lines of the document. It is the purpose of this paper to suggest some techniques which have proven useful in this regard. These suggestions by no means exhaust the field, but the author hopes that readers will be able to build upon them to resolve other issues.

24.2   Reconstructing a paragraph

Essential to a line-oriented analysis is TEX's \parshape command, which enables the exact specification of line lengths within a particular paragraph. Once the paragraph has been created, it can be sliced up and the pieces rearranged to form a desired layout, as we will illustrate. Recall that \parshape takes two arguments – the *number* of lines and a *length list*, which is the sequence of pairs of dimensions. Each pair in the list consists of an indentation and a line length.

It is possible to create the list of lengths for \parshape on the fly; that is why \parshape is so useful within a layout macro. That is, we can write

```
\parshape=n \the\parshapespec
```

where \parshapespec expands to be a list of the indentations and lengths that \parshape uses; \parshapespec will have been created by our layout macro using information passed to the macro by the designer.

The creation of `\parshapespec` occurs most often in the context of a `\loop`. It is useful to examine the structure of a typical such loop:

```
\def\z{0pt}  \newtoks\parshapespec
\count20=7  %% initialize \count20
\parshapespec={\z\hsize \z\hsize} %% initialize
\loop \parshapespec=\expandafter{\the\parshapespec
    \z .75\hsize} \advance\count20 -1
    \ifnum\count20>0 \repeat
\parshapespec=\expandafter{\the\parshapespec\z\hsize}
```

(When TeX executes this code, the command

```
\parshape=10 \the\parshapespec
```

will typeset a paragraph whose first 2 lines are normal `\hsize` width, whose next 7 lines are 75% of this, and whose remaining lines are of the normal `\hsize`.) The presence of the `\expandafter` command is crucial, and its presence can be appreciated by seeing what happens in its absence. In the above code, just before the `\loop` gets under way, the `\parshape` specification is `{\z\hsize \z\hsize}`. After the first iteration, *without* `\expandafter`, the command

```
\parshapespec={\the\parshapespec \z.75\hsize}
```

generates a token list whose first two tokens are `\the` and `\parshapespec`. That is not what we want; we need

```
\parshapespec={\z\hsize \z\hsize \z.75\hsize}
```

The action of `\expandafter` is to temporarily suspend the token-building until `\the\parshapespec` is expanded. (See also the answer to exercise 20.15 in *The TeXbook*.)

London. Michælmas Term lately over, and the Lord Chancellor sitting in Lincoln's Inn Hall. Implacable November weather. As much mud in the streets, as if the waters had but newly retired from the face of the earth, and it would not be wonderful to meet a Megalosaurus, forty feet long or so, waddling like an elephantine lizard up Holborn Hill. Smoke lowering down from chimney-pots, making a soft black drizzle, with flakes of soot in it as big as full-grown snow-flakes—gone into mourning, one might imagine, for the death of the sun. Dogs, indistinguishable in mire. Horses, scarcely better; splashed to their very blinkers. Foot passengers, jostling one another's umbrellas, in a general infection of ill-temper, and losing their foot-hold at street-corners, where tens of thousands of other foot passengers have been slipping and sliding since the day broke (if this day ever broke), adding new deposits to the crust upon crust of mud, sticking at those points tenaciously to the pavement, and accumulating at compound interest.

Figure 1. Paragraph with window.

Once TeX has created a paragraph, we can slice it apart using `\vsplit` and reassemble it in any which way. For example, we can typeset a window within a paragraph as in Figure 1 by creating the paragraph of Figure 2 with a `\parshape` of the form

$$\text{\texttt{\textbackslash parshape}=}n \underbrace{\text{\texttt{\textbackslash z\textbackslash hsize \textbackslash z\textbackslash hsize}}}_{A} \underbrace{\text{\texttt{\textbackslash z\textbackslash sidesize} }\cdots\text{\texttt{ \textbackslash z\textbackslash sidesize}}}_{B} \underbrace{\text{\texttt{\textbackslash z\textbackslash hsize}}}_{1}.$$

A and B represent numbers of pairs contained by the underbrace. A should be the number of lines above the window. B is *twice* the number of lines along the window sides. (Compare Figures 1 and 2.) We only need a single final pair of the form `\z \hsize` to set all the lines below the window since `\parshape` repeats this final length specification for the remaining lines of a paragraph.

We do our `\vsplitting` with a loop, an iteration of which might look as follows.

```
\setbox\leftbox=\vsplit\paragraphbox to\strutheight
\setbox\rightbox=\vsplit\paragraphbox to\strutheight
```
   <Now unbox and unskip to remove `\parshape` *finishing glue.>*
```
\setbox\myline=\line{\box\leftbox\hss\box\rightbox}
```
We build up paragraphs by adding `\myline` to the current paragraph:
```
\setbox\newpar=\vbox{\prevdepth=\savedprevdepth
   \unvbox\newpar \myline}.
```
Since TEX does not adjust `\prevdepth` when unboxing, we must do it 'manually' to ensure correct spacing between adjacent lines in the paragraph we are building.

It is possible to generalize the slicing operation, and we can generate windows of arbitrary shape within a paragraph, as in Figure 3. Although these macros have previously appeared elsewhere (Hoenig, 1987), they are included in Appendices 1 and 2 in a substantially rewritten form.

Knuth (1987) solves a very similar problem. Rather than relying on `\vsplit`, the centerpiece of his method is a temporarily-altered `\output` routine in which `\vsize` = `\strutheight`, the height of a strut. Thus, each 'page' consists of a single line of text, which his output routine than separately places in the window paragraph.

Use windows in your text sparingly. They are uncomfortable and difficult to read across. Furthermore, they increase the TEX compilation time substantially.

24.3   `\pageshape`: Specifying the shape of an entire page

The *page shape* of a document is a description of its left and right profiles. Most often, we all work with rectangular page shapes, but sometimes a designer requests a non-standard shape. If the layout designer knew the lines per paragraph for all paragraphs in the document, he or she could specify `\parshapes` for each paragraph. This solution is not acceptable – not only is it tedious, but in fact paragraph lengths will rarely be known. Knuth (in a letter to Berhard, 1987) has suggested a slick solution to the problem of extending the 'reach' of `\parshape` to embrace a sequence of paragraphs.

London. Michælmas Term lately over, and the Lord Chancellor sitting in Lincoln's Inn Hall. Implacable November weather. As much mud in the streets, as if the waters had but newly retired from the face of the earth, and it would not be wonderful to meet a Megalosaurus, forty feet long or so, waddling like an elephantine lizard up Holborn Hill. Smoke lowering down from chimney-pots, making a soft black drizzle, with flakes of soot in it as big as full-grown snow-flakes—gone into mourning, one might imagine, for the death of the sun. Dogs, indistinguishable in mire. Horses, scarcely better; splashed to their very blinkers. Foot passengers, jostling one another's umbrellas, in a general infection of ill-temper, and losing their foot-hold at street-corners, where tens of thousands of other foot passengers have been slipping and sliding since the day broke (if this day ever broke), adding new deposits to the crust upon crust of mud, sticking at those points tenaciously to the pavement, and accumulating at compound interest.

Figure 2. Paragraph before window.

To understand this solution, recall that `\parshape` uses the value of `\prevgraf` at the beginning of the paragraph as an index into the sequence of indentations and lengths that accompanies the `\parshape` command. Typically, TEX resets `\prevgraf` to 0 at a paragraph's beginning, so TEX starts reading the length list at entry $(0 + 1)$, which is normally what we need. In preparation for creating a `\pageshape` command, examine this section of code:

```
\let\oldpar=\par
\newcount\linesdone
\def\par{\endgraf \linesdone=\prevgraf}
\everypar={\prevgraf=\linesdone}
```

From the point where this code is implemented, `\prevgraf` maintains a running count of the lines that TEX has set. If `\prevgraf` has a value of, say, 7 at the beginning of a paragraph, TEX will begin with the eighth line indentation in the parshape length list.

But `\parshape` only 'lasts' for a single paragraph. If we could extend its reach, and at the same time use `\linesdone` to enhance the utility of `\prevgraf`, then we have effectively transformed the `\parshape` command to a `\pageshape` command.

To extend the reach of `\parshape`, we need to make a further change to `\par`. If the end-of-paragraph symbol were somehow invisible to TEX's mouth, `\parshape` would persist for several paragraphs. Yet the paragraph marker should be visible to the rest of TEX's digestive organs. Knuth's elegant solution is simply to surround the end-of-paragraph marker with a pair of braces.

```
\def\par{{\endgraf \global\linesdone=\prevgraf}}
```

As far as TEX's mouth is concerned, it does not 'taste' any paragraph endings, although it is there for the stomach and esophagus to process. Now, define a `\pageshape` command via

London.   Michælmas Term lately over, and the Lord Chancellor sitting in Lincoln's Inn Hall.   Implacable November weather.   As much mud in the streets, as if the waters had but newly retired from the face of the earth, and it would not be wonderful to meet a Megalosaurus, forty feet long or so, waddling like an elephantine lizard up Holborn Hill.   Smoke lowering down from chimney-pots, making a soft black drizzle, with flakes of soot in it as big as full-grown snow-flakes – gone into mourning, one might imagine, for the death of the sun.   Dogs, indistinguishable in mire.   Horses, scarcely better; splashed to their very blinkers.   Foot passengers, jostling one another's umbrellas, in a general infection of ill-temper, and losing their foot-hold at street-corners, where tens of thousands of other foot passengers have been slipping and sliding since the day broke (if this day ever broke), adding new deposits to the crust upon crust of mud, sticking at those points tenaciously to the pavement, and accumulating at compound interest.   Fog everywhere.   Fog up the river, where it flows among green meadows; fog down the river, where it rolls defiled among the tiers of shipping, and the waterside pollutions of a great (and dirty) city.

The area of a circle is a mean proportional between any two regular and similar polygons of which one circumscribes it and the other is isoperimetric with it. In addition, the are of the circle is less than that of any circumscribed polygon and greater than that of any isoperimetric polygon. And further, of these circumscribed polygons, the one that has the greater number of sides has a smaller area than the one that has a lesser number; but, on the other hand, the isoperimetric polygon that has the greater number of sides is the larger.

[Galileo, 1638]

Figure 3. Windows of arbitrary shape can be set. See Appendix 2 for the macros.

```
\def\pageshape{\linesdone=0 \parshape}
```
Normal typesetting may be resumed with the statement (for example)
```
\let\par=\oldpar.
```

For long pages, the parshape specifications may be quite lengthy.   The EPS Group at *TV Guide* have made good use of these macros and they have developed sets of software tools to make the preparation of these pageshapes reasonably trouble-free.

An example of typesetting with `\pageshape` appears in Figure 4.   The little circles in each paragraph indent make each new paragraph more visible. The shape command controlling the shape of these 6 paragraphs is
```
\def\h{\hsize} \pageshape=13
  0\h1\h   .1\h.9\h  .2\h.8\h
.3\h.7\h  .4\h.6\h  .5\h.5\h
.6\h.4\h  .5\h.5\h  .4\h.6\h
.3\h.7\h  .2\h.8\h  .1\h.9\h
  0\h1\h.
```
I inserted the `\pageshape` command after the first paragraph.

```
┌─────────────────────────────────────────────────────┐
│    o One one one one one one one one one one one one one one  │
│    one one one one one one one one one one one one one one   │
│    one.                                                       │
│    o Two two two two two two two two two two two two two two  │
│        two two two two two two two two two two two two two.   │
│                    o Three three three three three three three │
│                    three three three three three three        │
│                    three three three three three              │
│                    three three three three                    │
│                    three.                                      │
│                            o Four four four four               │
│                    four four four four four four              │
│                    four four four four four four four four     │
│                    four four four four four four four four.    │
│                o Five five five five five five five five five five five │
│    five five five five five five five five five five five five five     │
│    five five five five.                                       │
│        o Six six six six six six six six six six six six six six six six │
│    six six six six six six six six six six six six six six six six       │
│    six six six six six.                                       │
└─────────────────────────────────────────────────────┘
```

Figure 4. The pageshape macros in action. 'o' marks the beginning of each paragraph.

24.4 Determining the current page position

Line-oriented typographers have few problems working with commercial *wysi-wyg* programs. For all their shortcomings, they do let you see where you are on a page. A designer who wants a design to take effect half way down the page knows when this half way point is reached by simply looking at the monitor. The situation with TEX is ambiguous – TEX is not *wysiwyg* and is asynchronous. By the time page 100 is typeset, TEX may be well into reading page 101.

In a recent paper of great importance, Tom Reid (1987) addresses this issue. He realized that a relatively simply and temporary modification to the output routine can provide the current vertical page position. Between any two paragraphs, a call to this macro will return the current vertical position. Subsequent typesetting commands can access this information.

Crucial to this solution is a realization that the \output routine need not actually be used to perform output-like duties. TEX defers to \output whenever it thinks something has to be done with a full page. TEX thinks the page is full whenever it *is* full, but also at other times, such as when the \outputpenalty is given a critical value or when TEX encounters an \eject. The only restriction on \output seems to be that it do something with all of \box255, which contains the typeset material as TEX completes it.

For example, we might define a \newoutput routine as follows:

```
\newbox\partialpage \newtoks\savedoutput
```

```
\newdimen\currentheight
\def\newoutput{\setbox\partialpage = \vbox{\unvbox255}%
\global\currentheight=\ht\partialpage \unvbox\partialpage}
```

That is, the current position is determined by unboxing the current page (the contents of box255) and boxing it in a new box register, whose height is the current vertical position. After yielding this important information, the new box is unboxed, freeing the text for further typesetting. (Note that the unboxing of \box255 removes any glue from its bottom.)

A \WhereAmI macro to determine the current vertical position on a page should somehow incorporate \newoutput. Specifically, \WhereAmI should do 3 things:

- temporarily redefine \output as \newoutput;
- cause T_EX to execute \output (thereby learning the current height); and
- restore the original \output.

Here is one way to accomplish this.

```
\def\WhereAmI{%
\savedoutput=\output % save current output routine
\output={\newoutput}% redefine output
\par % end current paragraph
\penalty-10000 % huge reward for doing output
   % \newoutput is silently executed, returning a
   % value to \currentheight.
\output=\savedoutput % restore original output.
}
```

24.5 Simple newspaper page layout macros

We can use these ideas to design a modest set of macros for newspaper page-layout. To crowd more material on the front page, editors place only a portion of a story there. A message at the end of this portion invites the reader to continue reading on some interior page. We will call the front page portion the *lead*; its continuation is the *jump*. The lead and jump of a story contain references to each other, small injunctions to *Please see* **STOCKS** *on page 17* or **STOCKS** *continued from page 1*. The *keyword* **STOCKS** is a short-hand reference to the title, which may have been something like *WALL ST BLOODBATH: STOCKS PLUNGE TO RECORD LOWS.*

To be of any use, we need control over a few settings. We need to:

- prepare the *story* by specifying the title and keyword, and the beginning and end of the story;
- prepare the *lead* by specifying the \hsize and line count for it;
- prepare the *jump* by specifying the \hsize for the jump copy; and
- (finally) place the lead and jump sections on the printed page.

Man Bytes Dog: A Baudy Tail

Seriously, folks, this is offered to you as a demonstration of the page layout macros. We are capable of setting a story and continuing this story on *Please see* **doggy** *on page 169*

Dickens: Bleak House

London. Michælmas Term lately over, and the Lord Chancellor sitting in Lincoln's Inn Hall. Implacable November weather. As much mud in the streets, as if the waters had but newly retired from the face of the earth, and it would not be wonderful to meet a Megalosaurus, forty feet long or so, waddling like an elephantine lizard up Holborn Hill. Smoke lowering down from chimney-pots, making *Please see* **Dickens** *on page 169*

Figure 5a. Some lead stories; see Figure 5b for their continuations.

The line count for the lead should be optional. If we omit it, then TeX will decide how much space to allocate for the lead based on rules we build in to the macros. We do not need to provide TeX with any information about the length of the jump, since the jump will always contain everything that did not fit into the lead.

The system will automatically generate forward and backward references connecting the lead and the jump to each other. These references will contain page numbers, so we will need a 2-pass compilation, since TeX cannot know these page numbers the first time around. During the first compilation, TeX writes the pagination information to a file, which it reads on the second pass.

For each story, there shall be 2 page layout commands: one to process the entire story (typeset it, place it into \boxes, and place the lead on the page), and one for the jump. We will use the keyword as the argument for the \printjump command, since a layout may require the preparation of several stories before any one of them is placed on the page.

Caution! This set of macros requires a change to the \newbox macro of plainTeX. In plainTeX, \newbox is defined to be \outer; here it is redefined *not* to be \outer. This change allows us to create new boxes within our macros, but may result in box allocation problems if you are not careful.

There are two concerns in creating these macros. On the one hand is the *bookkeeping* – preparing the cross reference files properly, performing the file input/output consistently, and setting up the keyword as a pointer to the correct lead and jump. While these tasks are not necessarily trivial, they are straightforward, and the interested reader may consult the details in the macros themselves; they are in the third appendix to this paper.

On the other hand are the page *layout* considerations, which are of greater interest to us here. They follow directly from our previous observations.

We use \WhereAmI to help decide on the line count for the lead of the story. In the macros included in Appendix 3, I implemented the following rules. The user may directly specify the line count for the lead. If the line count is negative, then TₑX computes it for us as follows. If there is more than .5\vsize of vertical room on the space, then the lead may occupy half of that. Otherwise, the lead occupies all of the remaining space. (You may program any rule you care to in these macros.) Let n be the number of lines in the lead portion.

Once TₑX computes n, we use the \pageshape command to create a page containing the entire story. The first n lines of the story are set to the lead \hsize; the remaining lines are set to the jump \hsize.

Finally, we use the \vsplit command to chop this story in two portions. At that time, TₑX places the lead in position, but waits for a command from the designer to insert the jump in the document file. The user can use \printjump command, the argument for which is the keyword to the story.

All details appear in Appendix 3.

24.6   Conclusions

At least some line-oriented typesetting is possible with TₑX. The author hopes that these suggestions and demonstrations will serve as springboards to individuals with similar typesetting tasks to perform.

24.7   Acknowledgments

The author gratefully acknowledges the advice of David Ness, Elizabeth Barnhart, and their colleagues in the EPS Group, TV Guide, Radnor, Pennsylvania, USA. Many thanks are due to the TₑX Users Group in Providence, Rhode Island whose financial support was truly providential.

Bibliography

Alan Hoenig, 1987, *TₑX Does Windows – conclusion*, TUGboat, 8(2), 211–215.

Donald E. Knuth., 1987, *Saturday Morning Problem – Solution*, TUGboat, 8(2), 210.

Donald E. Knuth, letter to E. Barnhart, TV Guide, Radnor, PA, USA, dated June 11, 1987.

Thomas J. Reid, 1987, *Floating Figures on the Right, and Some Random Text for Testing*, TUGboat, 8(3), 315–320).

Dickens *from page 167*
a soft black drizzle, with flakes
of soot in it as big as full-grown
snow-flakes – gone into mourning,
one might imagine, for the death
of the sun. Dogs, indistinguishable in mire. Horses, scarcely better; splashed to their very blinkers. Foot passengers, jostling one
another's umbrellas, in a general
infection of ill-temper, and losing
their foot-hold at street-corners,
where tens of thousands of other
foot passengers have been slipping
and sliding since the day broke (if
this day ever broke), adding new
deposits to the crust upon crust of
mud, sticking at those points tenaciously to the pavement, and accumulating at compound.interest.
Fog everywhere. Fog up the river,
where it flows among green meadows; fog down the river, where it
rolls defiled among the tiers of shipping, and the waterside pollutions
of a great (and dirty) city.

doggy *from page 167*
a non-contiguous page.   These
macros (as currently written) can
permit selection of different hsizes
for the lead and jump portions of
the story.   Please note, though,
that if one portion is narrow, you
should 'up' TEX's tolerance parameter.   Otherwise, you encounter
mildly disconcerting underfull messages, and the real possibility of
unsightly overfull rules.

The final paragraph should explicitly end with a 'par' command,
following which should be the 'end-
story' command. The effect is to
first create a monstrous box containing the entire story, which is
then split in two. The first portion will contain the lead, and these
macros typeset that immediately.
The jump portion of the story remains in a second box, which you
typeset at will.

Figure 5b. The jump portions of the stories in Figure 5a.

Appendix 1: Macros for rectangular windows

```
%%
\def\z{0pt}
\newdimen\strutdepth \newdimen\strutheight
\strutheight=8.5pt \strutdepth=3.5 pt  % for cmr10
%%
%%
%%  WINDOW Macro
%%  ============
%%
%%  Use this macro to open a window within a single
%%  paragraph.   The window is rectangular & centered
%%  between the left and right margins.    The
%%  dimensions of the window are fixed by specifying the
```

```
%%  line at which it is to begin, how far it begins from
%%  the right, and for how many lines it is to persist.
%%  With this macro, you may wish to turn \tolerance up,
%%  especially if there are narrow sides.
%%
%%  \openwindow expects that \strut, \strutheight, and
%%  \strutdepth have been defined to work for the current
%%  font size.
%%
%%  The result of \openwindow will be the construction of
%%  \box\windowparbox.   It is up to the \TeX nician to
%%  typeset this box him/herself (eg., by including
%%  something  \boxit{\box\windowparbox}  in the document
%%  file).
%%
\newcount\n % use to create special \parshape
\newcount\oldvbadness
\newcount\top \newcount\window
\newdimen\shaveheight % for use with \vsplit
\newdimen\oldsplittopskip \newdimen\oldprevdepth
\newdimen\side % will contain parameter #1
\newdimen\leftside \newdimen\rightside
\newdimen\windowhsize % horizontal width of window
\newtoks\parshapespec % token for special \parshape
\newbox\windowparbox % holds the typeset paragraph
\newbox\leftbox \newbox\rightbox % holds left & right
\newbox\buildpar % holds window paragraph as it is built
%%
\def\openwindow[in:#1][down:#2 lines][deep:#3 lines]#4\par{%
%%  #1:  measurement in inches, pts, etc of the left side
%%  #2:  a number, the no.  of lines below the top line of
%%       the paragraph at which point the window begins
%%  #3:  a number, how many lines the window shall
%%       persist
%%  #4:  the actual text of the paragraph (NO display math)
%%
%%  First, construct the \parshape we will need
\oldvbadness=\vbadness \vbadness=10000 % suppress msgs
\top=#2 \window=#3 \side=#1
\leftside=\side \rightside=\side
\createparshapespec
\setbox\buildpar=\vbox{\parshape=\n \the\parshapespec
\strut#4}
\shaveheight=\top\baselineskip
\advance\shaveheight by-\strutdepth
```

```
\oldsplittopskip=\splittopskip % store splittopskip
\splittopskip=0pt
\global\setbox\windowparbox=\vsplit\buildpar to\shaveheight
\oldprevdepth=\dp\windowparbox
%%    \windowparbox now contains top part of par.
\count10=#3 % prepare to slice lines and reposition them
\shaveheight=\strutheight
\loop \setbox\leftbox=\vsplit\buildpar to\shaveheight
\setbox\rightbox=\vsplit\buildpar to\shaveheight
\advance\count10 by-1 \makeline[\leftbox,\rightbox]
\addlinetowindowpar \ifnum\count10>0 \repeat
%% \windowparbox now has the mid section--window sides.
%% now add bottom part to \windowparbox
\global\setbox\windowparbox=\vbox{\prevdepth=\oldprevdepth
\unvbox\windowparbox \box\buildpar}
\vbadness=\oldvbadness % restore vbadness setting
\splittopskip=\oldsplittopskip % restore splittopskip
}     %%% End of Macro \openwindow
%%
%%  CREATEPARSHAPESPEC Macro
%%  =========================
%%  This macro assumes that \top and \window have been
%%  defined.   Output is \n and the token list
%%  \parshapespec, which will be used by the calling
%%  macro \openwindow as \parshape=\n \the\parshapespec.
%%  \count10 is a scratch register
%%
\def\createparshapespec{%
\n=\top \multiply\window by2 \advance\n by \window
\advance\n by 1
\parshapespec={} % initialize
\count10=\top
\loop \parshapespec=\expandafter{\the\parshapespec \z\hsize}
\advance\count10 by-1 \ifnum\count10>0 \repeat
\count10=\window
\loop \parshapespec=\expandafter{\the\parshapespec
\z\side}
\advance\count10 by-1 \ifnum\count10>0 \repeat
\parshapespec=\expandafter{\the\parshapespec \z\hsize}
}     %% End of Macro \createparshapespec
%%
%%
%%  UNWRAP
%%  ======
%%  The argument to this macro is a box register.
```

```
%%  This macro unwraps the vertical glue, and removes the
%%  final glue.    Argument #2 is the width of the resulting
%%  hbox.    The material is stored in the \box#1.
%%
\def\unwrap#1#2{\unvbox#1 \setbox#1=\lastbox
\setbox#1=\hbox to#2{\strut\unhbox#1 \unskip}%
}    %% End of Macro \unwrap
%%
%%
%%  MAKELINE
%%  ========
%%  Macro to put to hboxes together to form one line with
%%  \hss in the middle.    The resulting \hbox is in box
%%  register \box0.
%%
\def\makeline[#1,#2]{%
\unwrap\leftbox\leftside \unwrap\rightbox\rightside
\setbox0=\line{\box#1\hss\box#2}%
}    %% End of Macro \makeline
%%
%%
%%  ADDLINETOWINDOWPAR
%%  ==================
%%  Macro takes \box0 and adds it to the end of the current
%%  \windowparbox.
\def\addlinetowindowpar{%
\global\setbox\windowparbox=\vbox{\prevdepth=\oldprevdepth
\unvbox\windowparbox \box0}%
\oldprevdepth=\dp\windowparbox
}    %%  End of Macro \addlinetowindowpar
%%
```

The text in figure 1 was prepared with the command

```
    \openwindow[in:15pc][down:4 lines][deep:5 lines]%
    London.  Mich\ae lmas Term...
        ...accumulating at compound interest.\par
```

The text was placed in the document with the command \box \windowparbox.

Appendix 2: Macros for arbitrarily-shaped windows

```
%%
\def\z{0pt}
\newdimen\strutdepth \newdimen\strutheight
\strutheight=8.5pt \strutdepth=3.5 pt  % for cmr10
```

```
%%
%%
%%   WINDOW Macro
%%   ============
%%
%%   Use this macro to open a window within a single
%%   paragraph.   The window is ARBITRARILY SHAPED, but
%%   placed between the left and right margins.   The
%%   dimensions of the window are fixed by specifying the
%%   line at which it is to begin,
%%   and specifying a SHAPESPEC, of the form
%%   \\l1\\r1\\l2\\r2\\...\\l n\\r n\\, where the l_i
%%   determine the length of the left side of line i of the
%%   cutout, and r_i is the length of the right side of
%%   the i^th line of the cutout.   Notice that the
%%   \shapespec begins AND ends with a double backslash.
%%
%%   When this macro, you may wish to turn \tolerance up,
%%   especially if there are narrow sides to the window.
%%
%%   \openwindow expects that \strut, \strutheight, and
%%   \strutdepth have been defined to work for the current
%%   font size.
%%
%%   The result of \OPENWINDOW will be the construction of
%%   \BOX\WINDOWPARBOX.  It is up to the \TeX nician to
%%   typeset this box him/herself (eg., by including
%%   something  \boxit{\box\windowparbox}  in the document
%%   file).
%%
\newcount\n % use to create special \parshape
\newcount\oldvbadness
\newcount\top \newcount\window
\newdimen\shaveheight % for use with \vsplit
\newdimen\oldsplittopskip \newdimen\oldprevdepth
\newdimen\side % will contain parameter #1
\newdimen\leftside \newdimen\rightside
\newdimen\windowhsize % horizontal width of window
\newtoks\parshapespec % token for special \parshape
\newbox\windowparbox % holds the typeset paragraph
\newbox\leftbox \newbox\rightbox % holds left & right
\newbox\buildpar % holds window paragraph as it is built
\newtoks\windowshape
%%
\def\openwindow[down:#1 lines][shapespec:#2]#3\par{%
```

```
%%  #1:   a number, the number of lines below the top line of
%%        the paragraph at which point the window begins
%%  #2:   the \shapespec (see above)
%%  #3:   the actual text of the paragraph (NO display math)
%%
%%  First, construct the \parshape we will need
\oldvbadness=\vbadness \vbadness=10000 % suppress msgs
\top=#1 \windowshape={#2}
\bgroup %% How many lines in window?
\expandafter\cardinality\the\windowshape0pt \to\window
\global\advance\window by-1
\egroup %% keep cardinality def'ns local
\createparshapespec
\setbox\buildpar=\vbox{\def\\{0pt}%
\parshape=\n \the\parshapespec \strut#3}
\shaveheight=\top\baselineskip
\advance\shaveheight by-\strutdepth
\oldsplittopskip=\splittopskip % store splittopskip
\splittopskip=0pt
\global\setbox\windowparbox=\vsplit\buildpar to\shaveheight
\oldprevdepth=\dp\windowparbox
%%    \windowparbox now contains top part of par.
\count10=\window % prepare to slice and reposition lines
\shaveheight=\strutheight
\edef\w{\the\windowshape} %% \lop expects this argument
\loop
\lop\w\to\mymeasure \leftside=\mymeasure
\lop\w\to\mymeasure \rightside=\mymeasure
\setbox\leftbox=\vsplit\buildpar to\shaveheight
\setbox\rightbox=\vsplit\buildpar to\shaveheight
\advance\count10 by-2 \makeline[\leftbox,\rightbox]
\addlinetowindowpar \ifnum\count10>0 \repeat
%% \windowparbox now has the mid section--window sides.
%% now add bottom part to \windowparbox
\global\setbox\windowparbox=\vbox{\prevdepth=\oldprevdepth
\unvbox\windowparbox \box\buildpar}
\vbadness=\oldvbadness % restore vbadness setting
\splittopskip=\oldsplittopskip % restore splittopskip
}      %%% End of Macro \openwindow
%%
%%  CREATEPARSHAPESPEC Macro for Arbitrary windows.
%%  =========================
%%  This macro assumes that \top and \windowshape have been
%%  defined.    \window contains the number of lines of the
%%  window.    Output is \n and the token list
```

```
%%  \parshapespec, which will be used by the calling
%%  macro \openwindow as \parshape=\n \the\parshapespec.
%%  \count10 is a scratch register
%%
\def\createparshapespec{%
\n=\top \advance\n by \window \advance\n by 1
\parshapespec={} % initialize
\count10=\top
\loop \parshapespec=\expandafter{\the\parshapespec \z\hsize}
\advance\count10 by-1 \ifnum\count10>0 \repeat
\parshapespec=\expandafter \expandafter
\expandafter{\expandafter \the\parshapespec
\the\windowshape}%
%%  See \TeX book, p 374; we want to expand
%%  \windowshape first, then \parshapespec, then the {
\parshapespec=\expandafter{\the\parshapespec \hsize}
}     %% End of Macro \createparshapespec
%%
%%
%%  UNWRAP
%%  ======
%%  Argument #1 to this macro is a box register.
%%  This macro unwraps the vertical glue, and removes the
%%  final glue.    Argument #2 is the width of the resulting
%%  hbox.    The material is stored in the \box#1.
%%
\def\unwrap#1#2{\unvbox#1 \setbox#1=\lastbox
\setbox#1=\hbox to#2{\strut\unhbox#1 \unskip}%
}     %% End of Macro \unwrap
%%
%%
%%  MAKELINE
%%  ========
%%  Macro to put to hboxes together to form one line with
%%  \hss in the middle.    The resulting \hbox is in box
%%  register \box0.
%%
\def\makeline[#1,#2]{%
\unwrap\leftbox\leftside \unwrap\rightbox\rightside
\setbox0=\line{\box#1\hss\box#2}%
}     %% End of Macro \makeline
%%
%%
%%  ADDLINETOWINDOWPAR
%%  ==================
```

```
%%  Macro takes \box0 and adds it to the end of the current
%%  \windowparbox.
\def\addlinetowindowpar{%
\global\setbox\windowparbox=\vbox{\prevdepth=\oldprevdepth
\unvbox\windowparbox \box0}%
\oldprevdepth=\dp\windowparbox
}      %%  End of Macro \addlinetowindowpar
%%
%%
%%  LIST PROCESSING Macros - see TeX book, pp 378 ff.
%%  Modifications to \cardinality necessary because the
%%  here is slightly different from \TeX book--no braces
%%  around each item, and the list is terminated with \\.
%%  We also know that each item in the list is a dimension.
%%
%%
\newdimen\specdimen   %% a ''dummy'' dimen variable
\def\lop#1\to#2{\expandafter\lopoff#1\lopoff#1#2}
\long\def\lopoff\\#1\\#2\lopoff#3#4{\def#4{#1}\def#3{\\#2}}
\def\cardinality#1\to#2{\global#2=0
\long\def\\{\global\advance#2 by 1
\afterassignment\relax\specdimen= }#1}
```

The text of figure 3 was prepared by invoking the command

```
\openwindow[down:1 lines][shapespec:\\ 168\x \\ 168\x \\
154\x \\ 154\x \\ 145\x \\ 145\x \\ 138\x \\ 138\x \\ 134\x
\\ 134\x \\ 132\x \\ 132\x \\ 131\x \\ 131\x \\ 132\x \\
132\x \\ 134\x \\ 134\x \\ 138\x \\ 138\x \\ 144\x \\ 144\x
\\ 154\x \\ 154\x \\ 168\x \\ 168\x \\ ]%
London.  Mich\ae lmas Term ...
    ...accumulating at compound interest.\par
```

This puts the typeset window into a special box, which can be placed on the
page with the further command \box\windowparbox.

Appendix 3: Macros for a newspaper page layout system

```
%%  STRUTS and miscellaneous macros.
\newdimen\strutheight \newdimen\strutdepth
\strutheight=\ht\strutbox \strutdepth=\dp\strutbox
\font\specialfont=cmbxsl10 scaled\magstep1 \def\z{0pt}
%%
%%  WHERE AM I?
%%    Macro a la Reid to determine current position
%%    on the page.    \newoutput is the temporary new
```

```
%%    output that we use in this macro to get position.
%%    Normal output routine is stored as \savedoutput.
%%
\newtoks\savedoutput  \savedoutput={\the\output}
\newbox\partialpage \newdimen\currentheight
\def\newoutput{\setbox\partialpage=\vbox{\unvbox255}%
\global\currentheight=\ht\partialpage \unvbox\partialpage}
%%
\def\whereami{\global\savedoutput=\output %
\global\output={\newoutput}%
\par \penalty-10000 % huge reward for doing output
\global\output=\savedoutput}
%%
%% COMPUTEGOALHEIGHT
%% =================
%%
%%    Computes space we want to allocate for page 1
%%    of story.    \goalheight stores the computed goal
%%    height.   This macro uses the following rule:    If
%%    the space left on page is > .5\vsize, then half of
%%    that will be the goal height.   Otherwise, all the re-
%%    maining space is allocated to \goalheight.   Users and
%%    editors can code their own space allocation scheme into
%%    this macro.   This macro has no arguments.
%%
\newdimen\goalheight
\def\computegoalheight{%
\goalheight=\vsize %%
\advance\goalheight by-\currentheight
\ifdim\currentheight>.5\vsize \else \divide\goalheight by2
\fi
\advance\goalheight by-2\baselineskip % adjust for title
\count10=\goalheight %% compute goalheight equiv in lines
\divide\count10 by\baselineskip
\advance\count10 by1 %% adjust for truncation in division
}
%%
%% \BEGINSTORY, \ENDSTORY Macros
%% =============================
%% Use these macros to typeset the article.    Begin
%% with \beginstory and frame the end with \endstory.
%%
\newcount\n %% used by \createparshapespec
\newbox\currentpage %% to hold the article lead
\newtoks\parshapespec %% used by \createparshapespec
```

```
\newtoks\keyword %% will contain keyword identifier
\newdimen\leadhsize % \hsize of lead
\newdimen\jumphsize % \hsize of jump
\newdimen\shortsize % width of last line of lead
%%
\def\beginstory[title:#1][key:#2][lead hsize:#3][lead
height:#4lines][jump hsize:#5]{%
%% #1:   the title of the story
%% #2:   a single word for ident purposes
%% #3:   width (hsize) of story lead
%% #4:   depth of first part of story in LINES (1line
%%       = \baselineskip); let it be -1 (or any negative num)
%%          if you want \TeX to compute it as the goalheight
%% #5:   width of second part (jump) of story
%% \BEGINSTORY will always typeset the lead part of the
%% story.  Complete the story with the command \ENDSTORY
%% You have to explicitly give the command to typeset the
%% JUMP.  Do this via ''\printjump[key]'' where the 'key' is
%% the parameter #2.
%%
%% Because the determination of the forward and backward
%% page references requires a 2-pass compilation, you will
%% have to typeset your story TWICE. Otherwise, the page
%% references will appear as question marks '???'.
%%
\setbox0=\hbox{\quad\it Please see {\bf #2} on page ??}
\shortsize=#3 %% to hold width of last line of lead
\advance\shortsize by-\wd0 %% reduce by space for xref
%%
\leadhsize=#3 \jumphsize=#5
\setbox0=\vbox to2\baselineskip{\hbox
to\leadhsize{\hss\specialfont #1\hss}\vss}%
%%  assume title occupies 2\baselineskip of space
\box0 %% typeset title info
\count10=#4 \advance\count10 by-2 %% adjust for title
%%
\ifnum\count10>0 %% User specified space for lead?
    \goalheight=\count10\baselineskip %% yes
    \n=\count10 %% set numerical argument for \parshape
    \else %% no
    \whereami \computegoalheight
    \n=\count10 %%set numerical argument for \parshape
\fi %\n is the number of lines in the lead
\advance\n by1 % \n is the parameter for \parshape
%% \box0 will contain title
```

```
\createparshapespec
\makeboxident{#2}%
\global\keyword={#2}%
\partoks=% will contain 'stuff' controlling typesetting
{\tolerance=5000 \hsize=#3 \pageshape=\n \the\parshapespec}
\putinvbox{#2}%
} %% END OF MACRO \beginstory
%%
%%
\newdimen\splitheight %% ht of article lead
\def\endstory{%% \ENDSTORY Macro
\shutbox %% close box containing lead
\splittopskip=\strutheight
\ifpasstwo %% then determine page reference
\def\pageident{\expandafter\csname\the\keyword
b\endcsname}%
        \else %% first pass; for explanation of weird
%%      \write convolutions, see TeXbook, ex 21.10
\def\pageident{???}%
{\edef\mywrite{\write\xrefout{\{\csname\the\keyword
a\endcsname:}} \mywrite}%
{\let\the=0\edef\mywrite{\write\xrefout{\the\pageno:\} }}
\mywrite}\fi
\advance\n by-1 %% num of lines in lead
\splitheight=\n\baselineskip %% how high will lead be?
\setbox\currentpage=\vsplit\allocationnumber to\splitheight
%% see TeXbook, pg 346 ff for \allocationnumber
\vbox{% keep \box\currentpage & reference together
\box\currentpage
\vskip-\baselineskip \vskip-\strutdepth
\hbox to\leadhsize{\hss\it \strut Please see
{\bf\the\keyword} on page \pageident}%
}% end of \vbox
}%% End of \endstory
%%
%%
%% CREATEPARSHAPESPEC Macro
%% =========================
%%
%% \n contains the numerical argument for \parshape.
%% This macro called by \beginstory only.
%%
\def\createparshapespec{%
\count10=\n %% use \count10 as scratch register
\advance\count10 by-2 \global\parshapespec={}%
```

```
\loop\ifnum\count10>0
\parshapespec=\expandafter{\the\parshapespec \z\leadhsize}
\advance\count10 by-1 \repeat
\parshapespec=\expandafter{\the\parshapespec \z\shortsize}
\parshapespec=\expandafter{\the\parshapespec \z\jumphsize}%
}
%%
%%  PAGESHAPE Macros
%%
\newcount\linesdone %% tracks \prevgraf for each par
\newtoks\oldeverypar \oldeverypar={}
\let\oldparshape=\parshape
\def\parshape{\prevgraf=0 \linesdone=0 \oldparshape}
\def\par{{\endgraf \global\linesdone=\prevgraf}}
\everypar={\the\oldeverypar \prevgraf=\linesdone}
\def\pageshape{\global\linesdone=0 \oldparshape}
%%
%%
%%  BOXIDENTS: How to use them.
%%  ===========================
%%    Any KEYWORD can refer to a box by first saying
%%    \makeboxident{KEYWORD} (e.g., \makeboxident{Story1},
%%    etc.).  TWO commands control placing text in the box.
%%    Start with the \putinvbox{KEYWORD} command.   KEYWORD
%%    should be the same as in the corresponding
%%    \makeboxident command.   Follow \putinvbox with
%%    the text.   Finish up with the \shutbox command (no
%%   arguments.)    \putinvbox starts by expanding a \partoks
%%    token list, so commands to control the text can be
%%    placed in this token (e.g., \partoks={\noindent \hsize
%%    3.5in \bf \parshape=3 0pt\hsize 0pt.75\hsize
%%    0pt.5\hsize}).   In these macros, ''a'' refers to the
%%    lead of an article, and ''b'' refers to the jump.
%%
%%    To typeset the material, enter the command
%%    \printjump{KEYWORD}, e.g.,
%%    \printjump{Story1}.
%%
%%  Redefine NEWBOX so as not to be OUTER.
%%  WARNING: This is a deviation from Plain.Tex.   If
%%  this offends you, please read no further.   If it
%%  doesn't offend you, please beware of possible box
%%  allocation problems that may arise.
%%
%%  See TeXbook, page 346 ff, for discussion of box and
```

```
%%  register allocation.
%%
\catcode'\@=11 %% make @ a letter temporarily
\def\newbox#1{%\alloc@4\box\chardef\insc@unt}
\global\advance\count14 by1
\ch@ck4\insc@unt\box% make sure there is still room
\allocationnumber=\count14
\global\expandafter\chardef#1=\allocationnumber
\wlog{\string#1=\string\box\the\allocationnumber}}
\catcode'\@=12
%%
\newtoks\partoks \partoks={}
%%
\def\makeboxident#1{\newbox{\csname#1box\endcsname}}
%%
\def\putinvbox#1{%
%% single argument is keyword identifier
%%
\gdef\myident{\csname#1box\endcsname}%
\setbox\myident=\vbox\bgroup \the\partoks  \strut%
}  %% End of \PUTINVBOX.
%%
\def\shutbox{\strut\egroup} %% \SHUTBOX closes box opened
%%  by \putinvbox.
%%
\def\printjump[#1]{%% to print the jump portion of article
\gdef\myident{\csname#1box\endcsname}%
\ifpasstwo \def\pageident{\csname#1a\endcsname}\else
\def\pageident{???}
{\edef\mywrite
{\write\xrefout{\{\csname#1b\endcsname:}}\mywrite}
{\let\the=0%
\edef\mywrite{\write\xrefout{\the\pageno:\}}}\mywrite}
\fi
\vtop{\hbox to\jumphsize{{\bf#1} {\it from page
\pageident}\strut\hss}\box\myident}}
%%
%%
%% INPUT, OUTPUT, CROSS_REFERENCE Section.
%% =====================================
%%
%%    In what follows, we provide the i/o and
%%    cross-reference machinery for replacing the
%%    '???' in the 'Please see...' and 'Continued
%%    from...' messages.  As before, everything will be
```

```
%%      keyed off the KEYWORD spec.
%%
%%
%%  Temporary redefinition of group symbols so we can
%%  redefine \{ and \} for use in output.
%%
\bgroup
\catcode`\{=11 \catcode`\}=11 \catcode`\[=1 \catcode`\]=2
\gdef\{[{] \gdef\}[}]
\egroup
%%
\newread\xrefin \newwrite\xrefout
\newif\ifpasstwo \passtwofalse
\openin\xrefin=\jobname.xrf
\ifeof\xrefin \passtwofalse \else\passtwotrue \fi
\ifpasstwo
\immediate\write16{*********************************}%
\immediate\write16{I AM NOW INSERTING PAGE REFERENCES IN
YOUR ARTICLES.}%
\immediate\write16{*********************************}%
\else
\immediate\write16{*********************************}%
\immediate\write16{PLEASE don't forget to typeset this a
SECOND time!}%
\immediate\write16{*********************************}%
\openout\xrefout=\jobname.xrf \fi
%%
\newtoks\mytok
\def\readxreffile{%
\read\xrefin to\mykey
\mytok=\mykey
\ifeof\xrefin \let\next=\relax \else
\expandafter\parse\the\mytok
\let\next=\readxreffile \fi \next}
%%
\def\parse#1:  #2:{\def#1{#2}}
%%
\ifpasstwo \readxreffile \fi
%%
\def\cleanup{\closein\xrefin \closeout\xrefout}
```

As an example, the second story in Figure 5a was typeset using the following sequence of commands. First, the entire story was prepared, and the lead portion was typeset via the commands

```
\beginstory[title:  Dickens:  Bleak
House][key:Dickens][lead hsize:\hsize][lead
height:8lines][jump hsize:.45\hsize]%
London.  Mich\ae lmas Term ...
        ⋮
    ...great (and dirty) city.  \par
\endstory
```

The jump portion was typeset later on in the document with the command `\printjump[Dickens]`.

Keywords should not contain any spaces or other special symbols. As always, TEX is case sensitive, so the keyword 'Dickens' is distinct from 'dickens.'

Alan Hoenig
John Jay College
City University of New York
New York City
USA

Chapter 25
Drawing Trees Nicely with T_EX

Anne Brüggemann-Klein & Derick Wood

Various algorithms have been proposed for the difficult problem of producing aesthetically pleasing drawings of trees (Reingold and Tilford (1981), Wetherell and Shannon (1979)), but implementations only exist as 'special purpose software', designed for special environments. Therefore, many users resort to the drawing facilities available on personal computers, but the figures obtained in this way still look 'hand-drawn'; their quality is inferior to the quality of the surrounding text.

In this paper we present an entirely new solution that integrates a tree drawing algorithm into one of the best text processing systems available. More precisely, we present a T_EX macro package TreeT_EX that produces a drawing of a tree from a purely logical description. Our approach has three advantages. First, labels for nodes can be handled in a reasonable way. On the one hand, the tree drawing algorithm can compute the widths of the labels and take them into account for the positioning of the nodes; on the other hand, all the textual parts of the document can be treated uniformly. Second, TreeT_EX can be trivially ported to any site running T_EX. Finally, modularity in the description of a tree and T_EX's macro capabilities allow for libraries of subtrees and tree classes.

In addition, we have implemented an option that produces drawings which make the *structure* of the trees more obvious to the human eye, even though they may not be as aesthetically pleasing.

25.1   Aesthetic criteria for drawing trees

One of the most commonly used data structures in computer science is the tree. As many people are using trees in their research or just as illustration tools, they are usually struggling with the problem of *drawing* trees. We are concerned primarily with ordered trees in the sense of Knuth (1973), especially binary and unary-binary trees. A binary tree is a finite set of nodes which either is empty, or consists of a root and two disjoint binary trees called the left and right subtrees of the root. A unary-binary tree is a finite set of nodes which either is empty, or consists of a root and two disjoint unary-binary trees, or consists of a root and one non-empty unary-binary tree. An extended binary tree is a binary tree in which each node has either two nonempty subtrees or two empty subtrees.

For these trees there are some basic agreements on how they should be drawn, reflecting the top-down and left-right ordering of nodes in a tree; see Reingold and Tilford (1981), and Wetherell and Shannon (1979).

1:   Trees impose a distance on the nodes; no node should be closer to the root than any of its ancestors.

2:   Nodes of a tree at the same height should lie on a straight line, and the straight lines defining the levels should be parallel.

3:   The relative order of nodes on any level should be the same as in the level order traversal of the tree.

These axioms guarantee that trees are drawn as planar graphs: edges do not intersect except at nodes. Two further axioms improve the aesthetic appearance of trees:

4:   In a unary-binary tree, each left child should be positioned to the left of its parent, each right child to the right of its parent, and each unary child should be positioned below its parent.

5:   A parent should be centered over its children.

An additional axiom deals with the problem of tree drawings becoming too wide and therefore exceeding the physical limit of the output medium:

6:   Tree drawings should occupy as little width as possible without violating the other axioms.

Wetherell and Shannon (1979) introduce two algorithms for tree drawings, the first of which fulfills axioms 1–5, and the second 1–6. However, as Reingold and Tilford (1981) point out, there is a lack of symmetry in the algorithms of Wetherell and Shannon which may lead to unpleasant results. Therefore, Reingold and Tilford introduce a new structured axiom:

7:   A subtree of a given tree should be drawn the same way regardless of where it occurs in the given tree.

Axiom 7 allows the same tree to be drawn differently when it occurs as a subtree in different trees. Reingold and Tilford give an algorithm which fulfills axioms 1–5 and 7. Although this algorithm does not fulfill axiom 6,

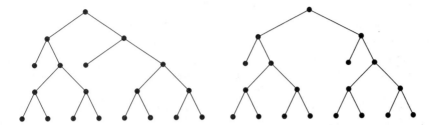

Figure 1. The left tree is drawn by the algorithm of Wetherell and Shannon, and the tidier right one is drawn by the algorithm of Reingold and Tilford.

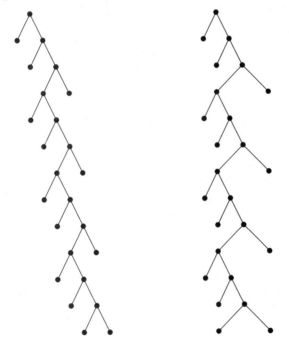

Figure 2. The left tree is drawn by the algorithm of Reingold and Tildford, but the right tree shows that narrower drawings fulfilling all æsthetic axioms are possible.

the aesthetic improvements are well worth the additional space. Figure 1 illustrates the benefits of axiom 7, and Figure 2 shows that the algorithm of Reingold and Tilford violates axiom 6.

25.2 The algorithm of Reingold and Tilford

The algorithm of Reingold and Tilford (hereafter called 'the RT algorithm') takes a modular approach to the positioning of nodes: The relative positions of the nodes in a subtree are calculated independently from the rest of the tree. After the relative positions of two subtrees have been calculated, they can be joined as siblings in a larger tree by placing them as close together as possible and centering the parent node above them. Incidentally, the modularity principle is the reason that the algorithm fails to fulfill axiom 6; Supowit and Reingold (1983). Two sibling subtrees are placed as close together as possible, during a postorder traversal, as follows. At each node T, imagine that its two subtrees have been drawn and cut out of paper along their contours. Then, starting with the two subtrees superimposed at their roots, move them apart until a minimal agreed upon distance between the trees is obtained at each level. This can be done gradually: Initially, their roots are separated by some agreed upon minimum distance. Then, at the next lower level, they are pushed apart until the minimum separation is established there. This process is continued at successively lower levels until the bottom of the shorter subtree is reached. At some levels no movement may be necessary; but at no level are the two subtrees moved closer together. When the process is complete, the position of the subtrees is fixed relative to their parent, which is centered over them. Assured that the subtrees will never be placed closer together, the postorder traversal is continued.

A nontrivial implementation of this algorithm has been obtained by Reingold and Tilford that runs in time $O(N)$, where N is the number of nodes of the tree to be drawn. Their crucial idea is to keep track of the contour of the subtrees by special pointers, called threads, such that whenever two subtrees are joined, only the top part of the trees down to the lowest level of the smaller tree need to be taken into account.

The RT algorithm is given in Reingold and Tilford (1981). The nodes are positioned on a fixed grid and are considered to have zero width. No labelling is provided. The algorithm only draws binary trees, but is easily extendable to multiway trees.

25.3 Improving human perception of trees

It is common understanding in book design that aesthetics and readability do not necessarily coincide, and – as Lamport (1986) puts it – books are meant to be read, not to be hung on walls. Therefore, readability is more important than aesthetics.

When it comes to tree drawings, readability means that the structure of a tree must be easily recognizable. This criterion is not always met by the RT algorithm. As an example, there are trees whose structure is very different, the only common thing being the fact that they have the same number of

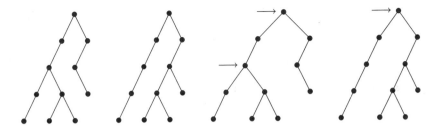

Figure 3. The first two trees get the same placement of their nodes by the RT algorithm, although the structure of the two trees is very different. The alternative drawings highlight the structure of the trees by adding additional white space between the subtrees of ($\longrightarrow$) significant nodes.

nodes at each level. The RT algorithm might assign identical positions to these nodes making it very hard to perceive the different structures. Hence, we have modified the RT algorithm such that additional white space is inserted between subtrees of *significant* nodes. Here a binary node is called significant if the minimum distance between its two subtrees is taken *below* their root level. Setting the amount of additional white space to zero retains the original RT placement. The effect of having nonzero additional white space between the subtrees of significant nodes is illustrated in Figure 3.

Another feature we have added to the RT algorithms is the possibility to draw an unextended binary tree with the same placement of nodes as its associated extended version. We define the *associated extended version* of a binary tree to be the binary tree obtained by replacing each empty subtree having a nonempty sibling with a subtree consisting of one node. This feature also makes the structure of a tree more prominent; see Figure 4.

25.4   Trees in a document preparation environment

Drawings of trees usually do not come alone, but are included in some text which is itself typeset by a text processing system. Therefore, a typical scenario is a pipe of three stages. First comes the tree drawing program which calculates the positioning of the nodes of the tree to be drawn and outputs a description of the tree drawing in some graphics language; next comes a graphics system which transforms this description into an intermediate language which can be interpreted by the output device; and finally comes the text processing system which integrates the output of the graphics system into the text.

This scenario loses its linear structure once nodes have to be labelled, since the labelling influences the positioning of the nodes. Labels usually

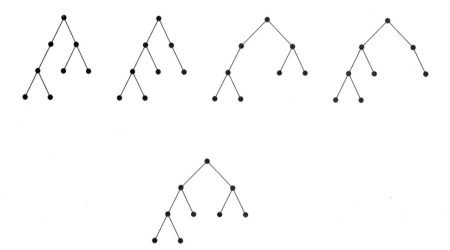

Figure 4. In the first two drawings, the RT algorithm assigns the same placement to the nodes of two trees although their structure is very different. The modified RT algorithms highlights the structure of the trees by optionally drawing them like their extended counterpart, which is given in the second row.

occur inside, to the left of, to the right of, or beneath nodes (the latter only for external nodes), and their extensions certainly should be taken into account by the tree drawing algorithm. But the labels have to be typeset first in order to determine their extensions, preferably by the typesetting program that is used for the regular text, because this method makes for the uniformity in the textual parts of the document and provides the author with the full power of the text processing system for composing the labels. Hence, a more complex communication scheme than a simple pipe is required.

Although a system of two processes running simultaneously might be the most elegant solution, we wanted a system that is easily portable to a large range of hardware at our sites including personal computers with single process operating systems. Therefore, we thought of using a text processing system having programming facilities powerful enough to program a tree drawing algorithm and graphics facilities powerful enough to draw a tree. One text processing system rendering outstanding typographic quality and good enough programming facilities is TₑX, Knuth (1984). The TₑX system includes the following programming facilities:

- datatypes:
  boolean variables (unrestricted), integers (256), boxes (256), token-lists (256), dimensions (512). Note that the term *dimension* is used in TₑX to describe physical measurements of typographical objects, like

the length of a word.

- elementary statements:

  $a :=$ const, $a := b$ (all types);

  $a := a + b$, $a := a * b$, $a := a/b$ (integers and dimensions);

  horizontal and vertical nesting of boxes.

- control constructs:

  if-then-else statements testing relations between integers, dimensions, boxes, or boolean variables.

- modularization constructs:

  macros with up to 9 parameters (can be viewed as procedures without the concept of local variables).

Although the programming facilities of TₑX hardly exceed the abilities of a Turing machine, they are sufficient to handle relatively small programs. How about the graphics facilities? Although TₑX has no built-in graphics facilities, it allows the placement of characters in arbitrary positions on the page. Therefore, complex pictures can be synthesized from elementary picture elements treated as characters. Lamport has included such a picture drawing environment in his macro package LATₑX, using quarter circles of different sizes and line segments (with and without arrow heads) of different slopes as basic elements; Lamport (1986). These elements are sufficient for drawing trees.

This survey of TₑX's capabilities implies that TₑX may be a suitable text processing system to implement a tree drawing algorithm directly. We are basing our algorithm on the RT algorithm, because this algorithm gives the aesthetically most pleasing results. In the first version presented here, we restrict ourselves to unary-binary trees, although our method is applicable to arbitrary multiway trees. But in order to take advantage of the text processing environment, we expand the algorithm to allow labelled nodes.

In contrast to previous tree drawing programs, we feel no necessity to position the nodes of a tree on a fixed grid. While this may be reasonable for a plotter with a coarse resolution, it is certainly not necessary for TₑX, a system that is capable of handling arbitrary dimensions and produces device *independent* output.

25.5 A representation method for TₑXtrees

The first problem to be solved in implementing our tree drawing algorithm is how to choose a good internal representation for trees. A straightforward adaptation of the implementation by Reingold and Tilford requires, for each node, at least the following fields:

- two pointers to the children of the node;
- two dimensions for the offset to the left and the right child (these may be different once there are labels of different widths to the left and right of the nodes);

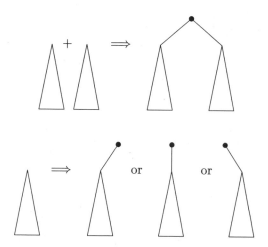

Figure 5. Construction steps 2 and 3

- two dimensions for the x- and y-coordinates of the final position of the nodes;
- three or four labels;
- one token to store the geometric shape (circle, square, framed text etc.) of the node.

Because these data are used very frequently in calculations, they should be stored in registers (that is what variables are called in TEX), rather than being recomputed, in order to obtain reasonably fast performance. This gives a total of $10N$ registers for a tree with N nodes, which would exceed TEX's limited supply of registers. Therefore, we present a modified algorithm hand-tailored to the abilities of TEX. We start with the following observation. Suppose a unary-binary tree is constructed bottom-up, in a postorder traversal. This is done by iterating the following three steps in an order determined by the tree to be constructed.

1: Create a new subtree consisting of one external node.
2: Create a new subtree by appending the two subtrees created last to a new binary node; see Figure 5.
3: Create a new subtree by appending the subtree created last as a left, right, or unary subtree of a new node; see Figure 5.

(A pointer to) each subtree that has been created in steps 1–3 is pushed onto a stack, and steps 2 and 3 remove two trees or one, respectively, from the stack before the push operation is carried out. Finally, the tree to be constructed will be the remaining tree on the stack.

This tree traversal is performed twice in the RT algorithm. During the first pass, at each execution of step 2 or step 3, the relative positions of the subtree(s) and of the new node are computed. A closer examination of the RT algorithm reveals that information about the subtree's coordinates is not needed during this pass; the contour information alone would be sufficient. Complete information is only needed in the second traversal, when the tree is actually drawn. Here a special feature of TₑX comes in that allows us to save registers. Unlike Pascal, TₑX provides the capability of storing a drawing in a single box register that can be positioned freely in later drawings. This means that in our implementation the two passes of the original RT algorithm can be intertwined into a single pass, storing for each subtree on the stack its contour and its drawing. Although the latter is a complex object, it takes only one of TₑX's precious registers.

25.6   The internal representation

Given a tree, the corresponding TₑXtree is a box containing the 'drawing' of the tree, together with some additional information about the contour of the tree. The reference point of a TₑXtree-box is always in the root of the tree. The height, depth, and width of the box of a TₑXtree are of no importance in this context.

The additional information about the contour of the tree is stored in some registers for numbers and dimensions and is needed in order to put subtrees together to form a larger tree. *loff* is an array of dimensions which contains for each level of the tree the horizontal offset between the left end of the leftmost node at the current level and the left end of the leftmost node at the next level. *lmoff* holds the horizontal offset between the root and the leftmost node of the whole tree. *lboff* holds the horizontal offset between the root and the leftmost node at the bottom level of the tree. Finally, *ltop* holds the distance between the reference point of the tree and the leftmost end of the root. The same is true for *roff*, *rmoff*, *rboff*, and *rtop*; just replace 'left' by 'right'. Finally, *height* holds the height of the tree, and *type* holds the geometric shape of the root of the tree. Figure 6 shows an example TₑXtree, with its corresponding additional information.

Given two TₑXtrees A and B, how can a new TₑXtree C be built that consists of a new root and has A and B as subtrees? An example is given in Figure 7.

First we determine which tree is higher; this is B in the example. Then we have to compute the minimal distance between the roots of A and B, such that at all levels of the trees there is free space of at least *minsep* between the trees when they are drawn side by side. For this purpose we keep track of two values, *totsep* and *currsep*. The variables *totsep* and *currsep* hold the total distance between the roots and the distance between the rightmost node of A and the leftmost node of B at the current level. In order to calculate *totsep* and *currsep*, we start at level 0 and visit each level of the trees until we reach the bottom level of the smaller tree; this is A in our example.

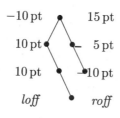

height	3
type	dot
ltop	2 pt
rtop	2 pt
lmoff	−10 pt
rmoff	20 pt
lboff	10 pt
rboff	10 pt

Figure 6. A TEXtree consists of the drawing of the tree and the additional information. The width of the dots is 4 pt, the minimal separation between adjacent nodes is 16 pt, making for a distance of 20 pt center to center. The length of the small rule labelling one of the nodes is 5 pt. The column left (right) of the tree drawing is the array *loff* (*roff*), describing the left (right) contour of the tree. At each level, the dimension given is the horizontal offset between the border at the current and at the next level. The offset between the left border of the root node and the leftmost node at level 1 is −10 pt, the offset between the right border of the root node and the rightmost node at level 1 is 15 pt, etc.

At level 0, the distance between the roots of A and B should be at least *minsep*. Therefore, we set *totsep* := *minsep* + *rtop*(A) + *ltop*(B) and *currsep* := *minsep*. Using *roff*(A) and *loff*(B), we can proceed to calculate *currsep* for the next level. If *currsep* < *minsep*, we have to increase *totsep* by the difference and update *currsep*. This process is iterated until we reach the lowest level of A. Then *totsep* holds the final distance between the nodes of A and B, as calculated by the RT algorithm. If the root of C is a significant node, then the additional space, which is 0 pt by default, is added to *totsep*. However, the approach of synthesizing drawings from simple graphics characters allows only a finite number of orientations for the tree edges; therefore, *totsep* must be increased slightly to fit the next orientation available.

Now we are ready to construct the box of TEXtree C. Simply put A and B side by side, with the reference points *totsep* units apart, insert a new node above them, and connect the parent and children by edges.

Next, we update the additional information for C. This can be done by using the additional information for A and B. Note that most components of *roff*(C) and *lroff*(C) are the same as in the higher tree, which is B in our case. So, if we can avoid moving this information around, we only have to access *height*(A)+*const* many counters in order to update the additional information for C. This implies that we can apply the same argument as in Reingold and Tilford (1981), which gives us a running time of O(N) for drawing a tree with N nodes.

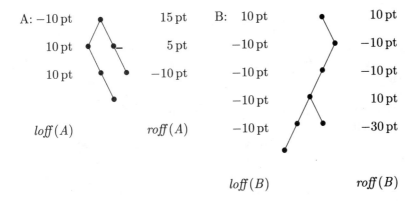

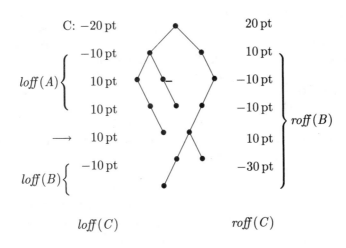

	A	B	C
height	3	5	6
type	dot	dot	dot
ltop	2 pt	2 pt	2 pt
rtop	2 pt	2 pt	2 pt
lmoff	−10 pt	−30 pt	−30 pt
rmoff	20 pt	10 pt	30 pt
lboff	10 pt	−30 pt	−10 pt
rboff	10 pt	−30 pt	−10 pt

level	*totsep*	*currsep*
0	20 pt	0/16 pt
1	25 pt	11/16 pt
2	40 pt	1/16 pt
3	40 pt	16 pt

Figure 7. The TₑXtrees A and B are combined to form the larger TₑXtree C. The small table gives the history of computation for *totsep* and *currsep*.

Therefore, we must carefully design the storage allocation for the additional information of TEXtrees in order to fulfill the following requirements. If a new tree is built from two subtrees, the additional information of the new tree should share storage with its larger subtree. Organizational overhead (pointers which keep track of the locations of different parts of additional information), must be avoided. This means that all the additional information for one TEXtree should be stored in a row of consecutive dimension registers such that only one pointer granting access to the first element in this row is needed. On the other hand, each parent tree is higher and therefore needs more storage than its subtrees. So we must ensure that there is always enough space in the row for more information.

The obvious way to fulfill these requirements is to use a stack and to allow only the topmost TEXtrees of this stack to be combined into a larger tree at any time. This leads to the following register allocation. A subsequent number of box registers contains the treeboxes of the subtrees in the stack. A subsequent number of token registers contains the type information for the nodes of the subtrees in the stack. For each subtree in the stack, a subsequent number of dimension registers contains the contour information of the subtree. The ordering of these groups of dimension registers reflects the ordering of the subtrees in the stack. Finally, a subsequent number of counter registers contains the height and the address of the first dimension register for each subtree in the stack. Four address counters store the addresses of the last treebox, type information, height, and address of contour information. A sketch of the register organization for a stack of TEXtrees is provided in Figure 8.

When a new node is pushed onto the stack, the treebox, type information, height, address of contour information, and contour information are stored in the next free registers of the appropriate type, and the four address counters are updated accordingly.

When a new tree is formed from the topmost subtrees on the stack, the treebox, type information, height, and address of contour information of the new tree are sorted in the registers formerly used by the bottommost subtree that has occured in the construction step, and the four address registers are updated accordingly. This means that this information for the subtrees is no longer accessible. The contour information of the new subtree is stored in the same registers as the contour information of the larger subtree used in the construction, apart from the left and right offset of the root to the left and right child, which are stored in the following dimension registers. That means that gaps can occur between the contour information of subsequent subtrees in the stack, namely when the right subtree, which is on a higher position on the stack, is higher than the left one. In order to avoid these gaps, the user can specify an option \lefttop when entering a binary node, which makes the topmost tree in the stack the left subtree of the node.

This stack concept has consequences for the design of the user interface discussed in Section 23.8.

25.7 Space cost analysis

Suppose we want to draw a unary-binary tree T of height h having N nodes. The height h and the number of nodes N refer to the drawing of the tree. N is the number of circles, squares etc. actually drawn, and h is the number of levels in the drawing minus 1. According to our internal representation, for each subtree in the stack we need:

- one box register to store the box of the TₑXtree.
- one token register to store the type of the root of the subtree.
- $2h' + 6$ dimension registers to store the additional information, where h' is the height of the subtree.
- three counter registers to store the register numbers of the box register, the token register, and the first dimension register above.

The following lemma relates to h and N the number of subtrees of T which are on the stack simultaneously and their heights.

Lemma:

- *At any time, there are at most $h + 1$ subtrees of T on the stack.*
- *For each set $\mathcal{T}$ of subtrees of T which are on the stack simultaneously we have*

$$\sum_{T' \in \mathcal{T}} (\mathrm{ht}(T') + 1) \leq \min(N, \frac{(h+1)(h+2)}{2}).$$

Proof:

- By induction on h.
- The trees in $\mathcal{T}$ are pairwise disjoint, and each tree of height h' has at least $h' + 1$ nodes. This implies:

$$\sum_{T' \in \mathcal{T}} (\mathrm{ht}(T') + 1) \leq N.$$

The second part is shown by induction on h. The basis $h = 0$ is clear. Assume this holds for all trees of height less than h. If $\mathcal{T}$ contains only subtrees of either the left or the right subtree of T, we have:

$$\sum_{T' \in \mathcal{T}} (\mathrm{ht}(T') + 1) \leq \frac{h(h+1)}{2} \leq \frac{(h+1)(h+2)}{2}.$$

Otherwise, $\mathcal{T}$ contains the left or the right subtree T_s of T. Then all elements of $\mathcal{T} - \{T_s\}$ belong to the other subtree. This implies

$$\sum_{T' \in \mathcal{T}} (\mathrm{ht}(T') + 1) \leq \mathrm{ht}(T_s) + 1 + \sum_{T' \in \mathcal{T} - \{T_s\}} (\mathrm{ht}(T') + 1)$$

$$\leq h + \frac{h(h+1)}{2} \leq \frac{(h+1)(h+2)}{2}$$

∎

Therefore, our implementation uses at most $9h + 2\min(N, (h + 1)(h + 2)/2)$ registers. In order to compare this with the $10N$ registers used in the straightforward implementation, an estimation of the average height of a tree with N nodes is needed. Several results, depending on the type of trees and of the randomization model, are cited in Table 1, which compares the number of registers used in a straightforward implementation with the average number of registers used in our implementation.

nodes	registers (straight-forward)	average registers		
		extended binary trees[1] $(\sqrt{\pi n})$	unary-binary trees[2] $(\sqrt{3\pi n})$	binary search trees[3] $(4.311 \log n)$
8	80	61.12	94.15	51.04
9	90	65.86	100.89	55.02
10	100	70.44	107.37	58.80
11	110	74.91	113.64	62.41
12	120	79.26	119.71	65.87
20	200	111.34	163.56	90.48
30	300	147.37	211.33	117.31
40	400	180.89	254.75	132.58
50	500	212.80	295.37	143.54

[1] de Bruijn, Knuth, and Rice (1972)
[2] Flajolet and Odlyzko (1982)
[3] Devroye (1986)

Table 1. The numbers of registers used by a straightforward implementation (second column) and by our modified implementation (third to fifth column) of the RT algorithm are given for different types of trees and randomization models. The formula in parentheses indicates the average height of the respective class of trees, as depending on the number of nodes.

25.8   The user interface

25.8.1   General design considerations

The user interface of TreeTEX has been designed in the spirit of the thorough separation of the logical description of document components and their layout; see Furuta, Scofield, and Shaw (1982), Goldfarb (1981). This concept ensures both uniformity and flexibility of document layout and frees authors from layout problems which have nothing to do with the substance of their work. For some powerful implementations and projects see Brüggemann-Klein, Dolland, and Heinz (1986), Beach (1985), Lamport (1986), Quint, Vatton, and Bedor (1986), and Reid (1980).

In this context, the description of a tree is given in a purely logical form, and layout variations are defined by a separate style command which is valid for all trees of a document.

A second design principle is to provide defaults for all specifications, thereby allowing the user to omit many definitions if the defaults match what he or she wants.

The node descriptions of a tree must be entered in postorder. This fits the internal representation of TEXtrees best. Although this is a natural method of describing a tree, a user might prefer more flexible description methods. However, note that instances of well defined tree classes can be described easily by TEX macros. In section 23.8.3 we give examples of macros for complete binary trees and Fibonacci trees.

TreeTEX uses the picture making macros of LATEX. If TreeTEX is used with any other macro package or format, the picture macros of LATEX are included automatically.

25.8.2   The description of a tree

The description of a tree is started by the command \beginTree and closed by \endTree (or \begin{Tree} and \end{Tree} in LATEX). The description can be started in any mode; it defines a box and two dimensions. The box is stored in the box register \TeXTree and contains the drawing of the tree. The box has zero height and width, and its depth is the height of the drawing. The reference point is in the center of the node of the tree. The dimensions are stored in the registers \leftdist and \rightdist and describe the distance between the reference point and the left and right margin of the drawing. These data can be used to position the drawing of the tree.

Note that the TreeTEX macros do not contribute anything to the current page but only store their results in the registers \TeXTree, \leftdist, and \rightdist. It is the user's job to put the drawing onto the page, using the commands \copy or \box (or \usebox in LATEX).

Each matching pair of \beginTree and \endTree must contain the description for only *one* tree. Descriptions of trees cannot be nested and new registers cannot be allocated inside a matching pair of \beginTree and \endTree.

As already stated, each tree description defines the nodes of the tree in postorder, that is, a tree description is a particular sequence of node descriptions.

A node description, in turn, consists of the macro \node, followed by a list of node options, included in braces. The list of node options may be empty. The node options describe the labels, the geometric shape (type), and the outdegree of the node. Default values are provided for all options which are not explicitly specified. The following node options are available:

- \lft{<label>}, \rght{<label>}, \cntr{<label>},
  \bnth{<label>}:

These options describe the labels which are put to the left of, to the right of, in the center of, or beneath the node (the latter only makes sense for external nodes). The arguments of these macros are processed in internal horizontal mode (LR-mode in L^AT_EX), but can consist of arbitrary nested boxes for more sophisticated labels. For each of these options, the default is an empty label.

- \external, \unary, \leftonly, \rightonly:
  These options describe the outdegree of the node. The default is binary (no outdegree option is specified).
- \type{<type>}:
  This option describes the type or geometric shape of the node. <type> can have the values square, dot, text, or frame. The default value is circle (no type is specified). A node of type square has a fixed width, while a node of type frame has its width determined by the center label. A node of type text has no frame around its center label. The center label can have arbitrary width.
- \leftthick, \rightthick: These options change the thickness of the left or right outgoing edge of a binary node. Defaults are thin edges (neither option is specified).
- \lefttop:
  The node option \lefttop in a binary node makes the last entered subtree the left child of the node (the right child is the default). This option helps to cut down on the number of dimension registers used during the construction of a tree. As a rule of thumb, this option is recommended when the left subtree has a smaller height than the right subtree, that is, in this case the right subtree should be entered before the left one and their parent should be assigned the option \lefttop.

25.8.3   Macros for classes of trees

Tree descriptions can be produced by macros. This is especially useful for trees which belong to a larger class of trees and which can be specified by some simple parameters. A small library of such macros is provided in the file TreeClasses.tex.

- \treesymbol{<node options>}:
  This macro produces a triangular tree symbol which can be included in a tree description instead of an external node. Labels for these tree symbols are described as for ordinary nodes. In addition, the options \lvls{<number>} and \slnt{<number>} are provided. \lvls defines the number of levels in the tree over which the triangle extends, and \slnt gives the slant of the sides of the triangle, ranging from 1 (minimal) to 24 (maximal). On the other hand, \treesymbol does not expand to a tree description, because a tree symbol cannot be built from subtrees, and, on the other hand, it is not a node, because it is allowed

to extend over several tree levels and therefore has a longer contour than an ordinary node.

- \binary{<bin specification>}:
  This macro truly expands to a tree description. It produces a complete binary tree, that is, an extended binary tree, where, for a given h, all external nodes appear at level h or $h-1$, and all external nodes at level h lie left of those at level $h - 1$. <bin specification> consists of the following options: \no{<number>} defines the number of internal nodes, with <number> greater than 0, and \squareleaves produces leaves of type square. Defaults are \no{1} and leaves of type circle.

- \fibonacci{<fib specification>}:
  This macro produces a Fibonacci tree. <fib specification> permits three options, \hght{<number>}, \unarynodes, and \squareleaves. Normally, a Fibonacci tree of height $h+2$ is a binary tree with Fibonacci trees of height h and $h + 1$ as left and right subtrees. The option \unarynodes means that the Fibonacci tree is augmented by unary nodes such that each two subtree siblings have the same height. These are examples of what has been called brother-trees in the literature; see Ottmann and Six (1976). Defaults are \hght{0}, the unaugmented version of a Fibonacci tree, and external nodes of type circle.

25.8.4   Style options for trees

The <style option> of the command \Treestyle{<style option>} contains all the parameter settings the user might want to change. Normally, the command \Treestyle appears only once at the beginning of the document and the style options are valid for all trees of the document.

The changes in the style options are global. A \Treestyle command changes only the specified style options; non-specified options retain the last specified value or the default value, respectively. The following style options are available:

- \treefonts{<font options>}:
  \treefonts is invoked by \beginTree, and it simply executes whatever is specified in <font options>. Defaults are \treefonts{\tenrm} (or \treefonts{\normalsize\rm} in LaTeX).

- \nodesize{<size>}:
  \nodesize defines the size of the nodes. <size> is a dimension and specifies the diameter of circle nodes. The width of square nodes is adjusted accordingly to be slightly smaller than the diameter of circle nodes in order to balance their appearance. Furthermore, \nodesize adjusts the amount of space by which the baseline of the labels is placed beneath the center of the node. The default value of \nodesize suits the default of \treefonts (taking into account the size option of LaTeX's

document style).
- \vdist{<dimen>}, \minsep{<dimen>}, \addsep{<dimen>}:
  vdist specifies the vertical distance between two subsequent levels of the tree. Default is \vdist{60pt}. \minsep specifies the minimal horizontal distance between two adjacent nodes. Default is \minsep{20pt}. \addsep specifies the additional amount of horizontal space by which two subtree siblings are pushed apart farther than calculated by the RT algorithm, if the level at which they are closest is beneath their root level. Default is \addsep{0pt}.
- \extended, \nonextended:
  With the option \extended in effect, the nodes of a binary tree are placed in exactly the same way as they would be in the associated extended version of the tree (the missing nodes are assumed to have no labels). The default is \nonextended, that is the usual layout.

Some examples of trees and their descriptions are given in the Appendix. A detailed description of the TreeT_EX macros is given in Brüggemann-Klein and Wood (1987).

25.9   Acknowledgement

This work was supported by a Natural Sciences and Engineering Research Council of Canada Grant A-5692 and a Deutsche Forschungsgemeinschaft Grant Sto167/1-1. It was started during the first author's stay with the Data Structuring Group in Waterloo.

Bibliography

Richard J. Beach, 1985, *Setting Tables and Illustrations with Style*, PhD thesis, University of Waterloo.

Anne Brüggemann-Klein, P. Dolland, and Alois Heinz, 1986, *How to please authors and publishers: a versatile document preparation system at Karlsruhe*, *in* J. Désarménien, *ed.*, T_EX for Scientific Documentation, Springer-Verlag.

Anne Brüggemann-Klein and Derick Wood, 1987, *TreeT_EX: Documentation and User Handbook*, Technical Report, University of Waterloo.

N.G. de Bruijn, D. Knuth, and S.O. Rice, 1972, *The average height of planted plane trees*, *in* R.C. Read, *ed.*, Graph Theory and Computing.

L. Devroye, 1986, *A note on the height of binary search trees*, Journal of the ACM, 33(3).

Ph. Flajolet and A. Odlyzko, 1982, *The average height of binary trees and other simple trees*, Journal of Computer and System Sciences, 25.

Richard Furuta, J. Scofield, and A. Shaw, 1982, *Document formatting systems: surveys, concepts, issues*, Computing Surveys, 14(3).

Charles F. Goldfarb,1981, *A generalized approach to document markup*, SIG-PLAN Notices of the ACM.

Donald E. Knuth,1973, *Fundamental Algorithms*, Addison Wesley Publishers, Reading, Mass.

Donald E. Knuth,1986, *The TₑXbook*, Addison Wesley Publishers, Reading, Mass.

Leslie Lamport,1986, *The LATₑX Document Preparation System*, Addison Wesley Publishers, Reading, Mass.

Th. Ottmann, H.-W. Six, 1976, *Eine neue Klasse ausgeglichener Binärbäume*, Angewandte Informatik, 9.

Vincent Quint, Irène Vatton & Hassan Bedor, 1986, *GRIF: An interactive environment for TₑX*, pp.145–158, *in* J. Désarménien, *ed.*, TₑX for Scientific Documentation, Springer-Verlag.

Brian K. Reid, 1980, *Scribe: A Document Specification Language and its Compiler*, PhD thesis, Carnegie Mellon University.

E. M. Reingold and J. S. Tilford, 1981, *Tidier drawings of tree*, IEEE Transactions on Software Engineering, 7(2).

K. J. Supowit and E. M. Reingold, 1983, *The complexity of drawing trees nicely*, Acta Informatica, 18.

Charles Wetherell and A. Shannon, 1979, *Tidy drawings of trees*, IEEE Transactions on Software Engineering, 5(5).

Appendix: Example trees

1   A complete binary tree

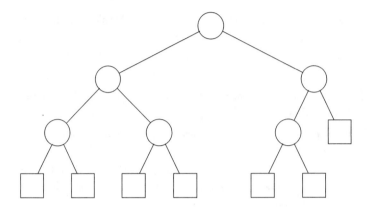

```
\beginTree
\binary{\no{6}\squareleaves}
\endTree
\hspace{\leftdist}\usebox{\TeXTree}\hspace{\rightdist}
```

2   A Fibonacci tree

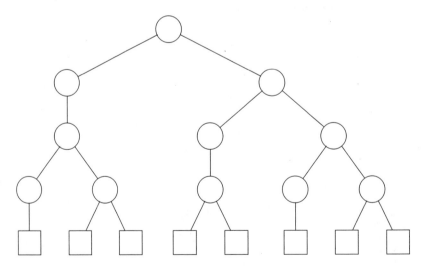

```
\beginTree
\fibonacci{\hght{4}\unarynodes\squareleaves}
\endTree
\hspace{\leftdist}\usebox{\TeXTree}\hspace{\rightdist}
```

3   A tree which includes labels

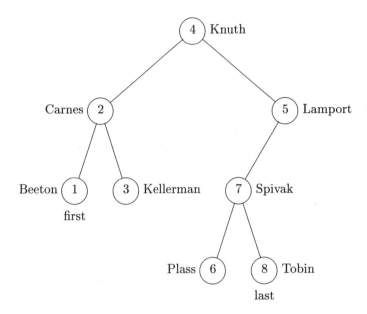

```
\beginTree
\node{\external\bnth{first}\cntr{1}\lft{Beeton}}
\node{\external\cntr{3}\rght{Kellerman}}
\node{\cntr{2}\lft{Carnes}}
\node{\external\cntr{6}\lft{Plass}}
\node{\external\bnth{last}\cntr{8}\rght{Tobin}}
\node{\cntr{7}\rght{Spivak}}
\node{\leftonly\cntr{5}\rght{Lamport}}
\node{\cntr{4}\rght{Knuth}}
\endTree
\hspace{\leftdist}\usebox{\TeXTree}\hspace{\rightdist}
```

4   A tree with framed centred labels

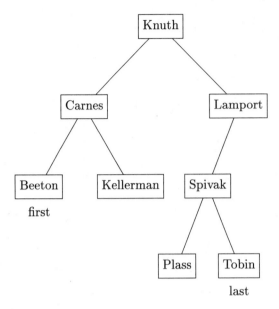

```
\beginTree
\node{\external\type{frame}\bnth{first}\cntr{Beeton}}
\node{\external\type{frame}\cntr{Kellerman}}
\node{\type{frame}\cntr{Carnes}}
\node{\external\type{frame}\cntr{Plass}}
\node{\external\type{frame}\bnth{last}\cntr{Tobin}}
\node{\type{frame}\cntr{Spivak}}
\node{\leftonly\type{frame}\cntr{Lamport}}
\node{\type{frame}\cntr{Knuth}}
\endTree
\hspace{\leftdist}\usebox{\TeXTree}\hspace{\rightdist}
```

Anne Brüggemann-Klein   and   Derick Wood
Institut für Informatik   Data Structuring Group
Universität Freiburg   Department of Computer Science
Rheinstraße 10–12   University of Waterloo
D-7800 Freiburg   Waterloo
FRG   Ontario, N2L 3G1
                                 Canada

Chapter 26
Electronic Publishing
and Chemical Text Processing

A C Norris & A L Oakley

There are impressive systems for the modelling and graphical display of chemical molecules but systems for the computer-based typesetting of chemical structures integrated with scientific text are less successful, especially where high quality is to be combined with ease of use and low costs. This paper evaluates strategies to meet these objectives and reports the results of interfacing an interactive chemical structure editor with PostScript and TEX.

26.1   Introduction

Electronic publishing is likely to have a significant impact on the way authors, research and commercial concerns and publishers produce and distribute information. This impact will be evident in books, journals and reports and, for chemistry, electronic publishing will be a vital component of laboratory information management systems.

High-quality, two-dimensional chemical diagrams are particularly expensive and surprisingly time consuming to produce by conventional methods. Both precision technical drawing skills and photoreduction of the original are necessary to achieve accuracy at final publication size. Further, positioning of the final diagram relative to text is still widely effected by 'cut and paste' into a gap left by the text processors. Costs in the region of £40 per page are quite common. The promise of reduced costs and shorter production times can only be realised following the development of computer techniques to draw and edit chemical structures and integrate them with typeset text.

Our current research (Norris & Oakley, 1988a, 1988b) has distinguished the requirements and stages of the publishing process for integrated chemical structures and developed an interactive icon-based package for the representation, screen display and editing of chemical structures. The distinctive features of chemical structure diagrams include a precise predefined geometry with consistent ring sizes and objects which tesselate, the correct relationship of characters (atoms) to lines (bonds), and the use of subscripts and specialised symbols. Since an object-based definition of structures has been selected, the output file of an image contains only defining points for lines and arcs and, optionally, calls to character font definitions, and translation to a page description language such as POSTSCRIPT is consequently straightforward.

Important design considerations in this work have included the requirement for a system that is responsive, interactive, simple to use and transparent. These criteria apply equally to the page makeup and output stages. However, the production of very high-quality mathematical and scientific text is achieved currently only by a limited number of command language/batch-oriented packages such as TEX (Tuthill, 1983; Knuth, 1984). Although such packages allow a high degree of control they are not simple or interactive. We therefore seek alternative strategies for the integration of chemical structures with text and production of hard copy. Several alternatives are considered:

- Drawings are produced using a command language based on a typesetting language such as LaTeX/TEX macros or the troff *pre*-pre-processor called **chem**. In this environment there is no problem integrating a graphic with the well-established text processing component.
- Both graphic structures and text are programmed in a high-level page or document description language (PDL or DDL) such as POSTSCRIPT.
- An interactive chemical structure editor is interfaced to a graphics-based scientific word processor.

- Text is produced using a typesetting language such as TEX or JustText and chemical graphics are created by an interactive drawing package. PDL files are then generated from both packages and integrated by a postprocessor.
- Graphics files from an interactive package and text files from a word processor are imported into a page makeup program such as Ventura.

The following sections consider these alternatives.

26.2 Command language preprocessors

Typesetting languages mimic the traditional method of markup in which formatting commands are embedded in the text. Examples of such typesetting languages include TEX (Knuth, 1984) and troff (Kernighan, 1981). JustText (Phillips, 1988) is a more recent addition designed to take advantage of POSTSCRIPT (Adobe, 1985a, 1985b).

These languages were originally intended for straightforward composition and to work with traditional text-oriented printers. They are very powerful, and allow considerable control, typographic precision and very high-quality output but they are difficult to use, especially for the novice or casual user. The language is often complicated and the juxtaposition of content and formatting commands makes either difficult to read. Additionally, since the whole document with the embedded commands must be processed, the system is batch oriented resulting in considerable delays between entering the document description and seeing the final result. This inhibits experimentation with different layouts and also makes the detection and correction of errors rather tedious. In a commercial environment, account must also be taken of the relatively long time and significant cost of training staff to use such systems.

However, these systems do not rely on graphics devices and they also allow device independence. For example, TEX is implemented on mainframes, minicomputers and 68000 and 8086-based microcomputers and is widely recognised for its powerful typesetting of mathematical and scientific text. Its output in ASCII form allows it to link via a range of specific drivers to a wide range of printers. These drivers may be PDLs.

The recent development of preview screens which give non-interactive viewing of output on-screen, partially offsets some of the disadvantages of delayed output. In general this approach subordinates ease of use to the quality requirement. Another advantage of these languages is that preprocessors can take advantage of the existing printing facilities. Descriptions of two such preprocessors for the typesetting of chemical structures have been reported recently (Haas & O'Kane, 1987; Bentley, Jelinski & Kernighan, 1987).

26.2.1   TEX-based preprocessors

One such system for chemical structure description and printing is a set of about 30 macros based exclusively on TEX and LATEX (Haas & O'Kane, 1987; Lamport, 1986). These macros produce some common structural fragments such as branching patterns and rings. A limited number of macros can produce a variety of structures by supplying variable structural parts as parameters and also by joining structures. The variables can include multiple bonds, substituent and aromatic rings, allowing a range of structures to be typeset.

This approach therefore allows the integration of mathematical and scientific text with chemical structures whilst it preserves device independence and can be used on a wide range of hardware. Certainly the approach is an appealing one to TEX enthusiasts.

However, TEX itself has no intrinsic graphics facilities and consequently the LATEX picture environment has a limited range of vector orientations and circle diameters. Although the authors of the chemical structure macros claim that this is not a severe limitation for structure diagrams, they themselves estimate that their macros cope with only about half the structure diagrams found in a typical organic chemistry text book. Features such as bonds at unusual angles, aromatic rings of various diameters and curly arrows may prove difficult to achieve. Also, scaling would be effective only at a discrete range of point sizes. Additionally, the structures demonstrated by the authors do not appear to be of full typographical quality (Haas & O'Kane, 1987). For example, some characters representing atoms appear too close to bond lines. It is not clear however, if this is a flaw in the use or design of the macros or a result of the limitations inherent in LATEX.

26.2.2   Chem preprocessor

Chem (Bentley, Jelinski & Kernighan, 1987) is a language to describe chemical structures and translate them into the pic graphics language which is a troff preprocessor running under the UNIX environment. Like the TEX implementation described above, the language comprises a set of macros. In contrast, however, chemical structures are normally connected in the order that they are written down, although these automatic connections can be overidden, and there are no parameters for substituents etc. Numbers as in the group CH_3 are automatically converted to subscripts. The quality of hardcopy is high although characters representing atoms are often too close to bonds on their immediate left (Bentley, Jelinski & Kernighan, 1987).

The ability to link a range of preprocessors to troff facilitates the development of 'little languages' (Bentley, 1986) to address specific domains and also allows several facilities to be brought together. For example, Greek symbols may be added to chem chemical structure diagrams via another troff preprocessor called eqn, and pic commands can be included in a chem document.

Since each preprocessor can build on facilities provided by other processors in the system, the development of new preprocessors like chem is relatively quick and easy.

26.2.3   Problems of the command language approach

Although the languages named above are impressive in terms of quality output and rapid development, they suffer from similar assumptions which are not always correct, and from problems of philosophy and design. For example:

- Although at first sight the basic commands appear quite simple, keeping track of position within larger molecules can present problems and building reaction sequences with small differences between each molecule and with correct alignment, arrow connections, brackets etc., might stretch the mind somewhat. It would be essential to work from a hand-drawn diagram. Also, where there are no macro facilities within the language, repeated structures must be specified individually, which at best involves copying blocks of text.

  Combining structures with the TeX/LaTeX macros, is not that easy. The user must determine the co-ordinates of points of attachment perhaps by placing individual structures into their own LaTeX picture box and combining these within an outer picture box. In chem, although brackets can be drawn around a structure, it takes several commands to define each bracket and these commands must be correctly placed within the commands defining the bracketed structure.

  Further, even the basic commands may appear complicated to someone who is not a computerate chemist or at least computerate. For example, with the TeX/LaTeX macros, the user must know the function of each parameter and how a structure will be oriented on the page. Since many of the macros contain nine parameters and a dummy 'Q' argument must be supplied if a particular option is not required, there is a lot of unnecessary typing to add to the confusion. The user must also be aware of the current ring position and associated numbering rules in order to provide substituent formulae in the correct sequence. For example, the sequence of characters representing the chemical group SO_3H should appear as HO_3S when attached to a six-membered ring at two positions but SO_3H at the remaining four positions.

  Again, in chem, the simple statements .cstart and .cend which surround structure definitions are a source of potential error and irritation since the dots must be in the first column of text! Further, although automatic connection of bonds to carbon atoms generally simplifies diagram construction, the user must be aware that this connection is not always appropriate and he must know when and how to override this facility. Finally, although bonds and rings can be scaled, text must be scaled separately using troff commands.

At best, in both languages there is considerable room for error which would be recognised only at preview if one exists, or more likely at printing.

- Both languages rely on other memory consuming software systems, particularly in the case of chem which depends on both pic and troff and can also need eqn. The ability to call other 'little languages' does assume that the user is already familiar with or is willing to learn them and has access to them. Further, troff is UNIX-based and hence is usually available only on workstations. Although UNIX can be implemented in a cheaper microcomputer environment it is still more expensive than other microcomputer operating systems both in terms of money and memory requirement.

- A modular approach has much to recommend it, but too many branched dependencies can lead to inefficient systems. This is so whether the modules be one procedure, small collections of procedures within one program, or whole packages.

- There appears to be an assumption that only chemistry authors will need to produce typeset chemical structures. The authors of chem state that the language attempts to capture the way that a chemist would describe a structural formulae to a colleague. Also, both languages require that the user has a knowledge of ring numbering conventions. However, the secretarial staff of academic institutions and industrial concerns are frequently required to produce the hardcopy submitted for publication. Even if this step is omitted and the author sends his document to a publisher in electronic form, it would be unlikely in practice that no further editing is required. Should the publishing staff be trained and happy to use a command language, they are likely to lack knowledge of chemical structures. Any typesetting system, even though geared to a particular domain, should be readily usable by those not skilled in that domain. Even if we assume that, in the best of all possible worlds, there is no need for editorial intervention between author and final hardcopy, there is yet another problem.

There is the further assumption that all chemists who might wish to publish chemical structure diagrams are familiar with the nomenclature and numbering conventions of organic chemical ring systems. However, non-organic chemists such as kineticists may not have this knowledge at their fingertips, yet wish to publish documents which include organic structures.

- The acceptability to users of simple command or interactive systems, is still a question for debate. We have recently conducted a pilot study in which a range of chemists, secretarial and publishing staff have been asked their preferences for creating chemical structure diagrams. 83% recognised a need for computer-based publishing of chemical structures, 78% preferred interactive software, 7% preferred a command language and 15% did not know or were indifferent. A large majority perceive interactive systems as preferable, while a small but significant minority seem to prefer a simple command language.

With any command language, the syntax and semantics must be learned and remembered. Since many chemists publish work only intermittently, there is ample scope for forgetting! Further, two separate command languages are likely to have different syntax and semantics and to be incompatible as are chem and the LaTeX macros.

Although there is a requirement for both interactive and command systems, there are further considerations in a production environment. Costs of training have been mentioned already but another point is that where employees have invested time and effort to gain expertise in a command language, if new easier methods are introduced there may well be a feeling that work interest and even jobs are under threat.

- The arguments in favour of a command language rest on two premises:
  - this is the only way to achieve full control and typeset quality; most known interactive software produces hardcopy that falls short of full typographic quality (Norris & Oakley, 1988a) and this is an inherent property of screen-based interactive systems; because of the low screen resolution compared with that of printers, it is not possible to obtain fine control of layout, line spacing and point sizes.
  - specialised and costly graphics terminals are essential to interactive systems but there is no such requirement where input is text based.

Whereas the first assumption may well be true for text it is not necessarily true for the construction of chemical structure diagrams. For example, the interactive chemical structure editor we have developed views chemical fragments as objects which relate spatially to each other. Hence the absolute screen position of a structure is largely immaterial. No essential distinction is made between text and graphics and any fine adjustment to the relative position of characters can be made at the output stage.

The use of a graphical interface allows a user to place and edit chemical fragments, characters and groups of characters and or fragments easily and precisely. There is no language to learn and reaction sequences are quickly built up (Norris, Oakley & Broadbent, 1988). The object descriptions, which are transparent to the user, translate directly into a page description language such as POSTSCRIPT and hence typeset output can be achieved. For example, characters can be placed correctly in relation to bonds, rings are correctly proportioned and without the small gaps sometimes seen on other interactive systems. Precise positioning to parts of a point on the printed page is achieved even though the screen representation can only be at integer pixel co-ordinates. The integration of these diagrams with text is discussed later in this paper, where we refer to this interactive chemical structure editor as DrawChem.

The second of these assumptions no longer holds great weight. For instance, the editor outlined in the previous paragraph can achieve very good quality hardcopy and an acceptable screen output that *looks* '*wysi-wyg*' (what you see is what you get) at a screen resolution of 600 by 400 pixels, i.e. at a resolution commonly found as standard on a PC or on a widely used and relatively low-cost graphics board such as the Hercules board. Although a larger screen is preferable to ease eye strain and a higher resolution screen will achieve a very small increase in hardcopy quality, neither is vital. Also, the previewers available to offset the disadvantages of the batch mode themselves require a graphics screen of at least similar resolution and, naturally, the VDU is required in text mode at least, to type in commands for command languages.

- Although a point in favour of the preprocessors of command languages is that, as extensions of existing systems, they are fairly quick and easy to develop, this is not a great recommendation unless the resulting system is also quick and easy for the user whilst still achieving the desired goal.

Overall, the strategy based on typesetting languages has much to recommend it in terms of ease of integration and quality of hardcopy but is difficult for many potential users.

26.3   Page description languages

Since programming in POSTSCRIPT is in ASCII text, it should be fairly straightforward to develop a chemical structure command language as a POSTSCRIPT preprocessor. This would also be possible for mathematical text and has to some extent already been accomplished, along with normal text processing, with JustText. POSTSCRIPT is easier to use than TEX, is more clearly documented and is excellent for both text and graphics.

In view of the portability, device independence, and power of POSTSCRIPT, this seems an attractive option. Further software might impose document structure and formatting on a completely integrated and powerful system to create mathematics, scientific text, diagrams, illustrations etc. However, the creation of chemical structure diagrams would still suffer many of the problems associated with command-driven systems discussed in the previous section. Also, POSTSCRIPT is at a lower level than TEX in that it has no inherent formatting and without further software, would not equal TEX's mathematical typesetting prowess. Perhaps POSTSCRIPT's greatest contribution will be as a common denominator as described in the following sections.

26.4   Scientific word processors

Although there is rapid change, at present scientific word processors do not provide the necessary typeset quality for scientific text (Norris & Oakley,

1988a) nor the range of page and document layout features of structure editor. However, the combination of word processor and page makeup program is useful where full typeset quality is not paramount. An example of such a combination is the interactive chemical structure editor called ChemWord (Norris & Oakley, 1988a) which interfaces to Microsoft's 'Word' word processor.

26.5   Interactive structure editor and typesetting language

This approach combines the power of a typesetting language with the ease of use of an interactive chemical structure editor. JustText and TeX are alternatives for a typesetting language in the non-UNIX world.

JustText is based on POSTSCRIPT; direct POSTSCRIPT commands are easily integrated by enclosing them in a '{ps} QQ' pair or a POSTSCRIPT file is included through the statement {INfilename}; thus anything POSTSCRIPT can do can be incorporated in a JustText document. However, JustText is confined to the Apple Macintosh world and since output is to laser printers only, in the current version, no proofing is available. Also, most importantly for scientific texts, it does not yet have the mathematical typesetting power of TeX, although in principle, there is no reason why it should not do so. Should this capability be developed then a JustText/DrawChem combination on the Macintosh would be an attractive option, allowing the combination of all elements of a chemistry text.

Therefore, the power of TeX has been coupled to our editor DrawChem, mentioned earlier. Since both packages can generate POSTSCRIPT files, these files are integrated as described below. When designing TeX Knuth had the foresight to include the \special command (Knuth, 1984) which allows sections of text within a TeX file to pass unprocessed into the DVI file, thus enabling interfacing to unknown future languages. Hence, in systems which convert the DVI file to a POSTSCRIPT file, any \special POSTSCRIPT commands are automatically merged with the TeX/POSTSCRIPT commands. For example, Arbortext's DVILASER/PS, converts TeX files to POSTSCRIPT. As in JustText, either a block of POSTSCRIPT code can be included in the original TeX file, using

   \special {ps::   *lines of* POSTSCRIPT *code*}

or a POSTSCRIPT file can be called, using

   \special {ps: plotfile filename} .

Similarly, on a Macintosh, *Textures* provides the calls

   \special{postscript   *lines of* POSTSCRIPT *code*}

for blocks of code and

   \special{postscript filename}

for POSTSCRIPT files.

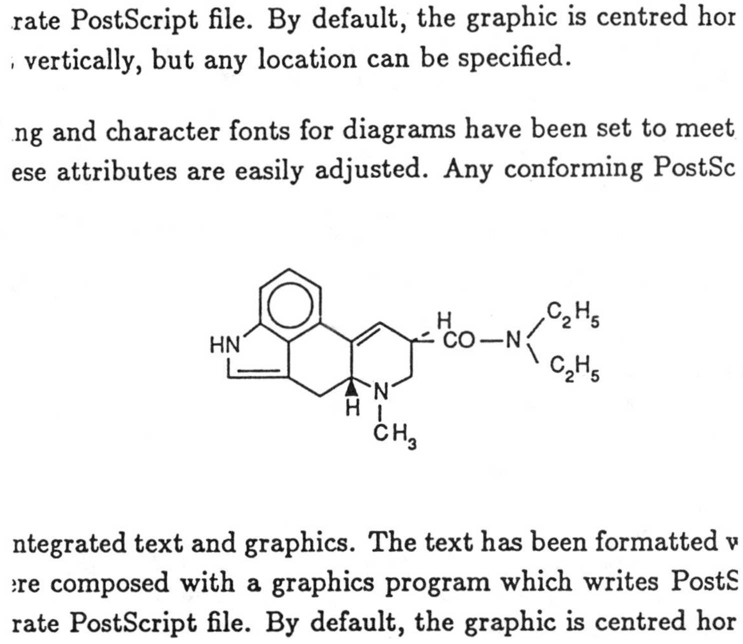

rate PostScript file. By default, the graphic is centred hor
, vertically, but any location can be specified.

ng and character fonts for diagrams have been set to meet
ese attributes are easily adjusted. Any conforming PostSc

ntegrated text and graphics. The text has been formatted v
:re composed with a graphics program which writes PostS
rate PostScript file. By default, the graphic is centred hor

Figure 1. Integrated text and graphics: the text was produced with TEX, and the chemical structure diagram with DrawChem.

Using the Arbortext software on an IBM compatible and a Laserwriter Plus, it has thus been relatively straightforward to develop simple TEX macros that are geared to integrate TEX text and POSTSCRIPT line-based graphics. POSTSCRIPT text files can also be called. This system replaces the time consuming conventional TEX process of reserving a space with \vbox and then using 'cut and paste' to insert a manually drawn graphic.

A summary of calls to these macros is shown in the Appendix. Calling these macros from within a TEX file is straightforward. Chemical structure diagrams created in DrawChem and saved as line-based encapsulated POST-SCRIPT files (EPS) are shown integrated with TEX formatted text in Figure 1. The ability to call text files as pictures is helpful where intermediate point sizes or special effects are required. All the power of POSTSCRIPT can be accessed. For example, one can change scaling independently horizontally and vertically, and alter linewidths, rotations, fonts etc.

By providing a range of macros with overlapping functions, almost automatic processing is possible in the publishing production environment whilst retaining flexibility. For example, all the macros can be available as a TEX

\input file but the most frequently called macro will be \figone (Appendix) which automatically centres a picture horizontally and relative to the latest text vertically on the page. This macro reflects the existing working practices at the scientific publishers John Wiley Ltd. who sponsored this work. However, the \placepict macro moves a picture any number of points in any direction, regardless of the position of any other element. Also, the scaling, linewidths and fonts of chemical structures are defined according to Wiley's publication requirements but are easily modified.

Although it is easy to scale a picture to a \vbox, this is not appropriate for chemical structure diagrams since these are needed at a given size. Therefore a \vbox must be sized to the picture rather than the other way round that is usual for illustrations and scanned images. Similarly, cropping is inappropriate for chemical structures!

Similar results, although geared to illustrations rather than chemical structures, have been achieved with the 'psfig' package (Brightly, 1988). Here too, small sections of code or whole PostScript files are accessed through TeX macros to provide a range of facilities. Also, with DVILASER/PS, MacDraw pictures can be incorporated into TeX documents (Varian & Sterken, 1986) and a set of extensions to LaTeX's picture environment has been effected (Maus & Baker, 1986).

Thus, the marriage of TeX and PostScript is very powerful, allowing the printing of high-quality, integrated scientific text and graphics. Apart from TeX, the system is easy to use. The development of interactive interfaces to typesetting languages (Cowan & De V Smit, 1986; Crisanti, Formigoni, Gazzano & La Bruna, 1985) could make even this aspect easy.

26.5.1   Problems of the interactive editor and TeX approach

What then are the problems with this route? Not surprisingly, the biggest drawback is speed. For example, the time taken to construct a toluene molecule in DrawChem is 28 seconds, the time to choose the save option and save it as an ASCII PostScript file is 15 seconds and the file thus created is only 35 lines long, including all built-in procedures and the usual pre- and post-ambles. Sending those lines character by character down a serial line to a Laserwriter Plus printing takes a total of only 3.9 seconds. However, the same file, integrated with only three lines of TeX text and sent through the same route takes 2 minutes 12 seconds in addition to 48 seconds to TeX the file and turn it into a PostScript file with DVILASER/PS. This is because the joint PostScript file is 1166 lines long! The reason for this is that the TeX to PostScript translation involves including all the PostScript calls embedded in the TeX macros (about 100 lines) and, more significantly, all the PostScript procedures provided by Arbortext in a prologue file supplied when a TeX to PostScript translation occurs. The straight ASCII PostScript commands become embedded in a welter of hexadecimal codes, resulting in a '.ps' file that is an order of magnitude larger than the original POSTSCRIPT file.

The second important limiting factor is the rate of translation of commands by the POSTSCRIPT interpreter. Arbortext provides a spooling program that is about twice as fast as the above serial method, but the interpreter returns spurious messages and no printing occurs when the rate of commands transmitted is too high.

A further problem is one of portability. On the Macintosh, the *Textures* POSTSCRIPT interface for calling whole files has within it graphics save and restore commands. This not only prevents unwanted knock-on effects but also precludes using TEX macros outside the POSTSCRIPT file to control attributes within the called POSTSCRIPT file. Thus, the TEX user must access the POST-SCRIPT code directly to set line widths etc. and also the y co-ordinate system is reversed.

Additionally, not only is an encapsulated POSTSCRIPT file (EPS) file a subset of a conforming POSTSCRIPT file (Adobe, 1985b), but an EPS file on an IBM system is *not* an EPS file on an Apple Macintosh! The latter must include Quickdraw commands so that structures can be displayed on the screen, whereas there is no such equivalent for PCs.

26.6   Interactive structure editor and page makeup program

Page makup programs now commonly allow output as a device-independent PDL or DDL thus providing transparency and ease of use, whilst achieving good quality hardcopy. Such software, although capable of adding text and graphics, is not generally designed for such; their function is page and or document layout. As a consequence, positioning and reading of characters is a strain unless 'snap to' features are used, and should be confined to small final editing functions. The text and graphics are better created elsewhere.

For example, we have successfully imported chemical structures created in **DrawChem** into both PageMaker and Ventura (Figure 2). The imported graphic can be moved, scaled and further edited, for example by the addition of a frame or text.

Text can be imported from powerful word processors, but at present, the best-quality mathematics is still likely to come from TEX. We have tried creating a POSTSCRIPT version of a TEX mathematics file and have called this as a POSTSCRIPT picture file in the DVILASER/PS environment and obtained a printout. The printing of a TEX-mathematics file via the page makeup program Ventura Publisher is also under development. The success of this approach could lead to a modular software system for chemical document creation and typesetting as outlined in Figure 3. Of course a powerful and efficient PDL is the common denominator.

This 'star' arrangement of modules is likely to be more efficient than the 'evolutionary' approach (Bentley, Jelinski & Kernighan, 1987; Bentley, 1986)

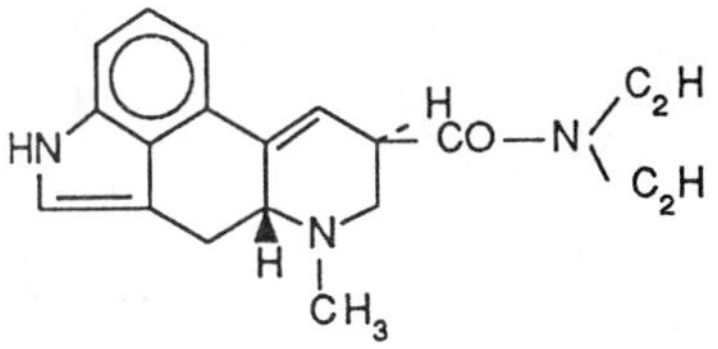

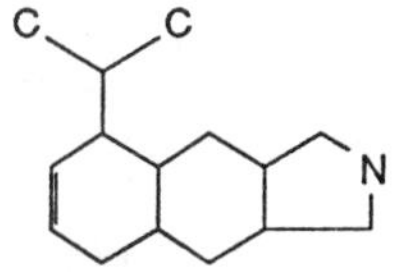

Figure 2. Chemical structure diagrams imported into, and scaled by, **Ventura**
Publisher.

of troff since there is no need for a chain of translations as found in **chem** →
pic → **troff** → **driver** and it is not essential for an individual to have access to
several other modules at once, again unlike the **troff** route.

26.6.1 Problems of the fully interactive approach

This route also has drawbacks. For example:

- Although we could create pages of low mathematical content in an interactive editor and page makeup program and the mathematical ones
  purely using TEX, there would be inconsistencies; for example, the same
  font names can give output with different appearance.

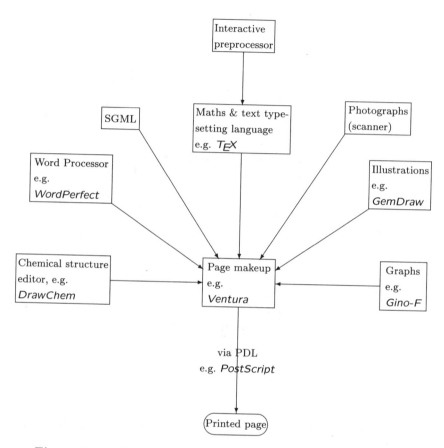

Figure 3. A scheme for creating a printed chemistry document.

- Ventura downloads a driver and fonts every time the PostScript print option is called, thus wasting time. However, this process takes only 23 seconds, and is therefore not over significant. The total print time to produce Figure 2 was only 34 seconds.
- A more significant disadvantage of Ventura for chemical structure diagrams is that if two graphics boxes are defined at the same size but the imported graphics have different bounding boxes, each structure is scaled differently to fit the graphic box as in Figure 4. This is totally appropriate to bit-map images but not to chemical structures where ring sizes etc. for separate diagrams would normally be the same on a given page or within a given document. As shown in Figure 2,

the diagrams can be scaled independently to match each other and achieve the required ring size, but this process is rather hit and miss. The independent scaling feature is disabled until a picture has actually been called, so it is not possible to fix the same scaling factor in advance. The DrawChem/TEX route does not have this disadvantage.

- Yet another problem with Ventura in particular is that it has a restricted definition of an EPS file and will not accept anything else. For example, EPS files accepted with no problem by PageMaker are not accepted by Ventura. The information to create EPS files accepted by PageMaker is readily available and not at variance with the standard POSTSCRIPT texts (Adobe, 1985b) but we have found it extremely difficult to obtain what turned out to be very trivial information for Ventura. Further, EPS files suitable for Ventura are fine for the DVI-LASER/PS route but not necessarily vice versa. The differences are as follows:
  - BoundingBox and DocumentFonts comment parameters must be at the top of the file; no '(atend)' is accepted;
  - the first line must have a dash between PS and Adobe thus: PS-Adobe; the PSAdobe accepted by other software will not do;
  - there must be one linefeed only after the %%Trailer comment.

So much for portability!

26.7   Conclusion

In summary, the important overall criteria in the typesetting of chemical structures integrated with scientific text are:

- ease of creating structure diagrams;
- ease of creating; scientific text;
- ease of integrating these diagrams and text;
- high quality of output;
- low costs.

Whereas the command languages for chemical structures meet the third and fourth and possibly the last of these criteria, it is our contention that the DrawChem/TEX route goes a long way towards meeting all these goals, despite the problems outlined. With an interactive front to TEX, especially for mathematics, all goals can be achieved. Other interactive chemical structure editor/typesetting language/page makeup combinations also have this potential.

Areas worthy of further investigation include an interactive front to one of the chemical typesetting languages and the improvement of non-TEX interactive mathematical software to TEX standards.

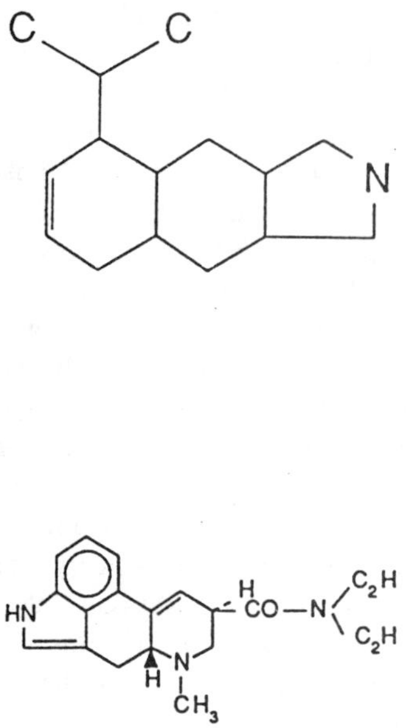

Figure 4. DrawChem structures automatically resized by Ventura Publisher to fit picture boxes of the same size.

26.8   Acknowledgements

One of the authors (ALO) gratefully acknowledges the award of an SERC CASE studentship in conjunction with John Wiley Ltd. The authors are also pleased to acknowledge financial support via a Collaborative Research Grant from SERC and John Wiley.

Bibliography

Adobe Systems Inc, 1985a, *The* POSTSCRIPT *Language Tutorial And Cookbook*, Addison-Wesley, Reading.

Adobe Systems Inc, 1985b, *The* POSTSCRIPT *Language Reference Manual*, Addison-Wesley, Reading.

J. Bentley, 1986, *Programming Pearls*, Comm. Assoc. Comput. Mach., vol.29(8), pp.711–721.

J. Bentley, L. W. Jelinski & B. W. Kernighan, 1987, *Chem - A Program for Phototypesetting Chemical Structure Diagrams*, Comput. Chem. vol.11(4), pp.281-29.

D. Brightly, 1988, *TEX and Graphics – the psfig package*, TEXline, no.7, pp.4–5.

D. D. Cowan & G. De V. Smit, 1986, *Combining Interactive Document Editing with Batch Document Formatting*, Proceedings of the Third International Conference on Text Processing And Document Manipulation, pp.140–153, Cambridge.

E. Crisanti, A. Formigoni, G. Gazzano, & P. La Bruna, 1985, *EasyTEX: An Integrated Environment for Scientific Document Preparation and an Interactive TEX Front End*, Proceedings of the Second International Conference on TextProcessing And Document Manipulation, pp.145–154, Cambridge.

R. T. Haas and K. C. O'Kane, 1987, *Typesetting Chemical Structure Formulas with the Text Formatter TEX/LATEX*, Comput. Chem. vol.11(4), pp.251–271.

Brian W. Kernighan, 1981, *A Typesetter-independent* troff, Comput. Sci. Tech. Report 97, Bell Laboratories, Murray Hill, N.J.

Donald E. Knuth, 1984, *The TEXbook*, Addison-Wesley, Reading.

Leslie Lamport, 1986, *LATEX, A Document Preparation System*, Addison-Wesley, Reading, Mass.

D. Maus & B. Baker, 1986, *Dvilaser/PS Extensions to LATEX*, TUGBOAT, vol.7(1), pp.41–47.

A. C. Norris & A. L. Oakley, 1988a, *Electronic Publishing and Chemical Text Processing – I. A Survey of Software for Two-dimensional Chemical Structure Editing*, Comput. Chem., vol.12, pp.245–251.

A. C. Norris & A. L. Oakley, 1988b, *Electronic Publishing and Chemical Text Processing – II. Character and Vector Representations of Chemical Structures*, Comput. Chem., vol.12, pp.253–255.

A. C. Norris, A. L. Oakley and S. E. Broadbent, 1988, *Electronic Publishing and Chemical Text Processing: The Design of a Chemical Graphics Editor*, Lab. Microcomput., vol.7, pp.103–108.

I. Phillips, 1988 (Feb.), *Just Text*, Desktop Publishing World, pp.28–32.

B. Tuthill, 1983, *Typesetting on the* UNIX *System*, Byte, vol.8(10), pp.253–262.

H. Varian & J. Sterken, 1986, *MacDraw Pictures in TEX Documents*, TUGBOAT, vol.7(1), pp.37–40.

Appendix: TᴇX macro calls to integrate drawings

The page origin is that of PostScript i.e. 0,0 is at the bottom left-hand corner

`\special {ps: landscape}`
provided by Arbortext; rotates the page clockwise through 90 degrees.

`\setlinewidth {`*appropriate* PostScript *value e.g. 0.3*`}`
draws all following lines with the thickness of the parameter.

`\scalepict{`*horizontal scale factor*`}{`*vertical scale factor*`}`
scales the picture horizontally and vertically.

`\hcentrepict`
automatically centres the diagram horizontally in the middle of the page.

`\vcentrepict`
centres the picture vertically on the page.

`\placepict{`*n points left (−) or right (+)*`}{`*n points up (+) or down (−)*`}`
moves the picture file relative to its current position.

`\absplacepict{`*n points left (−) or right (+)*`}{`*n points up (+) or down (−)*`}`
places the picture at the absolute point position on the page.

`\vertplacepict{`*number of points down page*`}{`*box depth*`}`
centres the picture in a box of depth 'box depth' starting at the specified number of points down the page.

`\pictatorigin`
automatically places the picture at the page origin.

`\vpictatorigin`
automatically places the picture at the bottom of the page.

`\insertplot{`*filename.eps*`}{`*box width*`}{`*vbox depth*`}{`*points left (−) or right (+)*`}{`*points up (+) or down (−)*`}{`*x scale factor*`}{`*y scale factor*`}`
reserves a `\vbox` and scales and moves the picture file relative to its current position.

`\figpone{`*figure no.*`}{`*caption*`}{`*width*`}{`*depth*`}{`*x scale*`}{`*y scale*`}{`*filename*`}`
saves a `\vbox` of width space *width* and depth space *depth* and at a fixed distance from previous text, draws a line at the top and bottom of the box for proofing, automatically scales and centres the picture file in this box, and sets a fixed linewidth.

`\figone{`*figure no.*`}{`*caption*`}{`*width*`}{`*depth*`}{`*x scale*`}{`*y scale*`}{`*filename*`}`
as `\figpone`, but without proofing lines.

`\gsave  \grestore`
this pair of commands ensures that there are no knock-on effects by changes to the graphics state that occurs between them.

`\pagesave   \pagerestore`
this pair of commands ensures that there are no knock-on effects by changes to any state that occurs between them; all states are reinitialised after the `\grestore` command to the condition prevailing before the `\gsave` i.e. they affect the POSTSCRIPT commands 'save' and 'restore'. They are best used to isolate each page and they also release any values stored in virtual memory.

`\scaletobox{`*filename.extension*`}{`*box depth*`}`
scales the named picture to a `\vbox` of depth *box depth*.

A C Norris
Department of Physical Sciences and Scientific Computing
South Bank Polytechnic
London SE1 0AA
UK

A L Oakley
Department of Chemistry
Portsmouth Polytechnic
Portsmouth PO1 2DT
UK

Chapter 27
Chemical Structure Formulæ and x/y Diagrams with TEX

Michael Ramek

TEX offers excellent tools for mathematical formulæ but lacks corresponding commands for most other fields of science. The purpose of this contribution is to present the macros \structure and \diagram, and a set of secondary macros which allow an easy (but not unlimited) generation of chemical structure formulæ and x/y diagrams. Portability should be guaranteed, since these macros are designed to work in the plainTEX environment. No additional font tables are required; instead the program converting the DVI file into the actual print file must be able to handle rules correctly.

27.1   Introduction and connection to TEX

In this contribution the usage and restrictions of two macros, \structure and \diagram, are described. Together with a set of secondary macros, these commands allow easy (but not unlimited) generation of chemical structure formulæ and x/y diagrams. The macros themselves will be described in detail elsewhere; they are available from the author upon request. Since the macros work in the plainTEX environment, no additional font tables are required. Instead the program converting the DVI file into the actual print file *must* be able to handle rules correctly.

With the exception of \nomorestructures, \nomorediagrams and \printsymbol, the secondary macros mentioned above should only be used inside the arguments of \structure and \diagram; outside use may cause severe troubles by changing registers, dimensions, and boxes. Additional macros are used by the secondary macros; the names of these further macros contain one uppercase vowel somewhere in the middle to avoid interference with other user defined macros.

Both \structure and \diagram will generate a \hbox, which can be used either immediately or saved by \newbox\name\setbox\name=... for a later \copy\name or \box\name. Also, both \structure and \diagram require a large amount of TEX's memory for macro definition. In case of memory shortage, most of this memory can be released by erasing those definitions, which are not in use at that time. This is achieved by either \nomorestructures or \nomorediagrams. (\nomorestructures was issued in this Chapter after Section 27.2 to prevent memory overflow in Section 27.3.)

27.2   Chemical structure formulæ

Chemical structure formulæ may be generated by the macro \structure, which should be called with one argument. The baseline of the \hbox generated by \structure is identical with the baseline of the first atom or bond entry in the argument of \structure, height and depth depend on the subsequent entries. The width of this \hbox is adjusted by \structure in processing the argument twice: once, without printing, to determine the amount of backspacing produced by all entries and a second time, after proper kerning, actually to do the print. This two step process combines correct positioning with the possibility to commence the structure formula definition at any atom. For testing purposes, or when starting with the leftmost atom, the first pass can and should be suppressed by issuing the command \nopositioncheck as the first entry in the argument of \structure.

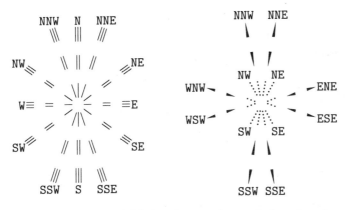

Figure 1. All available in-plane and out-of-plane bonds.

27.2.1 Atoms and bonds

Atoms are depicted in structure formulæ by their chemical symbol. It is easy to generate all possible symbols with TₑX's font tables at hand, quite contrary to their proper positioning. The latter is achieved by the \atom macro with the chemical symbol as the argument. 'Invisible' atoms (which are empty boxes with correct height, depth, and width for a given chemical symbol) can be generated by the \phantatom macro with that symbol as the argument.

Chemical bonding is symbolized in structure formulæ by lines connecting the atoms. These lines also bear additional information: electronic properties (single, double, or triple bonding), nuclear geometry (especially linear versus non-linear), and steric arrangement (in plane, above or below the plane). The bond macros available in \structure are named according to a system which combines all this information in a simple way: the direction of the bond (given in 'geographic' terms: n, nne, ne, ene, e, ese, se, sse, s, ssw, sw, wsw, w, wnw, nw, nnw) is followed either by single, double, triple, or phantom (meaning invisible) for in-plane bonds or, for out-of-plane bonds, by below, above, or evoba (a bond from above-plane down to in-plane). Directions for in-plane and out-of-plane bonds are not compatible: \nnwsingle, \nnwdouble, \nnwtriple, and \nnwphantom have one common direction; \nnwabove, \nnwevoba, and \nnwbelow have another common direction, which is slightly different from that of the \nnwsingle-group. Not all combinations of direction and bond type are defined. Figure 1 shows all available visible bonds with their direction codes. Bond macros have no argument.

For correct positioning, the last entry of \structure is expected to be either \atom or \phantatom. (The first entry may be an atom or a bond.)

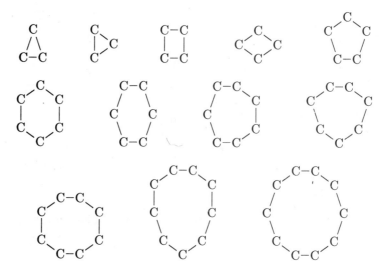

Figure 2. Three- to ten-membered carbon rings.

27.2.2 Rings

The in-plane bonds allow a variety of ring shapes; Figure 2 shows a sample collection. Rings built-up by identical atoms will close as perfectly as the ones in Figure 2: the $(n+1)$th atom in a n-membered ring is printed exactly at the same position as the first atom. For rings built up by different atoms, however, chances are high for a mismatch due to different widths of the atom symbols. In such cases it is advisable to begin a ring with an \atom and to end it with a \phantatom.

The perfect closure of all rings shown in Figure 2 is achieved by different lengths for bonds in different directions, which, however, leads to somehow irritatingly short bonds in the directions e, w, ene, ese, wnw, and wsw. If no rings (or only rings with an even number of ring atoms) are to be generated, the command \longerewbonds may be used to elongate bonds in these directions (as shown in Figure 10). The reverse command \shorterewbonds is also available to return to the default bond lengths shown in all other figures of this section.

Aromatic rings can be specified by generating four outmost ring atoms by \wmostaromatatom, \nmostaromatatom, \smostaromatatom, and \emostaromatatom instead of simply \atom. The order of these four atoms is arbitrary; they cannot be made invisible though.

Unusually long single bonds, connecting atoms across a ring, can be generated by using the macros \firstbicycloatom and \secondbicycloatom instead of \atom. Again, these atoms are always visible. As the names indicate, the \firstbicycloatom must be defined before the \secondbicycloatom.

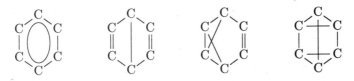

Figure 3. Four different benzene structures.

Nesting of such long bond definitions is impossible: a second or third bond across a ring cannot be specified before completion of the previous one.

Both of these groups of macros (aromatic rings and bicyclo bonds) use the same internal registers, so they can only be used one after the other. Chemists will not regret the impossibility to define a ring as both aromatic and bicyclic. They will, however, appreciate a facility to nest bridging bonds for the generation of tricyclic or polycyclic rings; the instructions used to generate Figure 3, which displays an aromatic, a bicyclic, a tricyclic, and a tetracyclic ring, show how to handle such problems.

Bicyclo bonds and the ellipses marking aromatic rings have more in common than just internal registers: they can never be predefined in a font table but have to be generated anew whenever needed by a sequence of partially overlapping squares. Only this method of generation makes them flexible enough to handle all possible situations (Figures 3 and 4 show how different aromatic rings may look). There is, however, a problem caused by this method of generation: it needs a large portion of TEX's memory. Pages full of aromatic rings or bicyclo bonds may require memory enlargement. (This section requires a main memory size of 50620.)

Due to their generation by a series of rule boxes, bicyclo bonds need considerably more computer time than ordinary bonds do. Whenever possible, bridging in bicyclic rings should therefore be specified by normal bonds, as it was done in Figure 4. Bicyclo bonds can also be used to close mismatching rings (as the one shown in Figure 5).

27.2.3   Side chains

Side chains are generated by the \side macro. (In this context, a 'side chain' is anything attached to the main chain of the molecule by some type of bond.) The \side macro argument is the sequence of bonds and atoms, which define the side chain. This sequence must begin with a bond and must end with an \atom or \phantatom.

\side has to be called immediately after the atom to which the side chain is bound. The definition of the main chain will be completely suspended while \side is processed, which is especially important for the definition of aromatic rings or bicyclo bonds: partially specified aromatic rings or bicyclo bonds will be saved when \side is entered and restored when \side is left,

Figure 5. Envelope form of the cyclo-

Figure 4. The azulene ring system.   pentane ring.

thus \side does not affect incomplete specifications of aromatic rings or bicyclo bonds at all. Furthermore, \side is able to generate aromatic rings or bicyclo bonds of its own, as long as all necessary specifications are part of its argument (Figure 6 was generated in this way).

Side chains often have side chains themselves. Therefore \side may be called from inside \side, the maximum nesting of side chains being 20: \side may be called from an outer \side, which in turn may be called from an outer \side, which in turn may be called from an outer \side, etc., etc. (Nesting side chains to that extent might need an enlargement of TₑX's input stack size; this section required an input stack size of 16.)

27.2.4 Larger structures

Structure formulæ of considerable complexity can be generated with the macros discussed so far. Figures 7–10 show a number of examples. These examples have also been included to point out the following details:

- \sseabove goes with \sebelow in Figure 6 and with \sswbelow in Figure 7 (as does \nneabove with \nnwbelow and \nebelow, etc.);
- bonds below the plane may also be used to symbolize weak bonds (Figure 9);
- \enspace and \thinspace can be used to compensate additional superscripts or subscripts (Figure 9);
- the choice of baseline, eventually with the help of invisible atoms and bonds, may be essential when structure formulæ are combined with text or other symbols (Figure 10).

For even larger structures like the ones shown in Figures 11 and 12 the four macros \wpin, \epin, \spin, and \npin may be of interest: these macros generate side chains, which are attached to the main chain without an explicitly drawn bond.

Figure 11 also illustrates the multiple use of substructures saved in boxes. Figures 6 and 7 employ intermediate saving of structures for correct caption positioning.

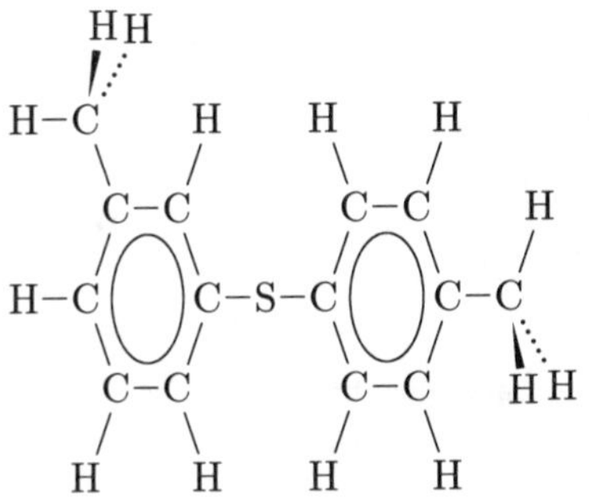

Figure 6. 3,4'-Ditolylsulfide.

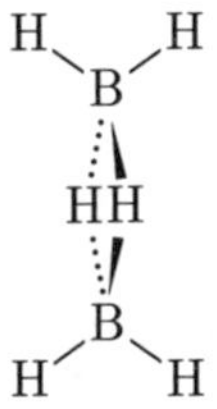

Figure 7. Diborane.

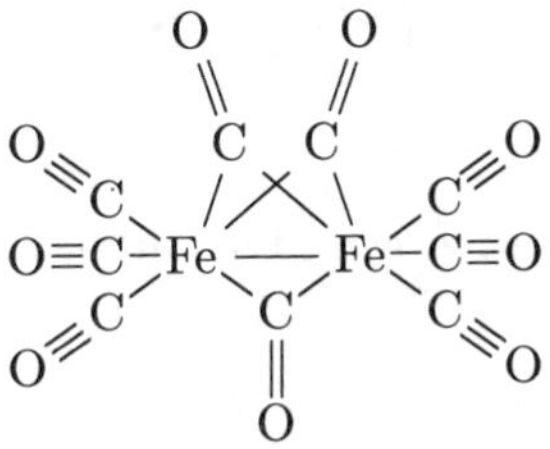

Figure 8. Tri-μ-carbonyl-bis(tricarbonyliron).

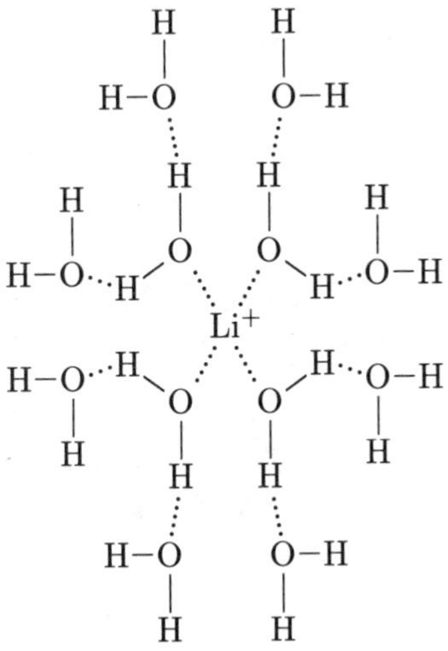

Figure 9. A lithium cation surrounded by two hydration spheres.

$$
\begin{array}{ccc}
\mathrm{H\,H} & & \mathrm{O{-}H} \\
\backslash & & / \\
& \mathrm{C{-}C} & \\
/ & & \backslash\backslash \\
\mathrm{N} & & \mathrm{O} \\
\end{array}
\qquad \rightleftharpoons \qquad
\begin{array}{ccc}
\mathrm{H\,H} & & \mathrm{O} \\
\backslash & & // \\
& \mathrm{C{-}C} & \\
/ & & \backslash \\
\mathrm{N} & & \mathrm{O{-}H} \\
\end{array}
$$

Figure 10. Two conformeres of neutral glycine in equilibrium.

$$
\begin{array}{cccccc}
\mathrm{CH_3} & \mathrm{CH_3} & \mathrm{CH_3} & \mathrm{CH_3} & \mathrm{CH_3} & \mathrm{CH_3} \\
| & | & | & | & | & | \\
\end{array}
$$
$-\mathrm{CH}{-}\mathrm{CH_2}{-}\mathrm{CH}{-}\mathrm{CH_2}{-}\mathrm{CH}{-}\mathrm{CH_2}{-}\mathrm{CH}{-}\mathrm{CH_2}{-}\mathrm{CH}{-}\mathrm{CH_2}{-}\mathrm{CH}{-}\mathrm{CH_2}{-}$

$$
\begin{array}{ccc}
\mathrm{CH_3} & \mathrm{CH_3} & \mathrm{CH_3} \\
| & | & | \\
\end{array}
$$
$-\mathrm{CH}{-}\mathrm{CH_2}{-}\mathrm{CH}{-}\mathrm{CH_2}{-}\mathrm{CH}{-}\mathrm{CH_2}{-}\mathrm{CH}{-}\mathrm{CH_2}{-}\mathrm{CH}{-}\mathrm{CH_2}{-}\mathrm{CH}{-}\mathrm{CH_2}{-}$
$$
\begin{array}{ccc}
| & | & | \\
\mathrm{CH_3} & \mathrm{CH_3} & \mathrm{CH_3} \\
\end{array}
$$

Figure 11. Isotactic and syndiotactic polypropylene.

27.3   x/y diagrams

Standard types of x/y diagrams can be generated by the macro \diagram.
\diagram expects two arguments: one containing all information about the
coordinate system, and one which specifies what to place in this coordinate
system. The secondary macros, which are available for use in these two
arguments, are described in the following sections.

The baseline of the \hbox generated by \diagram is below the x axis
labelling, so that the box will have zero depth.

27.3.1   Coordinate system

The coordinate system has to be specified in the first argument of \diagram
with the commands \xaxis, \yaxis, \noscale, \noaxis, and \nogrid.
Except for \noscale and \noaxis, the order in which these commands are
given is arbitrary: they only store the coordinate system information in
various registers. The real work is done after processing the first and before
processing the second argument of \diagram.

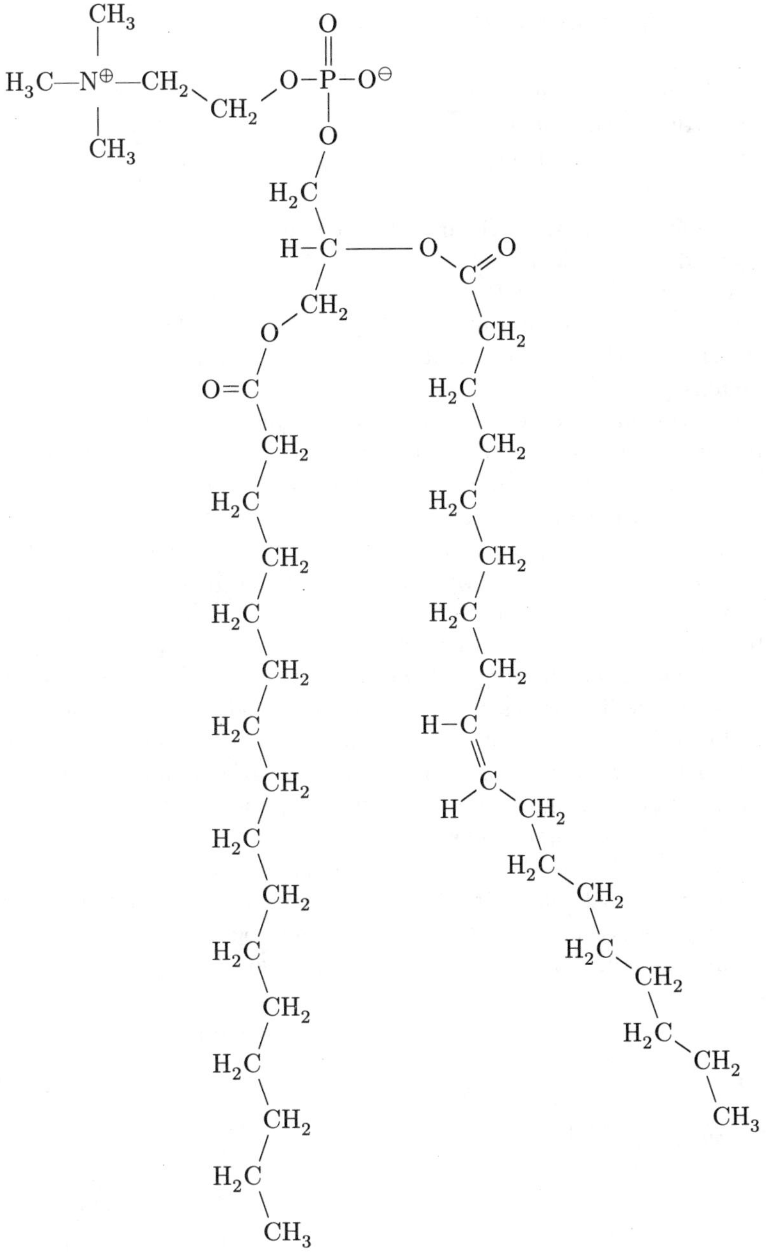

Figure 12. 1-Palmitoyl-2-oleoyl-3-*sn*-glycerophosphocholin.

The following arguments are required by both \xaxis and \yaxis:

- axis length,
- minimum coordinate,
- maximum coordinate,
- coordinate increment,
- axis label.

These arguments must be separated by commas and the axis label must be terminated by a semicolon.

'Axis length' specifies the length of this coordinate axis and may be given in any of TEX's dimension units. The total width or height of the diagram will be this length plus the amount of space required for scaling and labelling of the axis.

Axis scaling is done according to 'minimum coordinate', 'maximum coordinate', and 'coordinate increment'. These quantities must be real numbers containing a decimal point. (TEX can only do integer arithmetic, the decimal point therefore is essential as delimiter between integer and fraction part.) Due to TEX's integer arithmetic, no exponential form can be handled; exponents should be part of the axis label. 'Coordinate increment' must be positive, in other words: 'minimum coordinate' must be less than 'maximum coordinate'. Coordinate values are converted to dimensions (in points) during diagram generation; the range of coordinate values therefore is restricted by TEX's limits on dimensions and the necessity to calculate differences between these dimensions. The commands \noscale and \noaxis are only valid after an axis definition; \noscale supresses printing of coordinate values for this axis while still drawing the axis itself, whereas \noaxis supresses printing of both, axis and coordinate values.

The 'axis label' is placed left of the y axis or below the x axis, together with an arrow. It should contain the information about the quantity depicted on the axis. Anything except a semicolon may be given. A semicolon must terminate the label. If no label is specified, \diagram skips the arrow too.

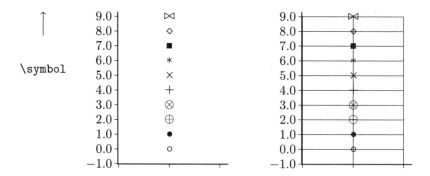

Figure 13. Ten symbols are predefined: o = \symbol0, • = \symbol1, ..., ⋈ = \symbol9.

By default, a grid according to the axis scaling will be drawn in the diagram. The command \nogrid, if given, suppresses this grid. Figure 13 shows two sample diagrams, with and without grid.

27.3.2   Diagram specification

The second argument of \diagram is expected to contain the specification of the material to be displayed. The primary commands for this specification are \values, \connect, \lsqline, and \curve. If more than one of these commands is needed, the command order is again arbitrary.

Single points in the coordinate system are marked by \values. For each of these points, the x and y coordinate must be given in the argument of \values following the identifier \point as real numbers with a decimal point, separated by a comma, and terminated by a semicolon. To mark these points, ten symbols are prestored; these are shown in Figure 13 and can be selected using the command \symbol succeeded by one of the ten digits before specifying the coordinates. Other symbols can be defined by the command \ownsymbol with the desired symbol as its argument. Symbols defined in this way may require small horizontal or vertical shifts to mark the desired coordinates exactly; the ten prestored symbols are correctly adjusted. Symbols may be changed as often as needed. Any new symbol definition will replace the previous one. If no symbol is selected, \values takes the properly shifted lower case x of the typewriter font as the default symbol.

Points in the coordinate system may be connected with straight lines by using \connect. Examples are shown in Figures 14–16. To specify these points and the symbols used to mark them, the commands \point, \symbol, and \ownsymbol are available inside the argument of \connect with the same meaning as in the argument of \values. In addition, the command \nosymbol is available to turn off point marking. If no symbol is selected, \connect does not mark points.

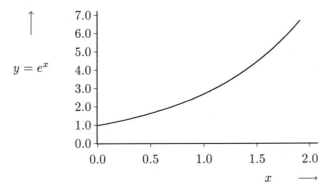

Figure 14. The function $y = e^x$.

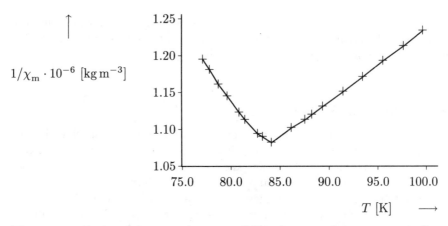

$1/\chi_{\mathrm{m}} \cdot 10^{-6} \; [\mathrm{kg\,m}^{-3}]$

$T \; [\mathrm{K}] \quad \longrightarrow$

Figure 15. Reciprocal magnetic susceptibility (measured at a magnetic flux density of 0.75 T) of superconducting $\mathrm{Tm}_{0.75}\mathrm{Sc}_{0.25}\mathrm{Ba}_2\mathrm{Cu}_3\mathrm{O}_{7-x}$.

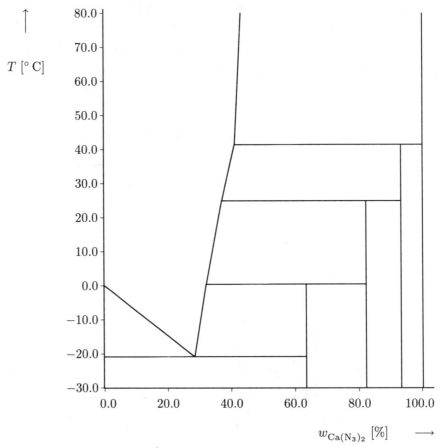

$T \; [^\circ \mathrm{C}]$

$w_{\mathrm{Ca(N_3)_2}} \; [\%] \quad \longrightarrow$

Figure 16. Phase diagram of the $\mathrm{H_2O} - \mathrm{Ca(N_3)_2}$ system (simplified).

Single points and the corresponding regression line are plotted using \lsqline. To specify the points and the symbols marking them, the commands \point, \symbol, and \ownsymbol are available as described in \values. If no symbol is selected, \lsqline takes the properly shifted lower case x of the typewriter font as the default symbol. An example is shown in Figure 17. \lsqline will yield an error if the slope of the regression line is too steep; in such cases, the points should be displayed with the command \values and the desired straight line should be generated via \connect using two properly calculated points on the regression line.

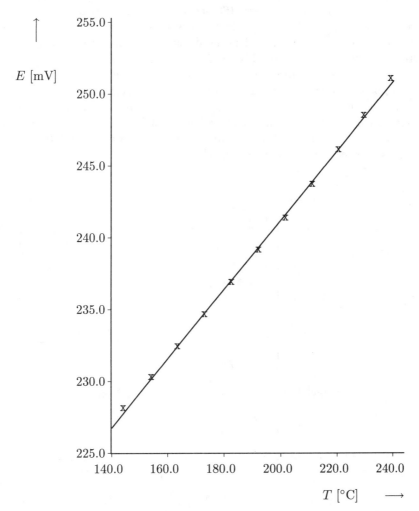

Figure 17. Temperature dependence of the electromotorical force E of the galvanic cell Pt/Ag/AgJ/Te(Ag),Ag$_5$Te$_3$/Pt.

The command \curve plots single points and a smooth curve connecting these points. Between any two points, this curve is calculated in an iterative process via the two circles, which are given by the two points and the preceeding and following point respectively. The total number of points used to approximate the curve is displayed in each step of this iteration. Since T_EX has a limited memory, two external files (named *jobname*.co1 and *jobname*.co2) are used to store intermediate results. (This section required a save size of 309.) Operating with these external files and the complicated computational procedure used to calculate the curve both require a large amount of computer time to generate a single curve. (The generation of Figure 18 needs 82 seconds of CPU time on a Vaxstation 3200, Figure 19 takes 168 seconds, whereas Figure 14 requires 17 seconds.) \curve therefore is by far the most costly command within \diagram; thus \connect should be used instead whenever possible. (The instructions used to generate Figure 20 exemplify this idea: the macros operate by connecting precomputed coordinate values.) In addition to the commands \point, \symbol, \ownsymbol, and \nosymbol, which have the same meaning as in the previously discussed commands, \hpoint and \vpoint are available to specify points, which must have horizontal or vertical tangents. Examples for such curves are shown in Figures 18 and 19. If no symbol is selected, \curve does not mark points.

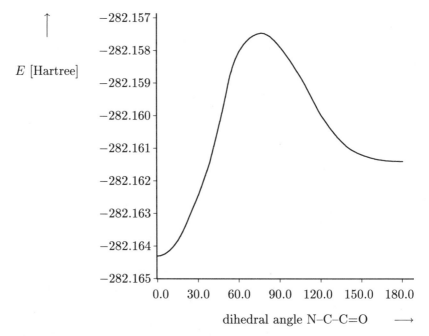

Figure 18. Energy profile for the neutral glycine equilibrium shown in Figure 10, obtained from *ab initio* SCF calculations with the 4-21G basis set.

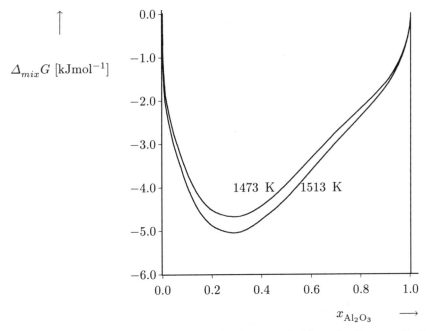

Figure 19. Integral Gibbs energy of solution of the α-$Cr_2O_3 - \alpha$-Al_2O_3 system at 1473 and 1513 K.

27.3.3 General remarks

To simplify printing of the ten predefined symbols in the caption, a command \printsymbol is available. Figure 13 gives an example. Figure 19 demonstrates the use of \values in combination with \ownsymbol and \point to place information into the diagram itself.

All of the commands \connect, \lsqline, and \curve make use of a common procedure, which connects two points by a straight line. The detailed action taken by this procedure is different for points which have an identical x or y coordinate, and for points which do not have identical coordinates: points with identical coordinates are connected by one properly positioned \vrule, whereas the connection of points without identical coordinates is achieved by a series of partially overlaping squares (which again are \vrules). TₑX's memory allows the handling of only a limited number of such rules; long non-horizontal and non-vertical lines in diagrams will soon exhaust the memory size. Two or more such diagrams should be placed on different pages. (This chapter was prepared with a main memory size of 65500, which is sufficient to handle Figures 18 and 19 on separate pages, but insufficient to place Figures 18 and 19 on one page. In contrast, Figure 16 causes no problem because most of the lines are horizontal or vertical.) In case of memory overflow, reduction of the total diagram size is the easiest way out.

In special applications, user defined macros may be helpful within the second argument of \diagram to extract coordinate values from given information. Figure 20 was generated in such a way. \count{100} to \count{200}, \dimen{100} to \dimen{200}, and \box{100} to \box{200} are available for such user defined macros.

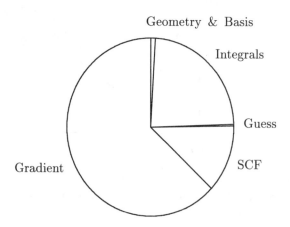

Figure 20. Distribution of CPU time for the first optimization cycle in an *ab initio* SCF geometry optimization of β-Alanine with the 4-31G basis set, using the program GAMESS on a CONVEX C1-XP. (Starting on top and proceeding clockwise: geometry and basis set definition: 38.9 s (= 1.1%), integral calculation: 778.1 s (= 23.0%), guess of initial density matrix: 16.5 s (= 0.5%), SCF iteration: 428.7 s (= 12.7%), gradient calculation: 2123.0 s (= 62.7%).)

27.4 Acknowledgement

The author is grateful to his colleagues at the Institut für Physikalische und Theoretische Chemie der Technischen Universität Graz, who supplied the 'real life' data presented in Figures 15–20. Continued support by the Zentrum für elektronische Datenverarbeitung der Technischen Universität Graz is also gratefully acknowledged.

Appendix: The TEX used to generate the figures

Figure 1:

```
\centerline{
\structure{\phantatom{C}
% The \phantatom just processed defines the central empty spot,
% from which all the bonds spray out; each one of the following
% \side{...} commands will generate one direction. The rules
% for \side are explained in chapter 27.3 .
\side{\wsingle\phantatom{C}\wdouble\phantatom{C}\wtriple
\atom{\tt W}}
\side{\esingle\phantatom{C}\edouble\phantatom{C}\etriple
\atom{\tt E}}
\side{\ssingle\phantatom{C}\sdouble\phantatom{C}\striple
\atom{\tt S}}
\side{\nsingle\phantatom{C}\ndouble\phantatom{C}\ntriple
\atom{\tt N}}
\side{\swsingle\phantatom{C}\swdouble\phantatom{C}\swtriple
\atom{\tt SW}}
\side{\sesingle\phantatom{C}\sedouble\phantatom{C}\setriple
\atom{\tt SE}}
\side{\nesingle\phantatom{C}\nedouble\phantatom{C}\netriple
\atom{\tt NE}}
\side{\nwsingle\phantatom{C}\nwdouble\phantatom{C}\nwtriple
\atom{\tt NW}}
\side{\nnwsingle\phantatom{C}\nnwdouble\phantatom{C}\nnwtriple
\atom{\tt NNW}}
\side{\nnesingle\phantatom{C}\nnedouble\phantatom{C}\nnetriple
\atom{\tt NNE}}
\side{\ssesingle\phantatom{C}\ssedouble\phantatom{C}\ssetriple
\atom{\tt SSE}}
\side{\sswsingle\phantatom{C}\sswdouble\phantatom{C}\sswtriple
\atom{\tt SSW}}
}
\hskip 1truecm
\structure{\phantatom{C}
\side{\wnwbelow\phantatom{C}\wnwabove\phantatom{C}\wnwevoba
\atom{\tt WNW}}
\side{\enebelow\phantatom{C}\eneabove\phantatom{C}\eneevoba
\atom{\tt ENE}}
\side{\wswbelow\phantatom{C}\wswabove\phantatom{C}\wswevoba
\atom{\tt WSW}}
\side{\esebelow\phantatom{C}\eseabove\phantatom{C}\eseevoba
```

```
\atom{\tt ESE}}
\side{\swbelow\atom{\tt SW}}
\side{\sebelow\atom{\tt SE}}
\side{\nebelow\atom{\tt NE}}
\side{\nwbelow\atom{\tt NW}}
\side{\nnwbelow\phantatom{C}\nnwabove\phantatom{C}\nnwevoba
\atom{\tt NNW}}
\side{\nnebelow\phantatom{C}\nneabove\phantatom{C}\nneevoba
\atom{\tt NNE}}
\side{\ssebelow\phantatom{C}\sseabove\phantatom{C}\sseevoba
\atom{\tt SSE}}
\side{\sswbelow\phantatom{C}\sswabove\phantatom{C}\sswevoba
\atom{\tt SSW}}
}
}
\medskip
\centerline{\bf Figure~1. \rm All available in-plane and
out-of-plane bonds.}
```

Figure 2:

```
\centerline{
\structure{\nopositioncheck\atom{C}\esingle\atom{C}\nnwsingle
\atom{C}\sswsingle\atom{C}}
\hskip 1truecm
\structure{\nopositioncheck\atom{C}\nsingle\atom{C}\sesingle
\atom{C}\swsingle\atom{C}}
\hskip 1truecm
\structure{\nopositioncheck\atom{C}\nsingle\atom{C}\esingle
\atom{C}\ssingle\atom{C}\wsingle\atom{C}}
\hskip 1truecm
\structure{\atom{C}\nwsingle\atom{C}\nesingle\atom{C}\sesingle
\atom{C}\swsingle\atom{C}}
\hskip 1truecm
\structure{\atom{C}\nnwsingle\atom{C}\nesingle\atom{C}\sesingle
\atom{C}\sswsingle\atom{C}\wsingle\atom{C}}
}
\medskip
\centerline{
\structure{\atom{C}\nwsingle\atom{C}\nsingle\atom{C}\nesingle
\atom{C}\sesingle\atom{C}\ssingle\atom{C}\swsingle\atom{C}}
\hskip 1truecm
\structure{\atom{C}\nnwsingle\atom{C}\nnesingle\atom{C}\esingle
\atom{C}\ssesingle\atom{C}\sswsingle\atom{C}\wsingle\atom{C}}
\hskip 1truecm
```

```
\structure{\atom{C}\nnwsingle\atom{C}\nnesingle\atom{C}\esingle
\atom{C}\sesingle\atom{C}\ssingle\atom{C}\swsingle\atom{C}
\wsingle\atom{C}}
\hskip 1truecm
\structure{\atom{C}\nwsingle\atom{C}\nnwsingle\atom{C}\nesingle
\atom{C}\esingle\atom{C}\sesingle\atom{C}\sswsingle\atom{C}
\swsingle\atom{C}}
}
\medskip
\centerline{
\structure{\atom{C}\nwsingle\atom{C}\nsingle\atom{C}\nesingle
\atom{C}\esingle\atom{C}\sesingle\atom{C}\ssingle\atom{C}
\swsingle\atom{C}\wsingle\atom{C}}
\hskip 1truecm
\structure{\atom{C}\nwsingle\atom{C}\nnwsingle\atom{C}\nsingle
\atom{C}\nesingle\atom{C}\esingle\atom{C}\sesingle\atom{C}
\ssingle\atom{C}\sswsingle\atom{C}\swsingle\atom{C}}
\hskip 1truecm
\structure{\atom{C}\nwsingle\atom{C}\nnwsingle\atom{C}\nnesingle
\atom{C}\nesingle\atom{C}\esingle\atom{C}\sesingle\atom{C}
\ssesingle\atom{C}\sswsingle\atom{C}\swsingle\atom{C}\wsingle
\atom{C}}
}
\medskip\centerline{\bf Figure~2. \rm
Three- to ten-membered carbon rings.}
```

Figure 3:

```
\centerline{
\structure{\nopositioncheck\wmostaromatatom{C}\nsingle\atom{C}
\nesingle\nmostaromatatom{C}\sesingle\emostaromatatom{C}\ssingle
\atom{C}\swsingle\smostaromatatom{C}\nwsingle\phantatom{C}}
\hskip 1truecm
\structure{\nopositioncheck\atom{C}\ndouble\atom{C}\nesingle
\firstbicycloatom{C}\sesingle\atom{C}\sdouble\atom{C}\swsingle
\secondbicycloatom{C}\nwsingle\phantatom{C}}
\hskip 1truecm
\structure{\nopositioncheck\firstbicycloatom{C}\nsingle
\phantatom{C}\nesingle\secondbicycloatom{C}\swphantom
\firstbicycloatom{C}\nephantom\phantatom{C}\sesingle\atom{C}
\sdouble\atom{C}\swsingle\secondbicycloatom{C}\nwsingle
\phantatom{C}}
\hskip 1truecm
\structure{\nopositioncheck\firstbicycloatom{C}\sesingle
\phantatom{C}\nephantom\secondbicycloatom{C}\swsingle
```

```
\firstbicycloatom{C}\nephantom\phantatom{C}\nsingle\phantatom{C}
\nwsingle\secondbicycloatom{C}\sephantom\firstbicycloatom{C}
\nwphantom\phantatom{C}\swsingle\secondbicycloatom{C}\ssingle
\phantatom{C}}
}
\medskip\centerline{\bf Figure~3. \rm
Four different benzene structures.}
```

Figures 4 & 5:

```
\hbox{\vbox{
\hbox to 0.5\hsize{\hss
\structure{\emostaromatatom{C}\swsingle\smostaromatatom{C}
\wsingle\atom{C}\nnwsingle\wmostaromatatom{C}\nnesingle
\nmostaromatatom{C}\esingle\atom{C}\sesingle\wmostaromatatom{C}
\nesingle\nmostaromatatom{C}\ssesingle\emostaromatatom{C}
\sswsingle\smostaromatatom{C}\nwsingle\phantatom{C}\nsingle
\phantatom{C}}
\hss}
\medskip\hbox to 0.5\hsize{\bf Figure~4. \rm
The azulene ring system.\hss}
}\vbox{
\hbox to 0.5\hsize{\hss
\structure{\longerewbonds\firstbicycloatom{C}\nnwsingle\atom{C}
\eneabove\atom{C}\eseevoba\atom{C}\sswsingle
\secondbicycloatom{C}}
\hss}
\medskip
\vbox{\hsize=0.5\hsize\noindent\bf Figure~5. \rm
Envelope form of the cyclo\-pentane ring.}
}}
```

Figures 6 & 7:

```
\vbox{% First: Save Fig. 6 and Fig. 7 in separate boxes.
\newbox\figsix\setbox\figsix=\structure{
\nopositioncheck\atom{H}\esingle\wmostaromatatom{C}
\nnesingle\nmostaromatatom{C}
\side{\nnwsingle\atom{C}\side{\nneabove\atom{H}}
\side{\nebelow\atom{H}}\wsingle\atom{H}}
\esingle\atom{C}\side{\nnesingle\atom{H}}\ssesingle
\emostaromatatom{C}\side{\esingle\atom{S}\esingle
\wmostaromatatom{C}\nnesingle\atom{C}
\side{\nnwsingle\atom{H}}\esingle\nmostaromatatom{C}
\side{\nnesingle\atom{H}}\ssesingle\emostaromatatom{C}
```

```
\side{\esingle\atom{C}\side{\sseabove\atom{H}}
\side{\sebelow\atom{H}}\nnesingle\atom{H}}\sswsingle
\smostaromatatom{C}\side{\ssesingle\atom{H}}\wsingle
\atom{C}\side{\sswsingle\atom{H}}\nnwsingle\phantatom{C}}
\sswsingle\atom{C}\side{\ssesingle\atom{H}}\wsingle
\smostaromatatom{C}\side{\sswsingle\atom{H}}\nnwsingle
\phantatom{C}}
\newbox\figseven\setbox\figseven=\structure{\atom{H}
\nnebelow\atom{B}\side{\nesingle\atom{H}}
\side{\nwsingle\atom{H}}\sseabove\atom{H}\sswevoba\atom{B}
\side{\swsingle\atom{H}}\side{\sesingle\atom{H}}
\nnwbelow\phantatom{B}}
% Second: Use the width of the saved structures for the
% figure captions, comment each end-of-line to avoid
% additional spacing.
\newbox\caption\setbox\caption=\hbox to\hsize{\hss%
\hbox to\wd\figsix{\hss\bf Figure~6. \rm %
3,4'-Ditolylsulfide.\hss}\hss\hss%
\hbox to\wd\figseven{\hss\bf Figure~7. \rm Diborane.\hss}%
\hss}
% Third: Print structures and captions.
\line{\hss\box\figsix\hss\hss\box\figseven\hss}
\medskip
\box\caption
}
```

Figure 8:

```
\vbox{
\centerline{\structure{\nopositioncheck
\atom{O}\etriple\atom{C}\esingle\firstbicycloatom{Fe}
\side{\nwsingle\atom{C}\nwtriple\atom{O}}
\side{\swsingle\atom{C}\swtriple\atom{O}}
\sesingle\atom{C}\side{\sdouble\atom{O}}\nesingle\phantatom{Fe}
\side{\esingle\atom{C}\etriple\atom{O}}
\side{\sesingle\atom{C}\setriple\atom{O}}
\side{\nesingle\atom{C}\netriple\atom{O}}
\nnwsingle\secondbicycloatom{C}\side{\nnedouble\atom{O}}
\ssephantom\firstbicycloatom{Fe}\swphantom\phantatom{C}
\nwphantom\phantatom{Fe}\nnesingle\secondbicycloatom{C}
\side{\nnwdouble\atom{O}}\sswphantom\firstbicycloatom{Fe}
\sephantom\phantatom{C}\nephantom\secondbicycloatom{Fe}}}
\medskip \centerline{\bf Figure~8. \rm
Tri-$\mu$-carbonyl-bis(tricarbonyliron).}
}
```

Figure 9:

```
\vbox{
\centerline{
\structure{\atom{\enspace\thinspace Li$^+$}
\side{\nwbelow\atom{O}
\side{\nsingle\atom{H}\nnwbelow\atom{O}\side{\wsingle\atom{H}}
\nsingle\atom{H}}\swsingle\atom{H}\wnwbelow\atom{O}
\side{\wsingle\atom{H}}\nsingle\atom{H}}
\side{\nebelow\atom{O}
\side{\nsingle\atom{H}\nnebelow\atom{O}\side{\esingle\atom{H}}
\nsingle\atom{H}}\sesingle\atom{H}\enebelow\atom{O}
\side{\esingle\atom{H}}\nsingle\atom{H}}
\side{\swbelow\atom{O}
\side{\ssingle\atom{H}\sswbelow\atom{O}\side{\wsingle\atom{H}}
\ssingle\atom{H}}\nwsingle\atom{H}\wswbelow\atom{O}
\side{\wsingle\atom{H}}\ssingle\atom{H}}
\side{\sebelow\atom{O}
\side{\ssingle\atom{H}\ssebelow\atom{O}\side{\esingle\atom{H}}
\ssingle\atom{H}}\nesingle\atom{H}\esebelow\atom{O}
\side{\esingle\atom{H}}\ssingle\atom{H}}}
}
\medskip
\centerline{\bf Figure~9. \rm A lithium cation surrounded by
two hydration spheres.}
}
```

Figure 10:

```
\vbox{
\centerline{
\structure{\longerewbonds\phantatom{H}\swphantom\atom{N}
\side{\sseabove\atom{H}}
\side{\sebelow\atom{H}}\nnesingle\atom{C}
\side{\nnwabove\atom{H}}\side{\nwbelow\atom{H}}
\esingle\atom{C}\side{\ssedouble\atom{O}}
\nnesingle\atom{O}\esingle\atom{H}}
\hskip 1cm{$\rightleftharpoons$}\hskip 1cm
\structure{\longerewbonds\phantatom{H}\swphantom\atom{N}
\side{\sseabove\atom{H}}\side{\sebelow\atom{H}}
\nnesingle\atom{C}\side{\nnwabove\atom{H}}
\side{\nwbelow\atom{H}}\esingle\atom{C}\side{\nnedouble\atom{O}}
\ssesingle\atom{O}\esingle\atom{H}}
}
\medskip
```

```
\centerline{\bf Figure~10. \rm
Two conformeres of neutral glycine in equilibrium.}
}
```

Figure 11:

```
\newbox\monomera\setbox\monomera=%
\structure{\nopositioncheck\esingle\atom{C}
\side{\nsingle\atom{C}\epin{H$_3$}}
\atom{H}\esingle\atom{CH$_2$}}}%
\newbox\monomerb\setbox\monomerb=%
\structure{\nopositioncheck\esingle\atom{C}
\side{\ssingle\atom{C}\epin{H$_3$}}
\atom{H}\esingle\atom{CH$_2$}}}%
\newbox\monomere\setbox\monomere=%
\structure{\nopositioncheck\esingle\atom{C}
\side{\nsingle\atom{C}\epin{H$_3$}}
\atom{H}\esingle\atom{CH$_2$}\esingle\phantatom{}}}%
\vbox{
\centerline{\copy\monomera\copy\monomera\copy\monomera%
\copy\monomera\copy\monomera\copy\monomere}
\medskip
\centerline{\copy\monomerb\copy\monomera\copy\monomerb%
\box\monomera\box\monomerb\box\monomere}
\medskip
\centerline{\bf Figure~11. \rm Isotactic and syndiotactic
polypropylene.}
}
```

Figure 12:

```
\centerline{\structure{
\atom{C}\epin{H$_3$}\nnwsingle\atom{C}\wpin{H$_2$}
\nnesingle\atom{C}\epin{H$_2$}\nnwsingle\atom{C}\wpin{H$_2$}
\nnesingle\atom{C}\epin{H$_2$}\nnwsingle\atom{C}\wpin{H$_2$}
\nnesingle\atom{C}\epin{H$_2$}\nnwsingle\atom{C}\wpin{H$_2$}
\nnesingle\atom{C}\epin{H$_2$}\nnwsingle\atom{C}\wpin{H$_2$}
\nnesingle\atom{C}\epin{H$_2$}\nnwsingle\atom{C}\wpin{H$_2$}
\nnesingle\atom{C}\epin{H$_2$}\nnwsingle\atom{C}
\side{\wdouble\atom{O}}
\nnesingle\atom{O}\nesingle\atom{C}\epin{H$_2$}
\nnesingle\firstbicycloatom{C}\side{\wsingle\atom{H}}
\nnwsingle\atom{C}\wpin{H$_2$}\nnesingle\atom{O}
\side{\nsingle\atom{P}\side{\esingle\atom{O$^\ominus$}}}
```

```
\side{\ndouble\atom{0}}
\side{\wsingle\atom{0}\swsingle\atom{CH$_2$}\nwsingle
\atom{~~H$_3$C---N$^\oplus$---CH$_2$}
\side{\nsingle\atom{C}\epin{H$_3$}}
\side{\ssingle\atom{C}\epin{H$_3$}}}}
\ephantom\phantatom{000}\ephantom\ssephantom\phantatom{0}
\sswphantom\secondbicycloatom{0}\sesingle\atom{C}
\side{\nedouble\atom{0}}
\ssesingle\atom{C}\epin{H$_2$}\sswsingle\atom{C}\wpin{H$_2$}
\ssesingle\atom{C}\epin{H$_2$}\sswsingle\atom{C}\wpin{H$_2$}
\ssesingle\atom{C}\epin{H$_2$}\sswsingle\atom{C}\wpin{H$_2$}
\ssesingle\atom{C}\epin{H$_2$}\sswsingle\atom{C}
\side{\wsingle\atom{H}}\ssedouble\atom{C}
\side{\swsingle\atom{H}}
\sesingle\atom{C}\epin{H$_2$}\ssesingle\atom{C}\wpin{H$_2$}
\sesingle\atom{C}\epin{H$_2$}\ssesingle\atom{C}\wpin{H$_2$}
\sesingle\atom{C}\epin{H$_2$}\ssesingle\atom{C}\wpin{H$_2$}
\sesingle\atom{C}\epin{H$_2$}\ssesingle\atom{C}\epin{H$_3$}}}}
\medskip
\centerline{\bf Figure~12. \rm
1-Palmitoyl-2-oleoyl-3-{\it sn\/}-glycerophosphocholin.}
```

Figure 13:

```
\def\Symbol{{\tt {\char'134}symbol}}
\vbox{\line{\hfil
\diagram{\xaxis3truecm,0.,1.0,0.5,;\noscale
\yaxis4truecm,-1.0,9.0,1.,\Symbol;\nogrid}
{\values{
\symbol0\point0.5,0.0;
\symbol1\point0.5,1.0;
\symbol2\point0.5,2.0;
\symbol3\point0.5,3.0;
\symbol4\point0.5,4.0;
\symbol5\point0.5,5.0;
\symbol6\point0.5,6.0;
\symbol7\point0.5,7.0;
\symbol8\point0.5,8.0;
\symbol9\point0.5,9.0;}}
\hfil
\diagram{\xaxis3truecm,0.,1.0,0.5,;\noscale
\yaxis4truecm,-1.0,9.0,1.,;}
{\values{
\symbol0\point0.5,0.0;
\symbol1\point0.5,1.0;
```

```
\symbol2\point0.5,2.0;
\symbol3\point0.5,3.0;
\symbol4\point0.5,4.0;
\symbol5\point0.5,5.0;
\symbol6\point0.5,6.0;
\symbol7\point0.5,7.0;
\symbol8\point0.5,8.0;
\symbol9\point0.5,9.0;}}
\hfil}
\vskip -\medskipamount
\noindent{\bf Figure~13.
\rm Ten symbols are predefined:
\printsymbol0 = \Symbol{\tt0},
\printsymbol1 = \Symbol{\tt1},
\dots,
\printsymbol9 = \Symbol{\tt9}.}}
```

Figure 14:

```
\vbox{\line{\hfill
\diagram{\xaxis6truecm,0.0,2.0,0.5,$x$;
\yaxis3.5truecm,0.0,7.0,1.0,$y=e^x$;\nogrid}
{\connect{
% Points were generated by the Fortran program
% DO 1 X = 0.0,1.9,0.15
% 1 WRITE(7,2)X,EXP(X),X+0.05,EXP(X+0.05),X+0.1,EXP(X+0.1)
% 2 FORMAT(3('\point',F4.2,',',F6.4,';'))
% END
\point0.00,1.0000;\point0.05,1.0513;\point0.10,1.1052;
\point0.15,1.1618;\point0.20,1.2214;\point0.25,1.2840;
\point0.30,1.3499;\point0.35,1.4191;\point0.40,1.4918;
\point0.45,1.5683;\point0.50,1.6487;\point0.55,1.7333;
\point0.60,1.8221;\point0.65,1.9155;\point0.70,2.0138;
\point0.75,2.1170;\point0.80,2.2255;\point0.85,2.3396;
\point0.90,2.4596;\point0.95,2.5857;\point1.00,2.7183;
\point1.05,2.8577;\point1.10,3.0042;\point1.15,3.1582;
\point1.20,3.3201;\point1.25,3.4903;\point1.30,3.6693;
\point1.35,3.8574;\point1.40,4.0552;\point1.45,4.2631;
\point1.50,4.4817;\point1.55,4.7115;\point1.60,4.9530;
\point1.65,5.2070;\point1.70,5.4739;\point1.75,5.7546;
\point1.80,6.0496;\point1.85,6.3598;\point1.90,6.6859;
}}
\hfill}
\medskip
\centerline{\bf Figure~14. \rm The function $y=e^x$.}}
```

Figure 15:

```
\vbox{\line{\hfill
\diagram{\xaxis7truecm,75.0,100.0,5.0,$T$ [K];\nogrid
\yaxis4truecm,1.05,1.25,0.05,%
$1/\chi_{\rm m}\cdot10^{-6}$ [kg$\,$m$^{-3}$];}
{\connect{\symbol4
\point99.6,1.234;\point97.6,1.213;\point95.5,1.193;
\point93.4,1.171;\point91.4,1.151;\point89.3,1.131;
\point88.2,1.120;\point87.5,1.113;\point86.1,1.102;
\point84.1,1.082;\point83.2,1.090;\point82.7,1.094;
\point81.4,1.113;\point80.8,1.123;\point79.6,1.145;
\point78.7,1.161;\point77.8,1.181;\point77.1,1.195;}}
\hfill}
\medskip \noindent{\bf Figure 15. \rm
Reciprocal magnetic susceptibility (measured at a
magnetic flux density of 0.75~T) of superconducting
Tm$_{0.75}$Sc$_{0.25}$Ba$_2\!$Cu$_3$O$_{7-x}$.}}
```

Figure 16:

```
\vbox{\line{\hfill
\diagram{\xaxis9truecm,0.,100.0,20.0,$w_{\rm Ca(N_3)_2}$ [\%];
\yaxis10truecm,-30.0,80.0,10.0,$T$ [$^\circ\thinspace C];
\nogrid}{\connect{\point0.0,-20.8;\point63.3,-20.8;}
\connect{\point63.3,-30.0;\point63.3,0.5;}
\connect{\point82.1,-30.0;\point82.1,25.0;}
\connect{\point93.2,-30.0;\point93.2,41.5;}
\connect{\point32.,0.5;\point82.1,0.5;}
\connect{\point37.,25.0;\point93.2,25.0;}
\connect{\point41.,41.5;\point100.0,41.5;}
\connect{\point100.,-30.0;\point100.0,80.0;}
\connect{\point0.0,0.0;\point28.3,-20.8;\point32.,0.5;
\point37.,25.0;\point41.,41.5;\point43.,80.0;}}
\hfill} \medskip
\centerline{\bf Figure~16. \rm Phase diagram of
the H$_2\!$O -- Ca(N$_3$)$_2$ system (simplified).}}
```

Figure 17:

```
\vbox{\line{\hfill
\diagram{\xaxis8truecm,140.,240.,20.,$T$ [$^\circ$C];
\yaxis11.5truecm,225.,255.,5.,$E$ [mV];\nogrid}
{\lsqline{\point239.1,251.06;\point229.5,248.5;
\point220.4,246.11;\point211.1,243.71;\point201.6,241.37;
```

```
\point192.1,239.14;\point182.6,236.9;\point173.1,234.65;
\point163.5,232.43;\point154.1,230.29;\point144.1,228.14;}}
\hfill} \medskip
\noindent{\bf Figure 17. \rm Temperature dependence of the
electromotorical force $E$ of the galvanic cell
Pt/Ag/AgJ/Te($\!$Ag),Ag$_5\!$Te$_3$/Pt.}}
```

Figure 18:

```
\vbox{\line{\hfill
\diagram{\xaxis7truecm,0.,180.0,30.0,dihedral angle N--C--C=O;
\yaxis7truecm,-282.165,-282.157,0.001,$E$ [Hartree];\nogrid}
{\curve{\hpoint0.,-282.164306;\point20.,-282.163403;
\point50.,-282.159406;\point70.,-282.157569;
\hpoint76.085,-282.157477;\point90.,-282.157919;
\point120.,-282.160011;\point140.,-282.160990;
\hpoint180.,-282.161409;}}
\hfill} \medskip
\noindent{\bf Figure~18. \rm Energy profile for the neutral
glycine equilibrium shown in Figure~10, obtained from {\it ab
initio\/} SCF calculations with the 4-21G basis set.}}
```

Figure 19:

```
\vbox{\line{\hfill
\diagram{\xaxis7truecm,0.,1.0,0.2,$x_{\rm Al_20_3}$;\nogrid
\yaxis7truecm,-6.0,0.0,1.0,${\mit\Delta}_{mix}G$ %
[kJmol$^{-1}$];}
{\connect{\point1.0,-6.0;\point1.0,0.0;}
\curve{\vpoint0.,0.;\point0.1,-3.687;
\point0.2,-4.527;\point0.3,-4.676;\point0.4,-4.426;
\point0.5,-3.929;\point0.6,-3.322;\point0.7,-2.723;
\point0.8,-2.183;\point0.9,-1.597;\vpoint1.,0.;}
\values{\ownsymbol{1473\enspace K}\point0.37,-4.;}
\curve{\vpoint0.,0.;\point0.1,-3.993;
\point0.2,-4.886;\point0.3,-5.046;\point0.4,-4.743;
\point0.5,-4.248;\point0.6,-3.605;\point0.7,-2.963;
\point0.8,-2.360;\point0.9,-1.698;\vpoint1.,0.;}
\values{\ownsymbol{1513\enspace K}\point0.64,-4.;}}
\hfill}
\medskip
\noindent{\bf Figure~19. \rm Integral Gibbs energy of solution
of the $\alpha$-Cr$_2$O$_3$-\alpha$-Al$_2$O$_3$
system at 1473 and 1513~K.}}
```

Figure 20:

```
% Circle diagram generation:
%
% Call: \Torte{arg1}{arg2} .
%
% arg1: Approximate diameter (in any of TeX's units) .
%
% arg2: Sector definition (in order) by \Sektor arg3,arg4; .
%
% arg3: Sector size in percent .
%
% arg4: Sector label .
%
% NOTE: Sector sizes MUST add up to 100 percent .
%
\def\Coo#1,#2;{%
\ifnum\count100=1 \point#1,#2;\fi%
\ifnum\count100=2 \point#2,#1;\fi%
\ifnum\count100=3 \point#2,-#1;\fi%
\ifnum\count100=4 \point#1,-#2;\fi%
\ifnum\count100=5 \point-#1,-#2;\fi%
\ifnum\count100=6 \point-#2,-#1;\fi%
\ifnum\count100=7 \point-#2,#1;\fi%
\ifnum\count100=8 \point-#1,#2;\fi}%
%
\def\Kreis{% Coordinates were generated by the program
% character*7 h
% real s(26),c(26)
% character*4 coo
% data coo/'\Coo'/
% pi=4.*atan(1.)
% do1i=1,26
% x=float(i-1)/100.*pi
% s(i)=100.*sin(x)
% 1 c(i)=100.*cos(x)
% write(7,2)(coo,s(i),c(i),i=1,26)
% 2 format(3(a4,f7.3,',',f7.3,';'),'%')
% end
\Coo 0.000,100.000;\Coo 3.141, 99.951;\Coo 6.279, 99.803;%
\Coo 9.411, 99.556;\Coo 12.533, 99.211;\Coo 15.643, 98.769;%
\Coo 18.738, 98.229;\Coo 21.814, 97.592;\Coo 24.869, 96.858;%
\Coo 27.899, 96.029;\Coo 30.902, 95.106;\Coo 33.874, 94.088;%
\Coo 36.812, 92.978;\Coo 39.715, 91.775;\Coo 42.578, 90.483;%
\Coo 45.399, 89.101;\Coo 48.175, 87.631;\Coo 50.904, 86.074;%
```

```
\Coo 53.583, 84.433;\Coo 56.208, 82.708;\Coo 58.779, 80.902;%
\Coo 61.291, 79.016;\Coo 63.742, 77.051;\Coo 66.131, 75.011;%
\Coo 68.455, 72.897;\Coo 70.711, 70.711;
}
\def\Adjust{\count100=1
\ifdim\dimen101>12.5pt \advance\count100 by1\fi%
\ifdim\dimen101>25pt \advance\count100 by1\fi%
\ifdim\dimen101>37.5pt \advance\count100 by1\fi%
\ifdim\dimen101>50pt \advance\count100 by1\fi%
\ifdim\dimen101>62.5pt \advance\count100 by1\fi%
\ifdim\dimen101>75pt \advance\count100 by1\fi%
\ifdim\dimen101>87.5pt \advance\count100 by1%
\advance\dimen101 by-25pt\fi\relax%
\ifnum\count100>1 \advance\dimen101 by-25pt\fi\relax%
\ifnum\count100>3 \advance\dimen101 by-25pt\fi\relax%
\ifnum\count100>5 \advance\dimen101 by-25pt\fi\relax%
\ifdim\dimen101<0pt \multiply\dimen101 by-1\fi\relax}%
%
\def\Vorbei{\dimen101=-1pt}%
\def\Sektor#1,#2;{\dimen101=\dimen100%
\advance\dimen100 by #1pt \ifdim\dimen100>100pt %
\message{Sector beyond 100 percent ignored}\else%
\advance\dimen101 by\dimen100\divide\dimen101 by2\Adjust%
\values{\ifnum\count100<5 \ownsymbol{\hbox to1em{#2\hss}}%
\else\ownsymbol{\hbox to1em{\hss#2}}\fi\relax%
% The following code was generated by the program
% dimension x1(41),x2(41),x3(41)
% pi=4.*atan(1.)
% i=0
% do1x=12.3,0.1,-.3
% i=i+1
% xx=x/50.*pi
% x1(i)=x
% x2(i)=120.*sin(xx)
% x3(i)=120.*cos(xx)
% 1 write(7,2)x,x2(i),x3(i)
% 2 format('\ifdim\dimen101>',f4.1,'pt \Coo',f7.3,',',f7.3,
% $';\Vorbei\fi\relax%')
% write(7,3)
% 3 format('\ifdim\dimen101<0pt \else\Coo0.,120.;\fi}%'/
% $'\dimen101=\dimen100\Adjust\connect{\point0.,0.;%')
% write(7,2)(x1(i),x2(i)/1.2,x3(i)/1.2,i=1,41)
% end
%
\ifdim\dimen101>12.3pt \Coo 83.780, 85.912;\Vorbei\fi\relax%
```

```
\ifdim\dimen101>12.0pt \Coo 82.146, 87.476;\Vorbei\fi\relax%
\ifdim\dimen101>11.7pt \Coo 80.482, 89.009;\Vorbei\fi\relax%
\ifdim\dimen101>11.4pt \Coo 78.790, 90.510;\Vorbei\fi\relax%
\ifdim\dimen101>11.1pt \Coo 77.070, 91.979;\Vorbei\fi\relax%
\ifdim\dimen101>' .8pt \Coo 75.323, 93.415;\Vorbei\fi\relax%
\ifdim\dimen101>10.5pt \Coo 73.549, 94.819;\Vorbei\fi\relax%
\ifdim\dimen101>10.2pt \Coo 71.749, 96.188;\Vorbei\fi\relax%
\ifdim\dimen101> 9.9pt \Coo 69.923, 97.523;\Vorbei\fi\relax%
\ifdim\dimen101> 9.6pt \Coo 68.072, 98.824;\Vorbei\fi\relax%
\ifdim\dimen101> 9.3pt \Coo 66.197,100.089;\Vorbei\fi\relax%
\ifdim\dimen101> 9.0pt \Coo 64.299,101.319;\Vorbei\fi\relax%
\ifdim\dimen101> 8.7pt \Coo 62.378,102.513;\Vorbei\fi\relax%
\ifdim\dimen101> 8.4pt \Coo 60.435,103.671;\Vorbei\fi\relax%
\ifdim\dimen101> 8.1pt \Coo 58.470,104.792;\Vorbei\fi\relax%
\ifdim\dimen101> 7.8pt \Coo 56.484,105.875;\Vorbei\fi\relax%
\ifdim\dimen101> 7.5pt \Coo 54.479,106.921;\Vorbei\fi\relax%
\ifdim\dimen101> 7.2pt \Coo 52.454,107.929;\Vorbei\fi\relax%
\ifdim\dimen101> 6.9pt \Coo 50.410,108.898;\Vorbei\fi\relax%
\ifdim\dimen101> 6.6pt \Coo 48.349,109.829;\Vorbei\fi\relax%
\ifdim\dimen101> 6.3pt \Coo 46.270,110.721;\Vorbei\fi\relax%
\ifdim\dimen101> 6.0pt \Coo 44.175,111.573;\Vorbei\fi\relax%
\ifdim\dimen101> 5.7pt \Coo 42.064,112.386;\Vorbei\fi\relax%
\ifdim\dimen101> 5.4pt \Coo 39.938,113.159;\Vorbei\fi\relax%
\ifdim\dimen101> 5.1pt \Coo 37.798,113.892;\Vorbei\fi\relax%
\ifdim\dimen101> 4.8pt \Coo 35.645,114.584;\Vorbei\fi\relax%
\ifdim\dimen101> 4.5pt \Coo 33.479,115.235;\Vorbei\fi\relax%
\ifdim\dimen101> 4.2pt \Coo 31.301,115.846;\Vorbei\fi\relax%
\ifdim\dimen101> 3.9pt \Coo 29.112,116.415;\Vorbei\fi\relax%
\ifdim\dimen101> 3.6pt \Coo 26.912,116.943;\Vorbei\fi\relax%
\ifdim\dimen101> 3.3pt \Coo 24.703,117.430;\Vorbei\fi\relax%
\ifdim\dimen101> 3.0pt \Coo 22.486,117.874;\Vorbei\fi\relax%
\ifdim\dimen101> 2.7pt \Coo 20.260,118.277;\Vorbei\fi\relax%
\ifdim\dimen101> 2.4pt \Coo 18.027,118.638;\Vorbei\fi\relax%
\ifdim\dimen101> 2.1pt \Coo 15.788,118.957;\Vorbei\fi\relax%
\ifdim\dimen101> 1.8pt \Coo 13.543,119.233;\Vorbei\fi\relax%
\ifdim\dimen101> 1.5pt \Coo 11.293,119.467;\Vorbei\fi\relax%
\ifdim\dimen101> 1.2pt \Coo 9.039,119.659;\Vorbei\fi\relax%
\ifdim\dimen101> 0.9pt \Coo 6.782,119.808;\Vorbei\fi\relax%
\ifdim\dimen101> 0.6pt \Coo 4.523,119.915;\Vorbei\fi\relax%
\ifdim\dimen101> 0.3pt \Coo 2.262,119.979;\Vorbei\fi\relax%
\ifdim\dimen101<0pt \else\Coo0.,120.;\fi}%
\dimen101=\dimen100\Adjust\connect{\point0.,0.;%
\ifdim\dimen101>12.3pt \Coo 69.817, 71.594;\Vorbei\fi\relax%
\ifdim\dimen101>12.0pt \Coo 68.455, 72.897;\Vorbei\fi\relax%
\ifdim\dimen101>11.7pt \Coo 67.069, 74.174;\Vorbei\fi\relax%
```

```
\ifdim\dimen101>11.4pt \Coo 65.659, 75.425;\Vorbei\fi\relax%
\ifdim\dimen101>11.1pt \Coo 64.225, 76.649;\Vorbei\fi\relax%
\ifdim\dimen101>10.8pt \Coo 62.769, 77.846;\Vorbei\fi\relax%
\ifdim\dimen101>10.5pt \Coo 61.291, 79.016;\Vorbei\fi\relax%
\ifdim\dimen101>10.2pt \Coo 59.790, 80.157;\Vorbei\fi\relax%
\ifdim\dimen101> 9.9pt \Coo 58.269, 81.269;\Vorbei\fi\relax%
\ifdim\dimen101> 9.6pt \Coo 56.727, 82.353;\Vorbei\fi\relax%
\ifdim\dimen101> 9.3pt \Coo 55.165, 83.408;\Vorbei\fi\relax%
\ifdim\dimen101> 9.0pt \Coo 53.583, 84.433;\Vorbei\fi\relax%
\ifdim\dimen101> 8.7pt \Coo 51.982, 85.428;\Vorbei\fi\relax%
\ifdim\dimen101> 8.4pt \Coo 50.362, 86.392;\Vorbei\fi\relax%
\ifdim\dimen101> 8.1pt \Coo 48.725, 87.326;\Vorbei\fi\relax%
\ifdim\dimen101> 7.8pt \Coo 47.070, 88.229;\Vorbei\fi\relax%
\ifdim\dimen101> 7.5pt \Coo 45.399, 89.101;\Vorbei\fi\relax%
\ifdim\dimen101> 7.2pt \Coo 43.712, 89.941;\Vorbei\fi\relax%
\ifdim\dimen101> 6.9pt \Coo 42.009, 90.748;\Vorbei\fi\relax%
\ifdim\dimen101> 6.6pt \Coo 40.291, 91.524;\Vorbei\fi\relax%
\ifdim\dimen101> 6.3pt \Coo 38.558, 92.267;\Vorbei\fi\relax%
\ifdim\dimen101> 6.0pt \Coo 36.812, 92.978;\Vorbei\fi\relax%
\ifdim\dimen101> 5.7pt \Coo 35.053, 93.655;\Vorbei\fi\relax%
\ifdim\dimen101> 5.4pt \Coo 33.282, 94.299;\Vorbei\fi\relax%
\ifdim\dimen101> 5.1pt \Coo 31.499, 94.910;\Vorbei\fi\relax%
\ifdim\dimen101> 4.8pt \Coo 29.704, 95.486;\Vorbei\fi\relax%
\ifdim\dimen101> 4.5pt \Coo 27.899, 96.029;\Vorbei\fi\relax%
\ifdim\dimen101> 4.2pt \Coo 26.084, 96.538;\Vorbei\fi\relax%
\ifdim\dimen101> 3.9pt \Coo 24.260, 97.013;\Vorbei\fi\relax%
\ifdim\dimen101> 3.6pt \Coo 22.427, 97.453;\Vorbei\fi\relax%
\ifdim\dimen101> 3.3pt \Coo 20.586, 97.858;\Vorbei\fi\relax%
\ifdim\dimen101> 3.0pt \Coo 18.738, 98.229;\Vorbei\fi\relax%
\ifdim\dimen101> 2.7pt \Coo 16.883, 98.564;\Vorbei\fi\relax%
\ifdim\dimen101> 2.4pt \Coo 15.023, 98.865;\Vorbei\fi\relax%
\ifdim\dimen101> 2.1pt \Coo 13.156, 99.131;\Vorbei\fi\relax%
\ifdim\dimen101> 1.8pt \Coo 11.286, 99.361;\Vorbei\fi\relax%
\ifdim\dimen101> 1.5pt \Coo 9.411, 99.556;\Vorbei\fi\relax%
\ifdim\dimen101> 1.2pt \Coo 7.533, 99.716;\Vorbei\fi\relax%
\ifdim\dimen101> 0.9pt \Coo 5.652, 99.840;\Vorbei\fi\relax%
\ifdim\dimen101> 0.6pt \Coo 3.769, 99.929;\Vorbei\fi\relax%
\ifdim\dimen101> 0.3pt \Coo 1.885, 99.982;\Vorbei\fi\relax%
%
\ifdim\dimen101<0pt \else\Coo0.,100.;\fi}\fi}%
%
\def\Torte#1#2{\diagram{\xaxis#1,-95.,155.,250.,;\noaxis%
\yaxis#1,-125.,125.,250.,;\noaxis\nogrid}{\dimen100=0pt\relax#2%
\advance\dimen100 by-100pt\relax\ifdim\dimen100<0pt %
\multiply\dimen100 by-1\fi\  .ax\ifdim\dimen100<0.01pt %
```

```
\count100=1\connect{\Kreis}\count100=2\connect{\Kreis}%
\count100=3\connect{\Kreis}\count100=4\connect{\Kreis}%
\count100=5\connect{\Kreis}\count100=6\connect{\Kreis}%
\count100=7\connect{\Kreis}\count100=8\connect{\Kreis}\fi}}
%
\vbox{\centerline{\Torte{6truecm}{
\Sektor1.1,Geometry\enspace\&\enspace Basis;
\Sektor23.0,Integrals;\Sektor0.5,Guess;\Sektor12.7,SCF;
\Sektor62.7,Gradient;}}
\noindent{\bf Figure~20. \rm Distribution of CPU time for
the first optimization cycle in an {\it ab initio\/} SCF
geometry optimization of $\beta$-Alanine with the 4-31G basis
set, using the program GAMESS on a CONVEX~C1-XP.
(Starting on top and proceeding clockwise: geometry and basis
set definition: 38.9\thinspace s~(=~1.1\%),
integral calculation: 778.1\thinspace s~(=~23.0\%),
guess of initial density matrix: 16.5\thinspace s~(=~0.5\%),
SCF iteration: 428.7\thinspace s~(=~12.7\%), gradient
calculation: 2123.0\thinspace s~(=~62.7\%)\thinspace.)}}
```

Michael Ramek

Institut für Physikalische und Theoretische Chemie

Technische Universität

Rechbauerstraße 12

A-8010 Graz

Austria

Chapter 28
Nontraditional Uses of METAFONT

Richard O. Simpson

METAFONT can be used with TEX for purposes other than the production of ordinary alphabets or even sets of special symbols. Using the TEX system based on the IBM 6150 (RT), the following functions have been implemented, employing METAFONT in a nontraditional fashion:

A plotting program, which graphs sets of numeric data as x-y plots or bar charts. A METAFONT program is created to draw the curves.

A conversion program which accepts the output of a mouse-based drawing program (Gremlin), converting the drawing commands into a METAFONT program.

A conversion program which accepts the output of an image processing program on the 6150 and converts raster images directly into characters in PK style TEX fonts.

In each case, the strategy is to produce a font containing only a single (very large) character. The character is not a letter or even a special symbol, but is an entire picture (a graph, a drawing, or a bit image). TEX knows how to deal with characters in fonts regardless of their size, and typesets them in the ordinary way. The result is a very flexible system which combines text, arbitrary data plots and drawings, and images, in a very natural and straightforward way.

28.1 Introduction

Most TₑX users know METAFONT merely as 'the program which makes fonts for TₑX'. Such people are not drawn to learn more about METAFONT because of the perceived esoteric nature of the font-making task and (if they have looked at the METAFONT specification for a font) by the complexity of the METAFONT language.

While METAFONT certainly does make fonts for TₑX, in the sense of alphabets of different sizes and shapes for the typesetting of text, it can be used for much more than just that.

If one considers TₑX's typesetting job in the abstract, all TₑX does is arrange rectangular boxes on a page in neat columns of horizontal rows. The boxes happen to contain character shapes, or glyphs, and the rules by which they are arranged are complex. There is no reason that the boxes must contain character shapes, however, and there is no practical restriction on the size of the boxes. For example, a LaTeX picture is a single large box which is typeset by TₑX just like any other box. If it is realized that the characters in TₑX's fonts are just boxes, and can be any size and contain arbitrary pictures, then one can see how METAFONT might be used to create special purpose fonts.

This paper describes several such uses of METAFONT, including images for use within LaTeX pictures, graphs of arbitrary sets of data, and figures and charts drawn interactively. In addition, a means of creating special TₑX fonts for the typesetting of photographic-style images is described.

28.2 Fonts shipped with TₑX

28.2.1 Alphabetic fonts

In the preface to *The METAFONTbook*, Knuth (1986a) says 'METAFONT is a system for the design of alphabets suited to raster-based devices that print or display text.' This has certainly been METAFONT's main use to date, and most of the features of the METAFONT programming language are there to assist in the task of creating sets of alphabetic characters which look good together. Within a font, the relationships between the characters are fairly obvious: all have serifs or not, all have the same kind of contrast between thick and thin lines, and so forth. Within a family of related fonts, for example Computer Modern family (Knuth 1986b), relationships between characters in different fonts are not so obvious but are there nonetheless: the characters in the boldface font must blend well with the ordinary font, so that an emphasized phrase in otherwise normal text does not appear jarring. Much of the complexity in METAFONT programs for real fonts is in the details that implement these relationships. It is fairly easy to write a METAFONT program to draw block letters of the type taught to children in early school years, but it is far more difficult to write the programs for fonts for true typesetting.

A METAFONT program is an abstract, algorithmic description of the set of shapes which make up a font. METAFONT's job is to execute the program and draw the shapes, taking into account such variables as the density of the output device in pixels per unit length and a scale factor for increasing or decreasing the size of the generated font. METAFONT programs are (almost) device independent; METAFONT's output is entirely device dependent, and in general a complete set of fonts is needed for each different type of output device. METAFONT thus has two major purposes: it realizes shapes by executing algorithms specified by METAFONT programs, and it handles details such as scaling for particular output devices.

Fonts produced this way and supplied with standard TeX distributions include the ordinary Computer Modern text faces (roman, *italic, slanted roman,* **boldface**, sans serif), some slightly more exotic faces such as Dunhill and **Fibonacci roman**, and the fonts containing mathematical symbols ($\sum \cong \nabla \oint \aleph \ldots$).

28.2.2   Non-alphabetic fonts

Some non-alphabetic fonts produced by METAFONT are supplied with TeX. LaTeX has `line10` for drawing lines:

$$\text{———} \diagup \diagup \text{///|||}\text{\textbackslash\textbackslash\textbackslash}\text{\textbackslash}\text{\char`\~\char`\~}$$

and `circ10` for circles:

$$\circ \circ O\text{\char`\~} \;\; \smallsmile \;\; \backsim \; r$$

These fonts are designed for use within `picture` environments, and the LaTeX user is not expected to refer to them directly. Rather, certain LaTeX macros (`\line`, `\circle`) make use of the fonts 'under the covers'.

28.3   Creating simple non-alphabetic fonts

The subject of non-alphabetic fonts created by METAFONT first came up when projection transparencies were being created for a presentation on TeX and METAFONT for the IBM 6150 (IBM RT Personal Computer). A large diagram being drawn as a LaTeX `picture` needed a symbol for a disk drive as it would appear in a flow chart:

The first attempt to draw this used LATₑX's quadratic splines to approximate an ellipse for the top of the disk and half an ellipse for the bottom, with straight lines for the sides. This worked, but it was slow – each point on the ellipse was calculated and plotted individually by a LATₑX macro. Worse, it was not easily extended: an attempt to make a chart containing five of the disk symbols exceeded TₑX's memory capacity.

At this point it was noticed that a powerful curve drawing program was readily available: METAFONT. Not only does METAFONT know how to draw an ellipse (a circle scaled differentially in x and y), but it can draw straight lines at arbitrary slopes, something that LATₑX cannot do. The METAFONT program needed to draw a disk flow chart symbol is very simple:

```
mode_setup;
font_size 10pt#;
wd# := 35pt#;
sideh# := 25pt#;
toph# := 15pt#;
define_pixels(wd,sideh,toph);
beginchar(0,wd#,sideh#+toph#,0);
```

$x_1 = x_4;$ $x_2 = x_5;$ $x_3 = x_6;$
$y_1 = y_2 = y_3;$ $y_4 = y_5 = y_6;$
$x_1 = 0;$
$x_2 = x_1 + (wd/2);$
$x_3 = x_1 + wd;$
$y_4 = toph/2;$
$y_1 = y_4 + sideh;$

```
pickup pencircle scaled 1pt;
draw fullcircle xscaled wd yscaled toph shifted(z₂);
draw z₁--z₄;
draw z₃--z₆;
draw halfcircle rotated 180 xscaled wd
    yscaled toph shifted(z₅);
labels (range 1 thru 6);
endchar;
end;
```

When METAFONT is run on this program, it produces a 'font' which contains only one character, numbered 0. Placing the disk file symbol into a LATₑX document is easy: just typeset character 0 of the font:

```
\newfont{\disk}{disk}
\disk\char0
```

METAFONT programs for simple geometric shapes such as this are not difficult to write. Related shapes can be collected into a font, just as the alphabetic fonts are. For example, the milstd font supplied with TₑX for the IBM 6150 contains the standard symbols for sc and, or, and other logic gates (milstd refers to MIL-STD-806, the standard which defines logic symbols used throughout the electronics industry). Using this font, simple logic diagrams can be produced using LaTeX pictures:

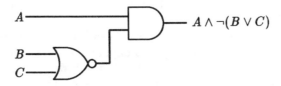

Fonts of this type have some common characteristics:

- they are generally based on simple geometric shapes;
- none of the nuances of alphabetic font design come into play – there are no serifs to worry about, and usually the lines need only be of one thickness;
- collections of related symbols can be grouped naturally into fonts;
- there are usually only a handful of symbols per font.

Because these fonts contain only a few characters, processing them with METAFONT can be very rapid, thus METAFONT can be used in an almost interactive mode in which it is easy to see results as the METAFONT program is changed. Because the characters themselves are simple, this is a good way to start learning how to use METAFONT. Even one who has never read *The METAFONTbook* and has not seen a METAFONT program can tell that the disk file program shown above:

- draws an ellipse at the top by drawing a 'fullcircle' which is scaled differently in the x and y directions;
- draws two lines at the sides;
- draws half an ellipse at the bottom using 'halfcircle'.

28.4   Machine-generated METAFONT programs

Once it was decided to treat METAFONT as a drawing engine and not just an alphabetic font generator, other ways in which METAFONT might be used were considered. Hand-coded fonts for special symbols work well if the symbols are to be used over and over again, as with the milstd font. However, it is desirable to be able to use METAFONT to draw arbitrary pictures in TeX documents, where the pictures vary from document to document and from instance to instance within the same document. Even restricting METAFONT's operations to 'simple geometric shapes,' it is too much to expect that the METAFONT programs for such pictures could be coded by hand. The process is too slow and error-prone to be used in any kind of production environment.

The solution was to write ordinary computer programs (in languages such as Pascal or C) which themselves write METAFONT programs. The user expresses what is wanted in some 'higher level language', or with a user interface quite unlike METAFONT's ASCII source files. This input is then converted into a METAFONT source program, and METAFONT is run to create a font containing only a single character. TEX then typesets the character at the location where the picture is wanted.

Two such conversion programs have been completed to date: a plotting program which graphs arbitrary sets of data and a conversion program which takes the output of an interactive window-based drawing package and permits it to be typeset as a picture in a TEX document.

28.4.1 Plotting graphs

This program lplot (LaTeX plot) came about because of the need ⁺ plot some performance graphs in a technical paper. It was obvious that t LaTeX **picture** environment is insufficient to plot arbitrary curves, even ¡ iecewise linear curves, since it is restricted to drawing lines of certain slopes. By this time it was clear that METAFONT could be used to draw the curves, but the logistical part of the task was daunting: drawing and labelling axes, scaling everything properly, and computing the points in METAFONT's coordinates for drawing the lines which connect the data points. It would not be too difficult to produce one graph, but more than a dozen were needed; besides, once the graphs were done, what if it became necessary to change their sizes or aspect ratios?

To handle all this, lplot was written. It accepts a simple language which specifies the characteristics of the desired graph (size, location of axes, ...), and writes two files:

- a .tex file which establishes a LaTeX **picture** environment, draws the graph's axes as horizontal and vertical \lines, typesets any annotations and axis labels as ordinary text, and typesets the single METAFONT-generated character which contains the graphed data;
- a .mf file which constructs a special font with one large character containing the graphed data.

Consider the input file for lplot (pop.lplot). This file is created with an ordinary text editor, just as TEX source files are. Note that while TEX and LaTeX commands appear in the text parts of the graph, no knowledge of METAFONT is needed since lplot handles the intricacies of METAFONT. The file describes a graph to plot the population of the State of Texas as a fraction of the United States population since 1850 (the first US census after Texas became a State). The graph itself is given as Figure 1.

```
%pop.lplot:    Texas population as fraction of US population
plot_type = xy
width = 4.5in
x_axis =
  description = "\shortstack{Texas population as
    fraction of US population\\
    \small Source:    World Almanac}"
  extent = 1845 1985
  ticks = yes
  labels = 1850 1860 "" 1870 "" 1880 "" 1890 ""
           1900 1910 "" 1920 "" 1930 "" 1940 ""
           1950 1960 "" 1970 "" 1980
y_axis =
  description = "\shortstack{P\\e\\r\\c\\e\\n\\t
    \\[1ex]o\\f\\[1ex]U\\S}"
  extent = 0 7.5
  labels = 0 1 2 3 4 5 6 7
curve =
  plot_symbol = none
  data =
    1850   0.918
    1860   1.922
      .   .   .
    1970   5.508
    1980   6.282
```

The entire process of creating the graph is controlled by a UNIX 'shell script' which runs lplot, METAFONT, and the gftopk utility to create the needed font files. These steps are shown in the diagram on the next page. This process appears complex, but the user is only concerned with the two files shown in heavy boxes: the source for the document (here, paper.tex) and the source for the graph (pop.lplot). To cause the graph to be typeset in the proper place, all that is needed in the LATEX source file is a single \input command:

```
\begin{center}
\input{pop}
\end{center}
```

To create pop.tex and the font files from pop.lplot, all that is needed is a single UNIX command:

```
lplot pop
```

When the pop.lplot source file is run through lplot, the files pop.tex and pop.mf are created. METAFONT then creates the pop.tfm file and two gf files, pop.118gf and pop.240gf. The gftopk utility converts the 'gf' files to

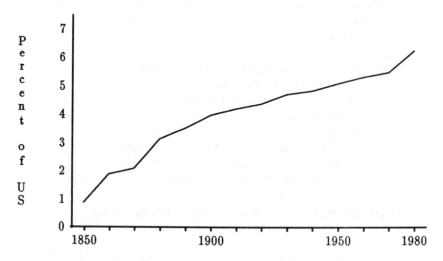

Figure 1. Texas population as fraction of US population
Source: World Almanac

pop.590pk and pop.1200pk for use by the TₑX previewer and printer driver on the IBM 6150. Figure 2 describes this process in a schematic form.

28.4.2 Drawing pictures

LATₑX has a `picture` environment that allows construction of simple line diagrams, subject to the constraints that lines must conform to a pre-specified set of slopes and that only straight lines and certain pre-generated circles and parts of circles may be used. As any who have used LATₑX `pictures` have found, these constraints are very restrictive. In addition, the need to calculate all positions explicitly and hand code them into `\put{}` statements means that `picture` construction can be very tedious.

Most modern computer systems have interactive drawing packages which allow the user to create line drawings essentially 'freehand', using a mouse or other locating device and a bit-mapped display. One such package which has been ported to the IBM 6150 is called '`gremlin`'. This program was originally developed at the University of California, Berkeley, and has been modified and updated for the 6150 by the University of Wisconsin and the IBM Almaden Research Center. Using `gremlin` it is easy to create charts and diagrams such as the flow chart earlier in this paper which describes how `lplot` works. Drawings can be saved as ordinary UNIX files, and can be retrieved and modified later or included as parts of larger drawings.

The `gremlin` program saves its drawings using its own internal data format. In order to use `gremlin` pictures in TₑX documents, it is necessary to

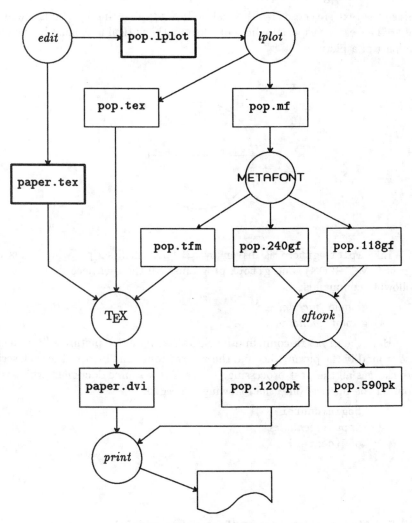

Figure 2. The lplot environment.

convert gremlin files into something that TEX can deal with. This is the purpose of the 'grtomf' (gremlin to METAFONT) program: it decodes gremlin's primitives such as 'draw line', 'draw arc', and 'typeset text' and writes two files just like the files written by lplot:

- a .tex file which establishes a LATEX picture environment, typesets any text specified in the gremlin picture, and typesets the single META-FONT-generated character which contains the gremlin drawing;
- a .mf file which constructs a special font with one large character

containing METAFONT versions of the `gremlin` drawing primitives.

Since the text is typeset by TEX, all of TEX's typesetting functions are available. This can be especially helpful when mathematical text must be included as part of a picture:

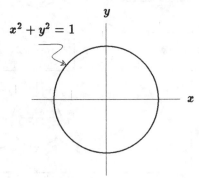

Like `lplot`, `grtomf` is driven by a UNIX 'shell script' which runs the `grtomf`, METAFONT, and `gftopk` programs. All the user need do is enter the following commands:

> gremlin *picname*.gr
> grtomf *picname*

Here the `gremlin` command invokes the interactive picture editor to create or modify the picture file, and the `grtomf` command invokes the shell script which does all the post processing. In the LATEX source document which is to contain the picture, only the following is needed:

> \begin{center}
> \input{*picname*}
> \end{center}

28.5   Non-METAFONT 'fonts' for special purposes

Anything which can be encoded as a two level raster image can be packaged as a 'character' in a font for TEX's use. All that is needed is:

- a means of converting the input data format (whatever that may be) into a font format such as PK that is usable by TEX DVI drivers;
- a means of creating a TEX font metric (TFM) file which describes the character's height, width, and depth so that TEX knows how it should be typeset.

Here METAFONT is bypassed entirely; the raster image to be used as a character comes from some external source rather than from the execution of a METAFONT program. Because METAFONT is not used, the two areas of de-

Figure 3. Gold Hill, Shaftesbury.

vice dependence that METAFONT handles must be taken care of in some other way:

- control over scaling of the raster image to fit different device densities is up to the external source. If only one size of image is available, such as for printing on a particular printer, then the image will appear a different size (or will not appear at all) on other devices;
- adjustment for device characteristics such a apparent pixel blackness and pixel overlap must also be handled by the external source or (more likely) ignored. This may or may not be important, depending on the characteristics of the image and the output device.

28.5.1   Example: Image typesetting

One conversion routine which takes raster images and converts them to fonts usable by TEX has been developed jointly by IBM Austin, Texas, USA, and by the IBM United Kingdom Scientific Centre at Winchester, Hampshire, UK. This program, called `imtopk`, converts the output of two-level images from the image-processing system known as IMPART on the IBM 6150 into a TFM file and a PK font file. The image becomes character 0 of a special font, and can be typeset very easily (Figure 3):

```
\newfont{\fontname}{fontname}
\begin{center}
\fontname\char0
\end{center}
```

The combination of the IMPART system to do image processing and TEX to do typesetting works very well. Each system is used for those functions that it is best at:

- IMPART:
  - handles image scaling, to allow for device pixel density;
  - does any filtering necessary for the particular output device (adjusts for pixel overlap, for example);
  - converts from n-level gray scale to two-level (black and white) by any means desired.
- TEX:
  - positions the image on the page;
  - typesets annotations around the image, or can superimpose them on the image;
  - handles all the rest of the typesetting for a technical paper.

28.6 Conclusions

From the examples given above, it can be seen how METAFONT can be used as a 'drawing engine' for TEX. Pictures have been shown which had their origins as sets of data points to be plotted, as interactively-drawn charts, and as raster-scanned images. It should be clear how programs can be written to take other sources of data and construct from them the appropriate TEX and METAFONT source files.

Combining text and pictures using TEX fonts in this way has certain advantages:

- no special support is needed in TEX or in dvi previewers and print drivers, other than the ability to handle large characters.
- drawings and images are independent of the final output device – such device dependencies are handled by METAFONT;
- no local TEX \special{} commands are used – these tend to inhibit transportability of TEX documents.

When lplot and grtomf are run, fonts are generated automatically for the IBM 6150's TEX previewer and its dvi print driver. Thus at any time anything which can be previewed can be printed and vice versa, which greatly enhances the utility of the previewer.

There are however some potential drawbacks to this approach.

- The fonts involved can be quite large. For example, consider an image which is 10 cm×10 cm on a device which prints approximately 100 pixels/cm. Then the image contains 1 000 000 pixels or 125 000 bytes (uncompressed). Memory space and file space for such a character is not much of a problem for a modern computer, but the transmission time to the printer can be significant.
- Some pictures can be too complex for METAFONT. This phenomenon was noticed when converting gremlin pictures which made heavy use of dashed lines into METAFONT programs – each dash became a separate METAFONT draw command, and METAFONT's memory capacity was

exceeded. The problem was solved by breaking the picture up into several separate characters and typesetting them superimposed on one another, but this aggravates the size and transmission time problems.

- Some DVI drivers and previewers 'know' that fonts contain text characters and thus cannot be larger than some arbitrary size. For the IBM 6150, care has been taken *not* to build in such size restrictions, and both the previewer and print driver will handle a character which covers the entire page. For other drivers, especially those on microcomputers, this may not be the case.

METAFONT does have limitations, and one obvious approach would be to use a drawing language such as POSTSCRIPT rather than METAFONT. In answer to this, note the advantages listed above: no \special{} commands are needed, and no special support is needed in the DVI drivers. All the METAFONT drawing and image work described here was done *after* the DVI previewer and print driver for the IBM 6150 were finished, and no changes in those programs were needed.

Bibliography

Jane D. Flatt, editor, 1984, *World Almanac & Book of Facts*, Newspaper Enterprise Association, New York.

Donald E. Knuth, 1986a, *The METAFONT book*, Addison Wesley Publishing Company, Reading, Mass.

Donald E. Knuth, 1986b, *Computer Modern Typefaces*, Addison Wesley Publishing Company, Reading, Mass.

Edward R. Tufte, 1983, *The Visual Display of Quantitative Information*, Graphics Press, Cheshire, Conn.

Richard O. Simpson
IBM Thomas J Watson Research Center
PO Box 218
Yorktown Heights
New York 10598
USA

Index